ב"ה

תשובה

RECLAIMING
THE SELF

ON THE PATHWAY
OF TESHUVAH

Rabbi DovBer Pinson

IYYUN PUBLISHING

Published by IYYUN Publishing
232 Bergen Street
Brooklyn, NY 11217

http:/www.IYYUN.com

Iyyun Publishing books may be purchased for educational, business or sales promotional use. For information please contact: contact@IYYUN.com

cover and book design: Rochie Pinson

pb ISBN 978-0-9786663-6-1

Pinson, DovBer 1971-
Reclaim the Self: The Path of Teshuvah / DovBer Pinson
1. Judaism 2. Spirituality 3. Self-help

IN GRATITUDE

TO MORDECHAI & HANNAH WOSK שיחי׳
Vancouver BC.

MAY THEY KNOW ONLY BLESSINGS
IN GOOD HEALTH
AND WITH EXPANSIVENESS OF MIND.

___

Many thanks to my students

REB MATTISYAHU YISRAEL BROWN שיחי׳
and
REB EDEN DANIEL PEARLSTEIN שיחי׳

for their tremendous effort with this text.

MAY THEY BE BLESSED WITH ALL
THAT THEIR HEARTS DESIRE.
AND MAY THEY RISE HIGHER AND DEEPER IN
AVODAS HASHEM, AND DO SO FROM A PLACE OF
INNER JOY AND CLARITY.

CONTENTS

CONTENTS

PREFACE

Every generation defines and expresses itself differently, from the literature it produces, to the songs it composes, to the technology it invents, to the wars it wages. While perhaps it was true that in years past, and especially during the dark ages, fear was used as a primary motivator to inspire people to live a moral and spiritually-oriented life, a more appropriate discourse today should be about love, healing, integration and harmony.

Teshuvah is one of the grand revelations and gifts of the Torah. It speaks of hope for a better today and empowers us to choose a brighter tomorrow.

But what is teshuvah? Often philosophical, psychological or even mystical terminologies seep into popular culture and take on connotations that are entirely different from their originally intended meanings. Teshuvah is one such word. Colloquially, the word *teshuvah* has become synonymous with the English word 'repentance', suggesting a relationship to 'sin'. 'Repentance', from the word 'penance', seems to imply remorse or guilt and an effort to alter one's behavior, while the implication of teshuvah is of a different order, as we will explore. As a result of such colloquial translations, the word teshuvah itself has been imbued with connotations far removed from its authentic meaning, until the word can seem stale and antiquated. A shift in perspective is required to recapture the true meaning and the transformative power of teshuvah. We need to re-contextualize this grand idea and create a fresh way of speaking about it.

Much like computers, our brains incline toward a binary system, and as a result, so does human language. Linguistic homeostasis depends on resolving cognitive dissonance caused by competing concepts and perceived contradiction. From the brain's normative perspective, there is either up or down, left or right, 0 or 1, but never both opposites at once. In other words, our minds operate in dichotomy and duality, within an either/or paradigm, also known as an Aristotelian worldview. We tend to use words such as good or bad, right or wrong, white or black, and forces of light or forces of darkness. Logically, then, our theological view can become 'God vs. evil', as if there were any real parity or any genuine independence of any creation in relation to its Creator. We imagine a 'Mighty Ruler' above who dictates to us what we should and should not do, who uses fear and intimidation as the primary motivators to do His bidding lest we be condemned and punished. To a thus conditioned mind, choosing God, who is the ultimate source of goodness, sadly seems the lesser of two evils. One must shift out of this primitive theology in order to have an authentic view of teshuvah.

Another outcome of the binary, finite, limited functioning of the brain is relegating God to a purely transcendent, heavenly realm. When pondering the reality of God, the brain attempts to grasp and measure that which cannot be measured. When it is realized that the Creator is immeasurable and infinite while the Creation is finite, the mind may seek to define the Creator as altogether separate and beyond any relationship to the earthly realm. This dualistic view also obstructs a full and subtle appreciation of teshuvah.

On the other hand, our brains can assist us in the realization that everything is rooted in Hashem's absolute and infinite unity. We can come to the view that Divine oneness embraces all realms. Although Hashem is unequivocally transcendent and beyond our grasp, Hashem is also manifest within the immanent earthly realm, and even within human thought. Hashem transcends and at the same time integrates all dualistic definitions: finite and infinite, form and formlessness, immanence and transcendence. Simply put, the unitary essence of Hashem is beyond infinity — beyond transcendence. Teshuvah is a movement of awareness towards a full recognition of all-embracing unity, towards ones own essential self, and towards the Source and Essence of all life.

Teshuvah is more a recalibration of consciousness rather than a mere apology or confession of mistakes — although the latter may be essential components of an authentic recalibration process. All kinds of activities, whether physical, emotional, mental or spiritual, can be vehicles of teshuvah. Overcoming emotional negativity and anxiety, or spiritually cleansing and ridding oneself of selfish urges and destructive desires, are acts of teshuvah. Dieting or exercising in order to return to a state of health and vitality can also be acts of teshuvah.

Acknowledging the essential unity of Hashem allows us to make conscious choices between wholeness and fragmentation; we can choose to have a healthy and empowered self or a disillusioned and weakened self. We can choose Divine presence or Divine absence — an emptiness filled with wholeness or an emptiness filled with emptiness. By declaring our intention to do teshuvah we immediately begin to return from fragmentation and confusion to a place of greater unity and wellbeing, to our authentic self. This process is a re-integration of all aspects of our self, and a reclaiming of the deepest, purest 'I' that exists from before birth. This pure 'I' actually remains intact throughout our life, and never departs, but at times it is eclipsed by circumstance or lack of consciousness. Teshuvah reclaims the manifest purity and luster of the pure 'I'.

When teshuvah is merely about *change*, it comes into direct conflict with any existing system that stands in resistance to that change. Yet real teshuvah is of a higher order, not just about change, but about genuine transformation. It is a major spiritual shift, through which the by-product of change occurs organically. Teshuvah directly transforms the believer within, and then by association, purifies and aligns the belief. For instance, if one were to just change their diet without a deep realization and commitment to whole-system health, then his new eating habits would run up against all his unchanged hungers, desires and subconscious validations for unhealthy behavior. It would turn out to be a schizophrenic enterprise, one which could end up causing more internal friction, contradiction and self-defeat. But if one came to the decision to eat healthier food through a profound revelation of the multi-dimensional benefits of a healthy lifestyle, then the decision would be an organic extension of a greater worldview or understanding. This, in turn, would lead to a stronger conviction and more holistic alignment between his actions and his ideals, without contradiction.

Personal transformation has a cosmic significance as well. Through our act of teshuvah and unifying with our true self, the whole world is repaired, returned from its seemingly splintered state of randomness to its primordial wholeness and revealed purpose. Every individual act of teshuvah inspires collective teshuvah. Conversely, a collective movement of teshuvah influences our own inner processes. Our sages say, *Adam olam katan; olam adam gadol* — "A human being is a small (microcosm of the) universe; the universe is a big (macrocosm of the) human being." All parts holographically reflect and represent the whole, and so the repair of one part benefits all others.

An existential challenge in being alive is to imbue our world with love, integration, honesty, spirituality and purity. In truth, these qualities are expressions of the spiritual condition into which we are born, and thus we need only unveil that which has always existed.

There are many people who still function from a disempowered state of being and can only respond to harsh and intimidating words. There are also many who have never relinquished their childish notions of God. With regard to every other subject matter, whether intellectual, emotional, or celestial, they may have highly evolved levels of understanding. But with regards to God, sadly, they stubbornly hold onto the primitive images they formed as children. God is envisioned, at least subconsciously, as an old man with a long white beard, who has a bag of goodies in one hand and a whip in the other. Do the right thing and you'll receive a reward, do the opposite and you'll suffer punishment.

This is why many people today wish to deny the existence of God. Indeed, their limited, unsophisticated ideas of God are foolish and unworthy of belief. Just remember that the 'God' that you don't or can't believe in really does not exist.

Whether such stagnant views can still serve a noble cause is beside the point, as the Torah's ambition is to infuse the world with a sense of freedom, maturity and responsibility. Towards those ends we must all continually seek out the true and living God, who animates, enlivens and inspires us to reach beyond ourselves, to evolve and to manifest ever higher degrees of love, light, and wholeness. The Torah acknowledges that for some, fear is the primary motivator for doing right, at least in the initial stages of growth. In any case, developing ourselves spiritually allows for a gradual spiritual maturation in which we become less fearful, meek or helpless, and less easily intimidated or manipulated. With maturity comes self-realization and empowerment in accomplishing our unique purpose in life.

Many of us live with a sense of insufficiency and constant need, and our thoughts are often at the service of mere survival. This anxiety is, in part, a psycho-spiritual symptom of being surrounded by a capitalist society where advertising is designed to seduce our desires, while industry simultaneously creates a false sense of scarcity and lack. A primary goal of Torah is to free us from such anxiety and constraint by restoring within us a mindset of security, sufficiency, faith and love. This freedom is expressed in the Torah's teachings on charity, the Jubilee year, and the first fruits offering, for example. Teshuvah is the key to activating our ability to fulfill the Torah's vision and teachings, and to return us to a conscious state of abundance on all levels.

FOREWORD

WHY *28* CHAPTERS?

T he first verse in the Torah (*Bereishis*, 1:1) has seven words containing a sum of twenty-eight letters. These letters correspond to the twenty-eight days of the month not including Rosh Chodesh, the 'head of the month' (*Da'as Z'keinim*, ad loc). The Book of Koheles (3:2-8) speaks of twenty-eight periods of life; the twenty-eight seasons in which "there is a time for everything." Every *chodesh* or month is a *chidush*, a 'novelty', bringing a new, never-before-seen revelation of Divine light into the world. Each month reveals a unique *tziruf*, or 'letter sequence', of the four-letter name of Hashem. Within every day of the month, and within every hour of the day, there is a new light and potential *ko'ach* or 'empowerment' that is revealed and manifest.

A finger has three bones, while the thumb has two, adding up to fourteen in each hand. The Creator used both 'hands', as it were, to form Creation: the right hand of *chesed*, 'Divine kindness', and the left hand of *gevurah*, or 'Divine severity'. These two hands represent the twenty-eight creative energies that are imprinted within the universe and within ourselves.

The numerical value of the word *ko'ach* is 28, alluding to the presence of a twenty-eight-day psycho-celestial cycle in which our inner energetic patterns and the phases of the moon interact and harmonize. We are compared to the moon in that the moon does not have any light of its own and only reflects the light of the sun. We recognize that our light and radiance comes from a source greater than ourselves: the Ultimate Light, the Light of the Infinite One. Like the moon, we also go through periods of waxing and waning. Both communally and individually, we are sometimes up, sometimes down, sometimes full and bright, and sometimes empty and dark. Our needs for empowerment are constantly in flux. The cycle of the moon is thus recognized as an external mirror of our internal processes.

To intermesh with our fluctuating spiritual needs, this book is divided into twenty-eight chapters, allowing you to read one chapter each day of the month until Erev Rosh Chodesh, the day before the new moon. Every Erev Rosh Chodesh is analogous to a miniature Yom Kippur, or *Yom Kippur Katan*, a day of *teshuvah*, or returning. The empowering, experiential course of learning offered in this book is relevant to any month of the year, and you are encouraged to repeat it through multiple monthly cycles. This cyclical spiritual practice is especially recommended during the month of Elul, as you prepare for Rosh Hashanah, the 'judgment day' of the New Year.

CHAPTER ONE

Being in
THE PRESENT

Following the passing of the early Nineteenth Century Rebbe, Reb Moshe of Kubrin, another Chassidic luminary, Reb Mendel of Kotzk, approached Reb Moshe's disciples and requested that they eulogize him and describe his special qualities. "There was no particular area of life in which he excelled," they said. "He was unique, however, in that whatever he was doing, at that moment he was completely present." Whatever occupied him at any given moment was all that was relevant to him. Wherever he was, he was fully there.

According to human nature, what we acquire easily and without exertion or difficulty is less valuable and exciting than that which we work hard to accomplish or obtain. Our sages say, "A person would rather possess one coin earned than nine coins granted" (Baba Metzia, 38a). This phenomenon extends beyond the realm of objects and into the realm of time as well. With the exception of peak moments, the present often feels less thrilling or relevant than the past or the future. We feel like we have 'earned' the past by 'going through it' or surviving it, and we have a sense that we have to 'earn' the future, by working towards it. We tend to look forward or backward, while the most important part of our reality, the present, appears less attractive. Even as we take it for granted, the present moment sits silently, waiting for us to fully inhabit it and recognize its significance.

While daydreaming or reminiscing we miss what is happening right in front of us. When life seems unsatisfying in the present, we may attempt to gain comfort by idealizing life in the past. Our minds restlessly roam through the maze of memory, searching for a richer or more promising reality. "Those were the days" is the universal cry of the disempowered spirit. Such nostalgia demonstrates an unwillingness to deal with what is, as it is.

Sometimes we may also resort to idealizing the potential future — how much more interesting or comfortable life will surely be one day. We are so busy ruminating over the past or planning our manipulation of the future that we are absent from the here and now. We are distracted by the fascination of what will become of us when we are older or even once we no longer embody physical form. Preoccupation with the future is a result of dissatisfaction with life, but when the present is regarded according to its actual significance, there is no need to look elsewhere for any form of confirmation or validation.

The Torah is a comprehensive and detailed divine blueprint of how to live in a spiritual and sensitive manner. It invites us in the form of *mitzvos* (plural of *mitzvah*, 'instruction', 'commandment', or 'connection'), to celebrate and fully experience life with a sense of nobility, compassion and Divine awareness. Performing mitzvos focuses our attention on the here and now so we can be fully alert and sensitive to the infinite spiritual potential in our lives. Vast groups of present-day mitzvos pertain to mundane human activities, such as how and when to sleep, use the bathroom, do business, and eat, how to care for others and even how to tie our shoes. These mitzvos in particular ground us in the time and space we presently inhabit, allowing us to sanctify it and bring a taste of the Infinite into the finite realm of space-time. These mitzvos elevate the seemingly ordinary into something extraordinary, the mundane into the miraculous, and the everyday into the unique and eternal.

We do not need to perform mitzvos with a sense of nostalgia or with the hopes of reward over punishment. The mitzvos are aimed at the center of our being and our present experience in order to connect us with the One who reveals the mitzvos. The essential Torah experience is therefore rooted in the here and now, and it empowers us to live mindfully — sensitive to the Divine Presence. We are given the awesome ability to transform 'mundane' actions performed in seemingly non-special moments, into divinized actions occurring in elevated, special moments.

> A prisoner in the Sixteenth Century was given a unique choice: one day of the year he would be allowed to act like a free man and practice Torah, as desired. This presented him with a great dilemma. Being a devout Jew, he did not know which day of the year to choose in order to perform the optimum quantity or quality of mitzvos. Should he choose Shabbos, so he could recite the Kiddush, a highly regarded prayer? Perhaps he should wait until Rosh Hashanah, the 'head of the year', which influences the whole year to come? Or better yet, maybe he should choose the holiest day of the year, Yom Kippur, the Day of Atonement. Unable to reach a decision, he sent letters to the leading sages seeking their counsel. Some time later, the Radbaz, a prominent Rabbi of the era, wrote and instructed him to choose the first opportunity that presented itself, whether it be Shabbos, a weekday, or a holiday.

In other words, the specific day is irrelevant — the most important thing is not to delay doing a mitzvah. According to Torah, the moment that is presenting itself *right now* is the most consequential moment of your life, for this is the only time when we are truly in contact with life and the Creator of life.

One of the names or attributes through which the Creator is known is *haMakom*, 'the Place' or 'the Omnipresent'. This implies that being fully present 'here' is what provides the greatest potential for spiritual connection to the Creator.

Hashem, 'the Name' of the Infinite and Ineffable One, sometimes called 'the Tetragrammaton', is made up of four Hebrew letters: *yud, hei, vav*, and *hei*. These four letters can be re-arranged and permutated to spell the words *haya* — 'was', *hoveh* — 'is', and *yihyeh* — 'will be'. The Name thus suggests that the Infinite encompasses past, present and future as one. Where is Infinity expressed? In the *hoveh*, the 'present moment'.

This Divine Name can also be read as *yud-hoveh*, meaning 'the *yud* of the present moment'. The letter yud is a small point, symbolizing the first infinitesimal point of manifestation that encompasses all further articulations. Yud therefore represents the pure potency of the present. Furthermore, when yud appears at the beginning of a word, it creates a grammatical sense of continuity. It is taught that the writing of every Hebrew letter begins with a small yud, the point where the quill first touches the parchment before the ink flows and expands, and only then continues into various horizontal or vertical lines to form other letters. Thus, one deeper meaning of the Name is 'the continuously unfolding potency of the present, the Eternal Now'.

The numerical value of the Name *Hashem* is 26: yud=10, hei=5, vav=6, and hei=5. Another way of calculating the numerical value, called the 'full value', involves multiplying each letter: (10 x 10) + (5 x 5) + (6 x 6) + (5 x 5) = 186. This is the same numeric value as the name *HaMakom*, mentioned above. This correspondence between the names *Hashem* and *HaMakom* suggests that the 'here and now' is omnipresent and includes all aspects of *haya* and *yihyeh*, past and future, in its unity. In other words, the Infinite reality, in which all space-time is unified, is expressed in the hoveh, in the immediacy of 'right here, right now'.

One of the questions incessantly asked in medieval Jewish thought is, 'Why is there no explicit mention in the Torah of an afterlife?' There is not a single verse or phrase in the entire Five Books that unequivocally indicates the existence of a 'beyond'. Nor is the concept of Heaven or an afterlife journey clearly indicated in the Written Torah. This has vexed the greatest minds throughout the ages. One of the prominent Jewish thinkers of Fifteenth Century Spain, the Abarbanel, offers a simple answer. He argues that the Torah does not mention the rewards of the World to Come because in the 'world of action', *today* is what is important. The rewards to be received in a future world shouldn't be a factor in our behavior today. The most relevant factor in life is life as it is *right now*.

Teshuvah means to believe that today is the first day of your life. You can access the deepest truth of teshuvah the moment you can truly tell yourself: 'Today is a new day. All of my past, the good and the bad, is in the past. Today I am choosing Hashem.' As Rabbeinu Yonah writes, "The foundation of teshuvah is considering today as the day you were born, the first day of your life, and you have no demerits or merits."

Just as our motivation in performing good and noble deeds need not be the attainment of rewards in an afterlife, we need not live our lives today in order to rectify actions done in a previous incarnation. Issues of previous lives or future worlds are not fully relevant to achieving mental or spiritual wellbeing today. In fact, a moment of diverting attention into the past or the future is a moment stolen from the extraordinary opportunity of making each moment special and worthwhile.

One way to serve Hashem, or perform the will of the Most High, is as a 'servant'. This is a laudable archetype or psychological stance, and it can allow us to develop a healthy sense of smallness and submission to something greater than ourselves; it is a way to deal with the phaorohic tyranny of the ego. This path is based on the spiritual quality called *yiras Hashem* or 'fear of God'. Not to be belittled at all, divine fear or awe is often a necessary stage of spiritual development. In fact, it is quite a lofty stage, and sufficient in and of itself as a form of divine service.

There are, however, other valuable ways to relate to Hashem: as a child, a relative, a friend, or even a lover. These roles represent different relationship dynamics, based on love rather than fear. When we can authentically relate to Hashem in these ways, our performance of mitzvos is not coming from a place of 'reward and punishment' or anxiety. Rather, the mitzvos become conscious expressions of our overflowing love and appreciation for the Infinite One who has given us the gift of life. In truth, Hashem is our closest and most responsive companion.

If we base our actions on love rather than on fear — or love balanced with healthy fear— we act to please our Beloved, rather than to gain salvation or spare ourselves from some vague sense of future torment. This is like leaving a note for your spouse or parents because you genuinely do not want them to worry about your whereabouts, rather than leaving them a note just so you do not get into trouble later. Ultimately, what matters most is leaving the note. But how and why you do it will have tangible psycho-spiritual effects on the quality of your connection with the other.

Teshuvah is about love. Through the path of love, we can enter the awesome dimension we call 'the now', reprogram our lives in the present, and by extension transform what was and what will be. It is being in the present moment that makes teshuvah possible. The present stands uninfluenced by past behavior and experiences, and to a degree, what may happen in the future. Teshuvah is about *you*, right now. Only by fully being *you*, right now, can you birth yourself anew at any given moment. Otherwise, you may be limited by or enslaved to fixed self-images, which block the possibility of real transformation.

The anomaly of the present moment is such: on one hand, everything exists in the now, and yet there is no such 'thing' as the now. Even though now is all there is, it is impossible to objectively know that we are in it because of its fluid and fleeting nature. As soon as you become aware of the present moment or acknowledge being in it, that moment is past and you are no longer in it.

Strictly speaking, one cannot go into the past or the future at all. Even if theoretically it were possible to do so, any 'past' or 'future' we could experience would be experienced in the present — it would be 'now'. Arguably, past and future do not exist; they are but fragments of memory and imagination that are appearing in the now. The only true moment is now, and we can never leave it or escape it.

The present is the one and only constant in life. It is the context in which the flow of life forms and transforms, appears and disappears. Whatever happens in our life and whatever changes we may undergo, we are always here, now. This moment is therefore not an action after which we must chase, but rather it is the eternal, pure, open field upon which all actions unfold.

We will now introduce two concepts that will be helpful in navigating the linguistically murky territory of human souls and spiritual psychology. These concepts are *yesh*, 'something' and *ayin*, 'nothing'. In cosmological terms, the universe is created '*yesh* from *ayin*' — something-ness manifesting out of no-thing-ness, out of the Creator's Light. When used within the framework of our individual, internal experience, the term *yesh* refers to our separate identity, ego or personality structures. *Ayin* correspondingly refers to our state of integral wholeness, true self, pure awareness or being-ness. *Yesh* is self-consciousness in which the self is viewed as a separate 'thing'. *Ayin* is a state of absorption in the Source, in which there is no sense of separate self — all appearances of separation are 'nothing' in the totality of infinite Oneness. There is no egoic 'I', only the One True 'I'.

The ego is a fixed self-image, and a fixed self-image can actually only exist in the past — it's already defined. Therefore, an ego-centered experience is one in which an entity 'in the past' is claiming to be experiencing things in the present. But the ego is an experience, not the experiencer. We are therefore not our ego.

When the ego pretends to be in the present moment, it really remains in a normative-identity-bound state of yesh and finite forms. It focuses on the *content* of the experience of the moment, rather than the timeless moment itself. This is merely exchanging a 'yesh' for a 'yesh' — trading the 'story' of a past or future for the finite 'story' of a so-called 'present moment'. Yet, even the egoic 'present' is much better than the ego's ruminating about the past or future. Although it does not approximate the infinite story-less space of ayin, at least it is a better 'story'.

Yesh is the sound that echoes against the background of our silent present-ness. That silence is ayin. We are in touch with our vast ayin-self when we are fully in the ever-unfolding formless moment, without superimposing labels or opinions, but just listening in deep stillness.

It is important to note that while ayin is our deeper level of self, there is an essence of self that is beyond both yesh and ayin. The ultimate goal of life is not to reject yesh and stay in the silent, unmoving selflessness of ayin, but rather to be the essence that is beyond both and inclusive of both. However, on the way to that ultimate goal — on the path of teshuvah — immersion in ayin is key. That is because to do teshuvah, or better, *to be in a state of* teshuvah, requires that we detach from being stuck in the past or attached to a seemingly inevitable future, and to be fully present in the infinite potential of this moment.

When we move out of the limited, rigid yesh-consciousness, and into the ayin of the formless present, we find ourselves in wide-open, limitless spaciousness. From this state of purity and flexibility, we can re-create and redirect our lives. We can then emerge as a new yesh, with a new understanding of the past and hope for a brighter future.

Feelings of being imprisoned by our past, or negative anxiety about a bleak future, can initially spark the flames of teshuvah. Such crises can motivate us to take the appropriate steps to challenge, if not completely relinquish, the haunt and grip of the past. However, if we desire to be in a state of teshuvah, we need to center ourselves in the eternal present which encompasses the past and the future. Only then can the past and future be fully transformed.

Similarly, says Reb Shalom Shachnah of Probisht, when a person searches his soul and begins to acknowledge past mistakes, his initial re-action may be to immediately mend what was broken — yet this may not be the wisest course of action. When garments are dirtied with mud, it is best to wait until the mud has dried before attempting to rub it off. In such close proximity to the unhealthy action or omission of action, any involvement, even with the most sincere intentions of rectification, may cause more damage. Often the best initial course of action is to disregard our successes or failures of the past, and to focus simply on the living, breathing present. Once we are empowered by the selfless energy and presence of ayin, we can then effectively fix the past.

Every new moment translates as an opportunity for exponential growth and spiritual advancement. It is through teshuvah that we have the ability to release ourselves from the imprints of the past, and untangle ourselves from automatic, programmed responses and deterministic beliefs. What's more, when we release the heavy baggage of our preconceived notions, more of life and more of who we truly are become accessible to us. What we have, in any case, is the now: the past is history and the future is mystery. The present is indeed a 'present', a gift of fresh energy and hope in beginning anew.

SYNOPSIS:CHAPTER 1
Be in the Moment

Learn to focus on the present. When we are preoccupied with our past or future, we are stealing a moment from the 'now'. The gift of life is the present. The past is memory and the future is imagination; the only true moment of life is the formless, eternal now.

PRACTICE

'Kavanah'
INTENTION

In order to be present, we need to cultivate mindfulness. Before taking any action, speaking any words or deliberately thinking any thoughts, pause and become mindful of what you are about to do or say.

Take an action, as simple as enjoying a drink of water. Before you say the *berachah* or 'blessing' over the water, pause for a moment and open fully to consciousness of gratitude. When someone is speaking with you, be fully present with the person, disregarding any thoughts that may come up that would try to define whom this person is. If asked a thoughtful question, resist formulating a response until you have heard what is being asked in its entirety. Think it through first. Then respond with caring and consciousness.

LIVING
with
CONTINUOUS RENEWAL

The *koach ha-hischadshus* or 'power of renewal' is present within every moment of Creation, as Creation manifests from an *ayin* state of non-being into a *yesh* state of being. Tapping into this recreation of being offers us the ability to instantaneously refresh our lives. We can unburden ourselves of past experiences, which are within the realm of *yesh* or 'something-ness', and enter into *ayin* or no-thing-ness, a fluid and formless moment within the present.

From the perspective of ayin, every moment and everything in it is new, there is only now, and at any point one can start life all over again. Yet without the awareness of yesh, where time is linear and flows from past into present, with the present impregnating the future, we would not take responsibility for our past actions. And why should we do so, if we have glimpsed that there is no past or future, no causality or responsibility? Ayin provides the spaciousness and freedom to transform, however our return to yesh reintroduces accountability. Ayin and yesh complement and complete each other. Yesh without ayin is self-referential and rigid, with no potential for actual change. Ayin without yesh is a dis-embodied state of limitless potential, without substance or any sense of tangible manifestation.

Teshuvah is awakening to the flow of life. The flow of life moves continually from ayin to yesh, and there is never a moment of repetition, inevitability or predictability. In the beginning of his book, the Prophet Yechezkel (Ezekiel) relates visions revealed to him during the beginning of the Exile, on the banks of the River Kvar. *Kvar*, in Hebrew, means 'already'. Subtly, the Torah is associating exile with the notion of '*already*', as in the 'been there, done that' attitude. One who 'already knows' cannot learn or grow. This person leaves no space for disengaging from his fixed patterns of the past and beginning anew. Exile is the burdensome clinging to the old with no freedom in the present for newness or movement. For the redemptive mind, nothing is kvar, 'already' or old; every thing is fresh and exciting.

Children live from within a place of wonder, since for them more of life is new and unexplored. When we are younger, a year seems to pass much more slowly than when we are older. This apparent stretching of time is because our perception of life is not yet fixed or routine. Our days are full. Most of our experiences are novel, and they leave strong impressions, forming deep and lasting memories. As our memories accumulate, however, our constant state of amazement and awe gradually diminishes. As years go by, we become more set in our ways. More and more experiences fall in the category of 'already', and time seems to speed up.

'It is prohibited to be old', say the Chassidic rebbes. Nothing in our lives and spiritual practices should be performed in an automatic or routine way. We should not fall into lethargic or stale perceptions and actions. Such would not be true to reality. In reality, all of Creation is being created out of no-thing-ness, continuously and at this very moment.

The letters that make up the word *tikkun*, 'rectification', can be rearranged to spell the word *tinok*, 'child'. This is a hint that part of our personal soul-tikkun may be to reconnect with our 'inner child'. When we live with childlike awareness, with wonder, awe, vigor and excitement, we can also contribute to the universal process of *tikkun*, the rectification of the entire universe. Teshuvah helps us discover this opportunity.

The Torah's promise of *orech yamim*, 'long days', doesn't necessarily mean long life, but rather 'long' or 'full' days. This is the meaning of "Avraham was old and *ba ba-yamim*, 'he came into his days'" (Bereishis, 24:1). He was 'old' only in the sense of spiritual maturity, and specifically because he "came into his days" — he came into each day as a completely new experience. His life was full, for he made every day a full day. Every day was a different experience and a different expression.

"…This mitzvah that I commanded you *today* — it is not hidden from you and it is not distant" (Devarim, 30:11). According to the Ramban and many other classic interpreters, "this mitzvah" refers to teshuvah, and regarding teshuvah, "today" is the most important element. According to Sifri, this verse implies that we should perform mitzvos as if they were given anew today. Even more importantly, perhaps, we should perform the mitzvah of teshuvah with a great sense of newness and excitement, in the *now* or 'today'. Teshuvah cannot be performed by rote, out of a sense of 'yesterday', 'distance' or 'already'.

'Seize the day' is the attitude to adopt when approaching teshuvah. We can seize the open opportunity of the present moment. Because this moment is unrelated to the past and it is yet to become a future, we begin again with a clean slate. Even within a single day we can 'begin anew' multiple times. Teshuvah delivers us into this realization: every instant is a complete *his'chadshus ha-briah* or 'renewal of Creation'. Philosophically speaking, if there is no real past, there is certainly no hindrance to our ability to be new, in the present.

A young man once entered the study of the Nineteenth Century Chassidic sage, Reb Asher of Stolin, and wept bitterly. "I truly desire to transform and mend my ways", he said, "but I am unable to. I have committed a deed for which it is written that teshuvah is not effective and the doer will forever lose his share in the world to come." The Rebbe looked deep into this boy's soul and responded, "Young man, why does this concern you? You should proceed with what you have to do. As to your concern regarding a share in the World to Come, this is a moot point. The Sages have already said, 'One hour of teshuvah and good deeds in this world is better than eternity in the world to come'" (Avos, 4:17). The point of life is found within the living itself, and not in whatever might come afterward.

Each day, we can explore our life as if for the first time. The simple act of awakening to a new day is an encounter with our great capacity for personal growth and enhancement. If we can make a genuine self-evaluation while staying in the present moment, we can inspire in ourselves a desire for teshuvah. Evaluating our spiritual status is not merely about judging our past, and teshuvah is much more than rectifying past behaviors. Self-evaluation and teshuvah are about coming to a sensitive understanding of how we can go forward and evolve into who we truly are. Yesterday may have been fulfilling for yesterday, but today is a new day, and we ourselves can be new. As Reb Pinchas of Koretz says, teshuvah is about beholding the present moment and viewing it as an initiation into a new and brighter life.

The word *aveira*, 'sin', has the same root as the word *avar*, 'past'. Sin is about staying stuck in the past, such as holding grudges or yearning for 'the good old days'. Images of our mistakes or faulty decisions may sometimes come back to haunt us. Our sins can thus chain us to our past and stand in the way of our freedom in the present. The process of teshuvah acknowledges this common mechanistic tendency of the mind, but it also provides us with an escape route. Our actions do have consequences, and our sins and traumas do have a magnetism that draws us back into our past; however, the state of teshuvah affirms, "I am not a slave to my past; Hashem is continually creating the world anew every second. I can tap into this perpetual renewal and begin again, right now!"

My grandfather, the famous *mashpia* or spiritual guide, Reb Avraham Mayorer, would say in jest that the Hebrew word *Amalek* is related to the Yiddish word *amol*, 'it once was.' A person thinking only about the past cannot move on. This is a hint in the Torah when it says that Amalek attacked Israel "from behind": our inner saboteur can attack us by using thoughts of the past, what is 'behind' us.

This spiritual force called *Amalek* can also attack with thoughts of a hopeless future. When all there is, is the past, the future is completely dependent upon it. With regards to Amalek the Torah says, "Go and wage battle with Amalek *tomorrow*" (Shemos, 17:9). We need to fight Amalek's idea that there is no hope for tomorrow. Mitzvos and specifically, the essential mitzvah of Teshuvah is the ultimate weapon. To be involved with mitzvos, in particular the *RaMaCH* or '248' positive mitzvos, is to believe that there is a *machar*, a 'tomorrow'. The letters of *RaMaCH* are the same as the letters of the word *machar*.

In numerical value *Amalek* is 240: ayin (70), mem (40), lamed (30), and kuf (100). This is the same gematria as the word *pa'amayim*, 'twice' as in 'repetition': pei (80), ayin (70), mem (40), yud (10), and mem (40). Amalek says, 'Why get excited or hopeful? Your future will be just a repetition of the past. You'll never really change much. Teshuvah is a fantasy.'

Teshuvah is not a fantasy, it is real and it does bring change, however it is not about change alone. 'Change' implies altering what already was. Teshuvah is more about calling forth a new beginning. If we have done something negative in the past, our joy in life will be impinged — genuine joy cannot be experienced if we are forever ruminating on the negativity of our past. Therefore, in order to call forth a new beginning, sometimes it is good to just forget the past. This can release the choke-hold that the past seems to have over us. Forgetting can allow us to come to life from a place of self-empowerment and joy. Then change comes easily. Reb Nachman of Breslov says, "The world thinks that forgetting is a negative quality. I, however, think it has great value."

The word *simcha*, 'joy', contains the letters that spell the word *emcha*, 'erase'. We experience more joy when we let go of resentments and erase grudges. First, we have to forget. Once negativity is erased, a healthy equilibrium can be restored, and then can we endeavor to transform our inner-state into joy.

We might assume that a main point of teshuvah is to make reparations, like fixing broken pipes. Indeed, teshuvah can include restoring what was marred. On this level, teshuvah is analogous to surgical operations on unhealthy limbs.

On another level, teshuvah may be compared to cosmetic surgery, albeit from the inside out. Some people in our society feel themselves to be younger than their chronological age; the image reflected in the mirror does not correlate to their internal image. They opt for cosmetic surgery, for better or worse. Similarly, spiritually sensitive persons may perceive a state of newness within, but wish for this inner 'appearance' to be manifested outwardly. These people opt for teshuvah, an 'operation' that aligns the inside and the outside.

In other words, the world is like a mirror. Ideally, our inner soul is re-

flected outwardly in the world. People see the external image of our mannerisms and behaviors and interpret them as who and what we truly are.
Yet, when we look deeply into this mirror, we may notice that our outer
appearances and behaviors are inconsistent with the true inner self we feel
ourselves to be. Our actions may not be in alignment with our spirit. Seeing this, we resolve to realign our behavior with our soul and unify the
two. We opt for a spiritual 'face-lift', so to speak, from the inside out.

On the other hand, at its highest level, teshuvah has little to do with
rectification, modification or even re-alignment of certain traits. Teshuvah is ultimately an elevation of the whole, not just parts or dimensions
of the self. It is a state of comprehensive integration, which even the
greatest of spiritual figures must strive for.

If we were to equate teshuvah with the process of healing, as the
Torah does, the best metaphor would be that of 'rebirth'. That is, rather
than see ourselves as someone who was sick and is now better, which implies that there was something wrong with us, we should see ourselves as
being completely reborn. Upon entering a state of teshuvah we are considered a new person, a new creation. This is an important interpretation,
for it will affect how we process our anxiety about our past behavior. Instead of perpetually beating ourselves up for how 'bad' or ignorant we
were, we can let the past be past. We can see ourselves in a positive light,
in the present, acknowledging that we have taken steps to live the way we
know to be right and true.

The idea of 'rebirth' is also connected to the Hebrew term *Eitz ha-
Chayim*. Most people translate this phrase as 'the Tree of Life', but it literally means 'the Tree of *Lives*'. This implies a multiplicity of incarnations
or identities within one 'tree' or living being. Indeed, many of us experience having been many different 'people' within a single lifetime. Think
about how many inner and outer changes you have gone through even in
the last ten years. The consciousness and opinions we had as small 'seeds'
are naturally much different from what we had as 'saplings', and even
more so as fully blossoming and fruit-bearing trees.

Teshuvah is always about rebirth, even when it is a response to a
past that was 'rotten' or 'infested'. All spiritually debased behaviors reduce
one's integrity, eclipse the soul and weaken the body. The word *aven*

(ayin, vav, nun) is one of the Torah's terms for 'transgression'. One *gematria*, or numerical value, of the word *aven* (when we spell out each letter and add them together) is 248: *Ayin* is spelled ayin (70), yud (10), nun (50). Vav is spelled vav (6), vav (6). *Nun* is spelled nun (50), vav (6) nun (50). Our sages say the body has 248 'limbs'. With every negative deed we alienate a part of our bodies from our deeper self, weakening the body and making it experience a sort of death. However, through the essential mitzvah of teshuvah — counted among the 248 Positive Mitzvos — we recreate and revitalize our 248 limbs. Not only that, we rebirth our whole existential reality.

As teshuvah is such a radical act of renewal and recreation, it is suggested that one who embarks on this path change his name. From this point forward, there is a new person. From a deeper perspective, the Hebrew letters are like the elements that make up a spiritual 'Periodic Table'. Therefore, to change your name is to alter your spiritual makeup, to change your inner chemistry. Shifting our inner dynamic so that we operate from a wholeness of being may actually create renewal on the level of physical chemistry, as well.

Modern medicine tells us that the power of the mind is such that the patient must believe in the remedy for healing to take effect. If consciously or unconsciously he denies the healing powers of the medicine, those powers may not manifest. The placebo effect works both ways. Similarly, our mind and heart determine the power of our acts of teshuvah. A person who truly desires to heal and begin life anew needs to place trust in the medicine of teshuvah. We should believe in the fact that teshuvah can and will heal us. The way we use our minds helps us 're-member' a splintered, broken or 'dis-membered' self.

The word 'heal' comes from an Old English word meaning 'to make whole'. The power of teshuvah is in acknowledging what is, and renewing our claim to intrinsic wholeness. When we align our outer self with our inner self, we can begin again to live in integrity with our deepest levels of soul.

SYNOPSIS:CHAPTER 2
Live With a Continuous Sense of Renewal

There is no room for growth, change or even movement, when we view our present as being the inevitable effect of our past deeds. There is no possibility for rebirth if our present is merely born of our history. The truth is that every moment is a new Creation, a new reality. Our lives are always beginning. When we live in a state of awe and wonder, we can tap into the spiritual opportunities that each moment brings, and start afresh.

PRACTICE
BREATH

A simple breathing meditation can allow us to deepen our awareness of continuous creation. With every exhalation we are emptying ourselves of our old yesh, *our old state of being; with every inhalation, we are filling ourselves with new yesh. This is an act of self-revival. Also, the momentary pause between each segment of the breath is the* ayin, *the refreshing stillness of 'nothingness'. Observing and contemplating the breathing process in this way can reawaken our life force, heighten our creativity, and reveal the beautiful possibility of beginning anew.*

Set aside a few moments each day for this practice. A good time to do so might be before your morning prayers, or the first few moments upon waking in the morning, or simply while walking down the street.

CHAPTER
THREE

A World of
ENDLESS POSSIBILITY

T eshuvah, our sages tell us, was fashioned even before the Creation of the world itself (Pesachim, 54a). The implication of this is twofold: first, that teshuvah stands above and is transcendent of time; second, teshuvah is deeply ingrained within the very fabric of the world. Teshuvah is the very foundation of Creation. It is an integral component of reality, a healing and reunifying force embedded within every atom, every moment and every thought form, drawing all of Creation back to its Divine root.

Teshuvah is the all-pervading desire and deepest will within each created being. In a sense, all of reality is constantly in a state of teshuvah, turning toward its true self and toward its Source, much like a plant turns towards the light while her roots extend toward the source of water. All forms of life are striving for evolution; they are all in a constant movement of teshuvah.

The Zohar, the primary text of the Kabbalah, offers that prior to creating the physical dimension, the Creator conceived the notion of teshuvah and spoke to teshuvah saying, "Soon, I am going to fashion a mortal human being of flesh — but on one condition. When they, because of their iniquities, turn to you, you must be prepared to expunge their iniquities" (Zohar, 3:69b).

Human beings are inclined to err. "There is no righteous person on this earth who does (only) good and does not err," writes the wise King Solomon (Koheles, 7:20). Even so, we need not ever despair, for the possibility of transformation is forever available. What was done yesterday is by no means an inevitable influence on what will be done today, and what may be done today does not indicate exactly what will be done tomorrow. The future is not an absolute consequence of the past, and time is not stuck in a linear flow. The future is not the explicit outcome of what was already implicit in the past. Spiritually as well as emotionally, there is always hope for a new beginning.

The possibility of healing our present behavior remains real and accessible, always. Without this built-in source of assurance, life could become quite disenchanting or hopeless. If there were no way to unshackle ourselves from the past, we would always be crushed by the burden of our errors. Without the power of disengagement, we would be resigned to a hamster wheel of inevitability and relentless motion without any real advancement.

If we were to think that there is no way out, we might just sink lower and lower into the abyss of our predicament. If everything that we ever did was permanently ingrained in the fibers of our being, and we dared not even dream of ever being free of it, we would fall into a deep hopelessness, and all zest for life would be drained. If not for the hope that we can alter the course of our own behavior, our lives would be one long slippery slope into despair. Conversely, life imbued with teshuvah is a life of optimism and vitality — a world of endless possibility. Regardless of our current state and imprints of the past, we always have the power to re-orient our life and leap over any obstacles.

Teshuvah offers us the freedom of rejuvenation, of beginning anew. The dynamics of self-transformation are essential for spiritual development and wellbeing. Reb Schneur Zalman of Liadi, affectionately known as the Alter Rebbe, teaches us that our soul descends into this realm of existence and is enclothed in a body only to experience the awesome phenomenon of human growth, evolution and refinement.

Teshuvah is an essential condition for our emotional and spiritual wellbeing and survival. To illustrate this, our sages speak of the universe as being created with the letter *hei* (Menachos, 29b). On a personal scale, *hei* represents our own place of continual creation and re-creation. The graphic design of this letter consists of three lines: ה. The full vertical line on the right connects with the full horizontal line on top. The shorter line on the lower left side does not connect with the top horizontal line, leaving a small gap like a passageway. The bottom of the letter is open; there is no floor, indicating that it is possible for someone to fall down and out of their *hei*. The gap, however, on the upper left side of the formation indicates that even if one falls, it is possible to leap up from one's circumstances, re-enter the *hei* through this gap, and return to the continuous renewal of life.

The gap in the hei is also seen as a window. This shows there is access to the 'beyond' and we can escape from our limitations.

The letter ches (ח) is quite similar to hei in construct, in that it has no floor. The main difference is that the ches has no gap, no open space for re-entering the place of newness. The impermeable walls of ches appear to trap a person and 'the only way to go is down.' In fact, ches is spelled the same as *cheit*, 'sin' or 'missing the mark'. We may feel trapped or fenced-in by our sins or mistakes, and this may bring us down. Through teshuvah, however, the fence of *ches/cheit* is transformed into the window of *hei*. We can thus free ourselves from the prison of our past and escape into the wide-open, ever-new wilderness of the present moment.

When one has drifted off course, the most effective route of return is often to take an entirely new route. In the quest for transformation and re-integration, it may be necessary at first to shift perspective and not to deal directly with the type of interaction that drove us off course. We need to find a new — and sometimes opposite — focal point, in order to proceed.

For example, a person who is suffering from emotional depression (as opposed to clinical depression, which is another issue) needs a radically new focal point. If we study the writings of notable personalities who have suffered from depression, we will see evidence of pre-occupation with the egoic self. One celebrated American author writes about himself: "I have made a captive of myself and put me into a dungeon, and now I cannot find the key to let myself out." In this one sentence, the author refers to himself no less than five times. A solution in this scenario would be to redirect his attention to the needs of others and develop compassion. Teshuvah includes transforming egocentricity into other-centricity and, ultimately, to theo-centricity or centering on the Transcendent Reality.

Redirecting our attention towards others brings feelings of productivity and vitality. This is the key to the dungeon of ego, and to the rediscovery of our true self. Even subtle positive feelings created by giving to others may awaken a genuine happiness. In the quest for self-rediscovery, the road that leads back home may be the direct opposite of the road that led you to alienation.

Following the brutal murder of his brother, the first murder recorded in the Torah, the Midrash says Cain was summoned to the Heavenly tribunal for judgment. After a brief deliberation it was decreed that Cain would be condemned to a life of wandering: "You shall become a vagrant and wanderer on earth" (Bereishis, 4:14). Acknowledging the gravity of his offense and accepting his sentence, Cain pleaded to the court for forgiveness, crying, "Is my iniquity too great to bear?" Indeed, the court mitigated his judgment.

In a state of great relief, Cain left the court. He soon met his father, Adam. Seeing his son's jubilant disposition, Adam asked Cain what had happened. When Cain told him of the power of pleading for forgiveness, Adam began to hit his head with excitement, and said, "Such is the power of teshuvah and I never knew it!" With holy inspiration he began to sing, and spontaneously composed Psalm 92: *Mizmor Shir l'Yom ha-Shabbos*, 'A Psalm, a Song for the Shabbos Day'.

Why specifically did Adam sing about Shabbos? What is the con-

nection between Shabbos and teshuvah? Shabbos and teshuvah are similar in that they both free us from our normal narrative of life. Shabbos
exists as a refuge in time. No matter how absorbed or preoccupied with
our activities we may be during the course of the week, there is an oasis
of sacred time when we can just *be* — we can stop and look within. Shabbos is a time when we can break free from our habitual behaviors, and
this is precisely what teshuvah is all about. As Shabbos is a refuge in the
dimension of time, teshuvah is a refuge in the dimension of consciousness
or soul. If we have become alienated from our deepest self, teshuvah is a
safe space where we can rediscover our soul and redefine our life.

The word *Shabbos* is comprised of three Hebrew letters: shin, beis
and tav. The same letters spell *tashev*, 'return', the root of the word *teshuvah*. Without Shabbos, we would toil without end, ultimately becoming
enslaved and stifled by the burdens of our labors and possessions. Intro-
ducing a period of respite from our materialistic involvement, a break
from creative activity, we are reminded of the spirit, the essential aspect
and integral essence of who we are. As we enter the Shabbos state of 'just
being', not doing, we are liberated from our natural materialistic focus.
With this firm and repeated rededication to spirituality, our lives change.
Both Shabbos and teshuvah are spiritual 'reset buttons' allowing us to
temporarily set the linear trajectory of yesh-consciousness to zero, and
immerse in the limitless stillness of ayin-consciousness. Both Shabbos
and teshuvah can be compared to a *mikvah*, a ritual bath from which one
emerges transformed and renewed. Shabbos is a mikvah in time, and
teshuvah is a mikvah of mind/heart/soul.

Parallels between Shabbos and teshuvah run even deeper. Shabbos is
a culmination of the six weekdays of toil, and an immersion in a peaceful
and perfect state of rest. It is thus the spiritual apex of the preceding
week and the foundation of the following days — 'the ray of light illuminating the anticipated week' (Zohar, 2:63b). Moreover, in addition to
looking at the week linearly, beginning with Sunday and culminating
with the seventh day, Shabbos can be envisioned as the mid-point of the
week. In this perspective, Wednesday, Thursday and Friday are the three
preceding days and Sunday, Monday and Tuesday are the three following

days (Pesachim, 106a). The focal point of every week is Shabbos; branching out in both directions are the three days before and after, with Shabbos as the middle pillar. In any case, like teshuvah, Shabbos simultaneously completes the past and impregnates the future; it is a positive conclusion to a less-than-positive past, and a positive commencement of a journey of infinite potential. Like Shabbos, teshuvah is a profound state of inwardness and beingness that radically shifts the way we project ourselves outward in thought, word or action.

When the philosophers of the world learned that the People of Israel had a seventh day reserved for rest, many promptly dismissed the idea as an indication of laziness. The Roman philosopher Seneca contended that doing nothing every seventh day would squander one seventh of a person's life. Others decided that dedicating a day of rest once a week would train the body and mind to become inactive, lethargic and sluggish. Challenging these philosophers, the First Century Jewish sage Philo of Alexandria argued that Shabbos was designed to free people from their labors in such a way that they would regain strength and be able to work more energetically throughout the following week. Philo's error was to interpret the purpose of Shabbos within a Greek-Hellenist world-view: that rest is only for the sake of further labor. This is clearly a materialistic slave-like mentality in which there is no intrinsic value in rest, enjoyment or spiritual development, insofar as the only value in life is enhancing production.

Shabbos is obviously much deeper than rest for the sake of future work. The state of *being* of Shabbos stands alone. It transcends time's rhythmic movement altogether, irrigating and permeating time with great blessing and spirituality. Shabbos helps us break our materialistic preoccupations and orients our focus on intellectual and spiritual matters and on togetherness with our families and loved ones. The spiritual pleasures of Shabbos are to be engaged without expectation of outcome, for "The reward of a mitzvah is the mitzvah itself" (Avos, 4:2), rather than for the sake of a future reward. However, the outcome of the practice of Shabbos is also transformative. It opens and maximizes opportunities rather than squandering them.

Only when life is lived automatically and unconsciously is the past a predictable prologue to the present, and the present a mere preparation for the future. Teshuvah is a source of blessing permeating all of time. When the state of being called *teshuvah* seemingly limits our activities, it is in order to open a panorama of spiritual opportunities. We are not locked into a world of misdeeds. The eternal present stands alone and allows us to *shav* or 'rest' from the confines of linear time, thus generating the gift of renewal every single moment.

SYNOPSIS:CHAPTER 3
Be Optimistic; Never Despair

There is never a valid reason to despair. No matter how difficult your past, each day brings the possibility for change. What you did yesterday does not automatically inform what you will do or who you will become today. Teshuvah is the bedrock of Creation, an always-accessible opportunity to begin again. Hashem is always with you, even in the times you feel trapped and helpless. Even in the deepest darkness there is Light. Never give up!

PRACTICE

RESOLVE

Whenever you are feeling weighed down by misdeeds, realize that if you were able to fall, you are able to arise.

If you have the power to destroy, you also have the power to repair. If you can wander astray, you can also return home. Cash in on this power to change; resolve to never give up. Before you go to bed at night, resolve that tomorrow will be better. If you feel loneliness and disconnection and cannot imagine life improving, focus on the facts: you are not here by accident. You are one-of-a-kind. Your life has purpose. Hashem is always with you.

CHAPTER
FOUR

The Nature of MISALIGNMENT

B efore the need for 'return' there occurs a misalignment or deviation; an internal disconnection in the fabric of a person. To master the process of realignment, it is helpful to understand the nature of misalignment. Why do certain activities and states of consciousness demand teshuvah?

A *mitzvah* is a deed that overtly connects the performer with his or her Source. Performing a mitzvah keeps us in sync with the Designer's inner purpose and intention for our existence. That intention is to continually re-establish and reveal our underlying unity, our intimate relationship with the Creator. An act that does not lift us higher and reveal our inherent bond with the Divine Self is an act that can lead in the opposite direction, causing disconnection and alienation.

A 'transgression' is therefore an *anti-mitzvah*, in which a misperception of reality leads a person to disengage from their ideal state. One of the most common terms the Torah uses for 'sin' is *cheit*. This word originates from a verb meaning 'to miss the target'. To function in the mode of cheit is to be off the mark, disconnected or out of alignment. Similarly, the English word 'sin' comes from the Latin word *absentia*, which means 'missing' or absence.

Every action or inaction can lead either to connection or disconnection, bonding or alienation, creation or destruction. The root letters of the word *bechira*, 'choice', are beis, ches, reish. We can reconfigure these letters to form the word *chaver*, 'friend' or 'connection', or *charav*, 'to destroy'. Every choice we make can enhance or destroy a friendship or connection. When a person deviates from his deeper integrity he disconnects himself, down to his very core, from the Source of Life. He also disconnects from other people and from himself. Fragmenting the connection with our Source causes fragmentation throughout the entire matrix of our reality.

Although there are many levels of cheit, ranging from seemingly benign to obviously hideous, their common denominator is that they are expressions of a temporary state of heresy (Midrash Rabbah). Transgressions are thus symptoms of an inner barrier, an underlying mistaken assumption that the Creator is disinterested with Creation, or even that the Creator does not exist. With such an outlook, the condition of separateness pretends to prevail, and one's true relationship with the ultimate Source is temporarily eclipsed. Whenever we forget who we really are, we imagine ourselves to be a substantially separate and independent entity. Reactive or negative behavior flows from this belief.

Hashem is to be found everywhere and anywhere, yet in terms of a paradigm of interactive duality, we as human beings sense the Presence of the Divine "wherever we allow Hashem to enter", as the Kotzker Rebbe said. When a person acts out of misalignment with the Divine Presence, he erects an imaginary barrier that keeps It from 'entering' or being sensed. In this confused state, his false sense of separation from the Divine is reinforced.

Through negative behavior one loses his focus and sense of destiny. It "closes the mind and shuts it off to wisdom" (Rashi on Yumah, 39a). To perpetuate negativity is to operate in a state of powerlessness. However, this powerlessness may not be clearly felt or recognized. On the contrary, there are countless documented cases of extremely negative acts where the perpetrator felt extremely powerful. When a person feels enslaved, insignificant or disempowered their entire lives, they may actually feel important, assured, or powerful while committing a crime or act of violence.

A distinction must be made here between genuine power and force. People tend to use these terms interchangeably when in fact they refer to two very different states. Power is an effect of deeper integrity and alignment with the Supreme Power of the universe. The use of force or coercion is a symptom of powerlessness and neediness. Those who demand to be served, obeyed or esteemed usually have low self-esteem. Incessant longing to be noticed or loved can be a psychological defense against lack of healthy self-love.

Subtler forms of coercive force include the use of persuasion and even using incentives or rewards for behavior. Depending on force can cause one to seek to accumulate wealth and influence. The core desire for domination is the same: that others conform to your will, admire your ideals, or make you feel comfortable. The use of force is inherently violent, impersonal, blind and neurotic. It gives birth to traits of intolerance and abusiveness. The powerless individual forever feels the need to control demonstrated in the behavior of seeking to accumulate as much wealth or influence as possible, always afraid of loss and losing. Life in this context is a quest to dominate, to impose upon others.

Conversely, truly powerful persons emulate the Creator by tolerating and supporting the abundant diversity of Creation. Power is not over others, but *for* others. Like the Infinite One who inhabits The Place, which created the empty space, through the mysterious and paradoxical act of *tzimtzum*, or constriction, which allowed for this finite universe to come into being with all its variety and abundance, those who emulate the Creator often allow, tolerate and even support diversity. The universe is designed to be interdependent, other-centered, and each being contributes its energy to the greater symphony of the performance of the Creator's will. The spark of Divine power within the bird's chirp, the ocean's roar, and the leaf's silent fall from the tree — each add to a cosmic harmony, seamless and unchallenged, power flowing into power. On the other hand, when a person chooses to use self-centered force over others, he deviates from this grand chorus. His notes are in discord with

the totality of existence, and he disconnects himself from the powerful
unity of Creation.

To a greater or lesser extent, most people are out of alignment with
what works in this world, namely the Designer's intention. There is a saying, 'it is easier to ride the horse in the direction in which it is going'.
Transgression is riding the horse in the wrong direction. This is not the
'wrong' defined by human institutions that distort power, rather it is
merely going against the grain, against the flow of the river, like spitting
into the wind. If a ship is veering off course, adjustments must be made
to move it back into the right direction, or it will soon be lost. When a
person is veering away from the design and intention of the universe, and
does not correct his course, he loses conscious connection and transgresses against his own power and wholeness.

One of the allusions to teshuvah in the Torah is regarding a case of
theft (Bamidbar, 5:7). The act of stealing is not only an offense against
Heaven and against the rightful owner of the object, but the thief also
hurts himself. The thief deprives himself of being who he really is and
could be. Whenever one transgresses in any way, says Rabbi Yehudah
Aryeh Leib of Ger, he is denying and depriving himself of his true potential and capability.

As long as a modicum of their inner integrity remains intact, almost
all human beings will occasionally feel the pang of misalignment. With
an honest evaluation of who we are and what we have accomplished in
life in comparison to what we could have been or done so far, some level
of turbulence will probably arise in our conscience. A person who listens
to this inner turbulence may be bothered and desire transformation, but
his attachment to the status quo may still be greater. Even if the notion
of change may be of intellectual interest, his fixed sense of identity, his
ego, will stubbornly resist.

"All the ways of man are straight in his eyes" (Mishlei, 21:2). In a
transgressor's own eyes, his actions were justified, as if they were the only
option, necessary for survival, an automatic result of trauma, or another
reason. Even the most hideous of criminals have found defenses for their
crimes. Human beings, like nearly all other creatures, do have strong sur-

vival instincts. However, we also have a subjective mind that can misconstrue reality and obscure the objective reasons for our behavior. This is why the news media is often full of people's justifications for their ethically questionable acts.

"Man does not commit a transgression unless a *ruach shtus* or a 'spirit of folly' enters him" (Sotah, 3a). Thoughtless behavior can occur when we do not take into consideration the consequences of our actions. Lack of responsibility is the mark of a fool. In the words of the Gemarah, a fool is "one who loses whatever is given to him" (Chagigah, 4a). Spiritual alienation fosters negligence, and is rooted in restriction wherein the individual thinks in the short-term only, with little understanding of his motives and certainly with no regard for the ramifications of his actions.

The word *aveirah*, 'transgression', means crossing a boundary, entering forbidden territory, being dislocated and in a place one should not be. There are natural consequences to dislocating and distancing ourselves from our authentic self. The harsh judgments detailed in the Torah for certain sins can be understood as simply the physical and psychological results of a harmful mindset and behavior. Both collective and individual exiles are experiences of the spiritual effects of distorted ways of living. Transgressions themselves, writes Rabbi Chaim of Volozhin, are their own worst punishments; the act itself contains its reprisal.

Aveirah, has the same letters that spell the word *areivah*, 'sweet', or pleasant. Selfish pleasure may appear to be sweet and gratifying for a few moments, yet, the aftertaste is truly bitter. In contrast, when someone who has attained a higher spiritual state experiences gratification from a permissible object, it is experienced from a place of pre-existing completeness and joy. There was no neediness, so there is no bitter aftertaste, nor attachment dragging him toward future gratification.

The harshest consequence of vice is spiritual suffocation that slowly overwhelms a person. Without teshuvah, a deep sense of constriction, emptiness and loss gradually creep in, until one is all but closed off to the life giving 'oxygen' of spirituality. Every negative act births another. The ripple effect of transgression is that it often leads to doing more of the same. One should not agonize over the single harmful act, says the

Midrash, but rather over how that act opens the door to more, leading the person down a slippery slope of increasing folly and self-suffocation.

Once the choice to compromise internal integrity is made, the door is open to habit formation. Habitual negativity starts to narrow a person's perspective while desensitizing him to the good. The universe gradually seems more and more threatening, and one's life therefore becomes increasingly survival-based and ego-projected.

Such patterns can ultimately enslave a person. Once a course of behavior is established, it is difficult to shake free. Newton's First Law tells us that bodies at rest tend to stay at rest, while bodies in motion tend to stay in motion in the direction in which they are moving, unless perturbed by an external force. Actually, unchecked negative patterns continue to accelerate. A desire fulfilled is not a desire quenched. Empirical evidence shows, rather, that fulfillment of selfish desire only inflames greater yearning, implanting in one a loop of addiction and increasing entrapment.

In the realm of cause-and-effect, each action, whether positive or negative, causes an effect. According to the laws of nature, every vibration emanated generates a ripple effect throughout the entire universe. An echo is born, whether heard or not. Once they are established, the effects of the spreading ripples of negativity cannot be easily avoided.

Even on subtler levels, the ripples sent out by our actions affect how we perceive ourselves, how others perceive us, and, subsequently, how they choose to interact with us. Expressions of anger and irritation towards others surround one with a negative aura, setting up the conditions for others to respond in the same unpleasant manner. Thus a chronically angry individual will be disliked by his peers and, ultimately, will come to loathe himself. When we choose to see the good in others and act in ways that send out ripples of kindness, a positively charged environment is created, a safe space that magnifies love and good feelings. What we project is what becomes real for us.

The Ten Commandments — more accurately translated as the Ten Utterances — begin with "I am Hashem Your God," and concludes, "Do not covet." These two directives are linked. Not coveting, in this context, says Reb Michel of Zlotchov, is not so much a commandment as an end result, a positive consequence of adhering to the previous nine. Otherwise, how could there be a commandment with regards to covetous feelings? The connection between the first and last of the utterances is obvious: Where consciousness of Hashem, which is wholeness, is lacking, there will be a void and a craving to fill this void. One will then seek false satisfaction in coveted objects or experiences. On the other hand, when we make Hashem present in our lives, the resulting satisfaction and wholeness will outshine any covetous feelings.

When accumulating objects for accumulation's sake, one's happiness becomes dependent on owning things. Then things actually own the person and not the other way around. But happiness can only be derived from who we are, not what we have. Simply put, satisfaction wells up in a life of integrity, being at one with our authentic self and letting our actions flow according to its inner guidance.

SYNOPSIS:CHAPTER 4
Take Control

Mitzvah means 'connection'; cheit means 'missing' or disconnecting from one's true self, from others, and from the Divine Source of power. With the first choice to compromise one's integrity, one opens the door to a habit of poor decision-making. This can prove quite challenging to overcome. Destructive actions gradually erode one's integrity, narrow one's perspective and desensitize one to goodness.

We can turn all of this around and sense the true goodness in life, when we begin to master ourselves through the path of teshuvah.

PRACTICE

CONTROL YOUR INTAKE

Thoughts, words and actions of a given kind lead to more thoughts, words and actions of the same kind. In order to focus or harness our instincts and desires, we must regain control of ourselves on the deep level of our psyche where habit becomes ingrained.

Patterns of alienation that inform our thoughts and actions can be sparked by images and sounds in our environment that we unknowingly ingest. One way to nurture positive patterns in your subconscious mind is to filter the messages coming in, whether they are seen, heard or sensed. This means protecting your eyes and ears from unwanted and harmful images and sounds.

A positive and holy image or sound is one that brings you to a place of deeper connection with yourself, with others and with Hashem. Harmful images and sounds sow seeds of alienation, strife, separation between people and a lack of mindfulness of the presence of the Creator. Stop and consider the real inner effects of images and messages you imbibe from the media you use, whether it is newspapers, the internet, advertisements, books or music. Experiment with ways of minimizing your exposure to negative content.

EGO & TRANSCENDENCE:
The Nature of Who We Are

T here is a measure of insanity within each of us, which steers us into places and situations that promise momentary satisfaction. In the language of the Gemarah, this driving force is called a *ru'ach shtus*, 'spirit of folly'. This state of temporary insanity has room to function where there is an underlying belief in *pirud*, 'separation'. A ru'ach shtus can create for us a false self-image and drive us to act as someone we are not. It is a distortion of the human ego.

If something is 'foolish' it strays from what is 'normal'. A clown, for example, makes us laugh with his 'foolish' dress, mannerisms and actions, because they contrast sharply or unexpectedly with what we consider normal. *Keri* means 'involuntary act', and is a common term in Torah implying 'unintentional transgression' (e.g. Vayikra, 26:21). A *keri* is an unexpected, unpremeditated act that strays from the normal, healthy course of life.

When our sages equate a negative act with foolishness it is hinting to us that sin deviates from our essential nature. Negativity is antithetical to the reality of the soul; it is not normal for a creature of Hashem. One word for 'transgression' is *aveirah*, which is derived from the root *avar*, 'to pass over', to go to the other side. When doing an *aveirah*, a person 'changes sides' or crosses a boundary within himself. To trespass the borders of your innate sanity is to enter into a foreign and dangerous realm of dissociation. It is extremely foolish to act in conflict with your inner essence, to defect from the Divine spark of your soul.

The inclination to surrender to the automaton-like life of the ego is part of the fabric of a human being. If a person organizes his life around survival instincts, his behavior will conform to the selfishness of the ego, that superficial layer of self which tends to interpret everything and everyone as an extension of itself. If, by contrast, we organize our life around the Infinite Source of Life then our behavior will follow the transcendent dimension of self. This behavior will have beneficial effects on everything and everyone. The choice is ours whether to approach life from an egocentric basis, or from a place of holistic and integrative transcendence.

Traditionally, these two states or dimensions of self are referred to as the *yetzer ha-ra*, 'the negative inclination' or selfish impulse, and the *yetzer ha-tov*, the 'good inclination' or selfless impulse (Berachos, 61a). The word *yetzer* is from the root word *yatzar*, 'to form or construct', and is related to the faculty of the 'Will' — as in freewill. We continuously form the person we are through the choices we make.

In the Genesis of our world, the Torah tells us that the Creator beheld Creation, and "it was very good" (Bereishis, 1:31). The sages of the Midrash interpret "very good" as a reference to our egocentric impulse, for this inclination is what urges us to do good things such as build our home, marry, and raise a family. Indeed, it is quite healthy and adaptive to make provisions for our own survival, and to secure material abundance and safety for ourselves and for our loved ones. Such activities are especially appropriate in the earlier decades of life. If we refused to give expression to this natural inclination, survival responses and anxiety would debilitate us by holding us hostage to the lower levels of physical, mental and spiritual functioning.

Once our needs for survival have been met, we are able to explore the subtler, more spiritual realms of our being. The Vilna Gaon, writes that a good preservative for fine wine is the dregs, when they settle to the bottom of the barrel and do not rise up; similarly, the *yetzer*, when settled and secure, serves as a reservoir of energy for our lives in this world. If the task of this inclination is to help sustain life, it is the task of the higher self to harness, limit it, and steer it towards supporting our higher functioning. Ultimately, we should make the ego transparent to the soul, so it will function as an instrument of our transcendent inclination.

If the converse occurs, and we meekly surrender to the ego, the laws of inertia dictate that our uncontrolled selfishness will lead first to seemingly innocuous vice, and finally to obviously pernicious behavior. When a totally selfish person needs to eat and does not have the means or the will to properly acquire food, he will think nothing of stealing or threatening another's wellbeing to meet his needs.

Again, evil is not intrinsic to the nature of the ego. The ego only has an inclination for survival. The exaggeration, misalignment or stagnation of its survival instincts is what transforms the ego into an instrument of evil. When tamed and directed toward fulfilling our spiritual needs, the *yetzer* is not 'ra', rather it is a tool that can help generate an abundance of strength and striving. Another name for this level of self is 'the animal soul', in that it acts instinctively and reflexively, seeking to protect and promote its own life and genetics. The animal soul is like an ox that we need to muzzle and yoke.

In order to protect the self from others, the ego emphasizes the perception of 'otherness'. Unchecked, this perception becomes contrived, projecting an experience of reality as a series of separate entities, unrelated to each other and independent of the Creator. This is the paradigm of *tzimtzum*, the opaque prism of 'contraction', concealment, limitation and *pirud* or 'separateness'. When separation is the only mode of consciousness available, one is fundamentally in conflict with others and even within oneself. One can experience an inner eclipsing of the transcendent.

The transcendence-centered *yetzer ha-tov* beholds reality the way it truly is. It sees that the diversity of the physical universe is interconnected and permeated by *achdus*, the 'oneness' of the Creator. In this mode of consciousness, it is seen that *tzimtzum lo k'peshuto*, 'the concept of Divine concealment is not literal.' Concealment and separation appears on the surface, but is transparent to an underlying awareness of the absolute unity both above and within Creation.

These two forces are the root cause of the seemingly inner duality and strife that exists within each one of us. One force instructs the person to seek that which seems rewarding in the moment. It is the consciousness that observes reality through the prism of a three-dimensional apparatus and, therefore, it pursues the image, the immediate and the materialistic. While the other force is connected to the Transcendent, thus beholding the entire picture, peering into past, present and future and the vastness of all of reality.

The quintessence of separation-consciousness is *avodah zarah* or 'idolatry'. In idol worship, one takes a 'something' to be the 'Everything'; an individual image or concept is separated from reality and held up as the whole. The Tanya says every sin or negative act is embedded in *avodah zarah*. This is because such an act serves an immediate impulse or desire, without consideration for the fact that every cause has an effect and everything is interconnected. The doer's scope is limited to the moment, and there is a blind disregard for oneself and others.

To clarify: limiting one's scope to the present moment is the opposite of the liberating spiritual condition of 'being in the now' that we mentioned in earlier chapters. There are two distinct ways of living in the now, with a vast difference between the two. One is to live '*for* the now', and the other is to live '*in* the now'. To live *for* the now is to be limited to the now. This may mean to act spontaneously, yet with no consideration for the motivation or outcome of one's actions. It is to discard intentionality, openness, awareness and responsibility. To live *in* the now is to behold the eternally expansive present, which transcends but also encompasses past and future, cause and effect. This authentic presence includes and integrates mindful clarity, morality, responsibility and accountability.

'Living in the now' is deeper than merely being with what is *happening* in this moment. It is being present with the fullness of the 'now' itself. Happenings are the content, which occurs in the space of the context —

which is now. The now is an infinite openness that contains all finite expressions, experiences and occurrences. Now-ness is a portal into all-inclusive wisdom, love and aliveness.

Idol worship can also be understood as 'idle' worship; meaning a form of attention and attachment which does not serve our growth, refinement or evolution, but merely serves to reinforce our constricted status quo. An 'idle worshipper' idles his time away, not going anywhere, stuck in a limited 'now' that excludes past and future. In this condition of closed consciousness and functioning, one seeks to satisfy any and every urge as it appears. Gratifying selfish urges may sometimes feel satisfying, but only fleetingly. Ultimately, grasping for passing phenomena is counterproductive and detrimental to the wholeness of the self.

A classic work on ethics, the *Sheivet ha-Musar*, suggests that the way we can know whether the motive of an act is positive or negative is to observe how we feel after the act. If we feel empowered and filled with a sense of inner peace, it indicates that the act emanated from a pure, selfless source, our truer self. Even if we feel jubilant while engaged in an act, if we feel disillusioned or disempowered afterwards, it usually indicates that the act came from an ungodly motive, sourced in our superficial egoself.

Reb Levi Yitzchak of Berdichev taught that during the act itself we should make an honest observation whether or not we sense a heightened and expansive cognition. This would indicate the activation and engagement of our higher soul. If we feel shrunken and more constricted during the act, it would indicate ego involvement. Taking note of the source of our actions helps with decision-making. These litmus tests can help us gauge whether or not we are being true to ourselves or not.

When we do not know whether or not we should to do something, and if there is no clear direction in the Torah, says the Ramban, we should try to remove from the picture any consideration for our personal pleasure. Then we can more easily evaluate the decision from an impartial and open intelligence. We could ask ourselves: "Aside from the sensory or immediate pleasure I will experience from this action, is it for the best? Does it serve the greater good? Does it bring me closer to my highest self and to Hashem? Does it make me more sensitive and available to the needs of others? Or does it merely satisfy a temporary desire, and ultimately separate me from where, who, how and what I want to be?"

Selfishness breeds contempt for anyone who stands in the way of its goals. It creates an inability to deal with other people, except as utilitarian extensions of its own will. Ultimately, selfishness gives rise to loneliness and depression. Even when negativity does not seem to lead to confusion, anguish, or to an absence of inner tranquility, it still limits one's perspective and does not allow one to appreciate the whole of life. Selfishness disables the opportunity to experience life from a place of transcendence, where everything is wonderfully interwoven and connected to its Creator.

What is remarkable about all of this is that so-called 'inner strife' is to a large degree illusory and self-generated. Even the egotistic inclination is, in reality, nothing more than a Divine messenger hiding behind a mask of darkness (Zohar, 2:163a). The ego's purpose is to challenge us in our commitment to righteousness and thereby strengthen our resolve for goodness.

Let us understand this through a parable offered by Reb Yakov Yosef of Polnoye:

> Once, a mighty king who ruled over the entire world desired to test his subjects' loyalty. So he sent one of his trusted servants to go around to the various lands and pretend to stir up a revolution. In some of the countries he was successful, while in lands more loyal to the king, they fought him until he left. Yet, in one wise land the people saw through their beloved king's scheme and realized that it was only a ploy to test their loyalty.

'Faker' would be the best way to describe the negative inclination. There are those who welcome it and go along with the revolt, foolishly surrendering to the ego. Others view the evil inclination as an enemy and declare war against it, hoping to destroy it. The wise sense the ruse and recognize their beloved King's scheme. For them, the 'war' is won without a battle. By revealing the identity of the enemy, the enemy vanishes.

When we turn on a light, the darkness dissolves.

What we choose to believe in is real for us. If, through belief, we endow our ego with an independent substance, we will be forced either to give into it or struggle against it. Rather than view the ego as an adversary, we can begin to realize that there is 'only You', only the One. All of our challenges and struggles are merely masks on the face of Oneness, and the moment we recognize this truth, they disappear.

There are no independent forces in the universe. In fact, there is no real separate, independent and autonomous 'I'. The 'I' of '*Anochi Hashem*, 'I am Hashem', alone is expressed through the individual 'I' of human consciousness. There is only one 'I', for *Anochi* is all there is. By coming to the realization that the Divine Self is the only real self, we recognize that the egoic 'I' is a minor, but vital, actor in the play of life. When recognized as a mere supporting role, the ego can become a useful tool in opening us up to the magnificence of being human.

This recognition is a deeper level of teshuvah, a return to the true 'I'. We were laboring under the false premise of separation, assuming that ourselves and others have separate, independent existences. Now our consciousness returns to the world of Unity. The ego is not destroyed in this process, however. It is only the ego's identification as a separate, alienated entity that is destroyed or nullified. The self is real, but through teshuvah it becomes transparent to its true Identity, as an expression of the Unity of Hashem, *Anochi*.

SYNOPSIS:CHAPTER 5
Don't Fool Yourself

Whenever we do something harmful to ourselves or others, especially if we do it deliberately, there is a rending of the fabric of our lives. The natural consequence is that we begin to suffocate spiritually. The harshest 'punishment' is not *for* the act, but *by* the act itself. Over time, a sense of deep loss and loneliness can creep in; we can feel completely cut off from life. These consequences are alarms, calling us to realize that their cause is the ego, the seemingly separate 'I'. The ego operates under false pretenses to prompt us to fall or regress. In reality, however, there is no separate 'I', there is only the One Divine 'I' living through each one of us. When we realize this truth, the possibility of teshuvah opens to us.

PRACTICE

MEDITATE ON THE DIVINE 'I'

Contemplate the revealed phrase, Ein od mi-l'vado, *'There is nothing else but Hashem alone,' (Devarim, 4:35): It is all 'You' — all One — all G-d!*

These words can resonate through your consciousness at all times. To begin, set aside at least a few moments a day to concentrate on this truth, perhaps as you are reciting the *Shema* or unwinding from the day. Certainly, whenever you feel yourself drawn toward negativity, meditate on *Ein od mi-l'vado*, and dissolve your separate self into the Divine Self.

CHAPTER SIX

The Meaning of
TESHUVAH

T he Hebrew word *teshuvah* has traditionally been translated as 'repentance' or 'penitence'. Like all translations, these are only partially
correct. The meaning of teshuvah includes and transcends these definitions. It is difficult to compress its vast implications into one English
word or phrase, but more accurate translations would be 'returning',
'turning', 'integrating' or even better, 'reintegrating'. Teshuvah restores the
human being to the state of *being human*, to the state of integration within
oneself and with the Source.

When translated as 'returning', teshuvah implies that there is an origin from which one was exiled, and to which one can return. What is this
origin? It is one's own deepest self. While being led down into exile, the
master Prophet says, "And *I* was within the exile" (Yechezkel, 1:1). The
most devastating forms of exile are the estrangement from the 'I' — oneself, and estrangement from the 'I' or heart of the community. Teshuvah
begins when we decide to reclaim our rightful place in relation to 'I'.

The Zohar divides the word *teshuvah* into two parts: *tashuv*, 'return', and the letter *hei* which is an abbreviation of the name of Hashem (Zohar, 3:122a). When we consider what it means to 'return the *hei*' to our lives, we can appreciate the discrepancy between the terms teshuvah and 'repentance'. While the latter is concerned with iniquity, i.e. recognition of error, regret and changing one's course of action, *teshuvah* is primarily concerned with the inner process of reintegrating Hashem's Presence more deeply within our consciousness. Teshuvah's embrace thus includes individuals who are upright, noble and righteous. The path of return to greater authenticity is without end or limit.

All souls embodied within physical form yearn for teshuvah. Enfolded within body and ego, the soul longs for transcendence, to return to its Divine root. Yet the soul acknowledges the body's purpose, and so the souls return is not through expiring from the physical realm and soaring upwards. On the contrary, the soul returns to the spark of Divinity *within* and through the body, permeating all layers of self, embracing physical existence as a vehicle to actualize the infinite powers of its Essence.

Turning away — cultivating alienation or abandoning authenticity — is the opposite of teshuvah. The journey of teshuvah alleviates the dreadful feeling of not being the right person or not being in the right place, and restores a sense of authenticity. However, in the initial stages, teshuvah may seem to increase a person's feelings of loneliness and discord. Aligning our thoughts, feelings and actions with the protocol of our truest self is not easy. This realignment requires profound sensitivity, awareness, and honesty regarding our inner desires, intentions and needs. One often needs to sift through many competing desires and demands emanating from the disparate parts of one's personality structure. This penetrating and fluid sense of self-consciousness is difficult enough, and it is only the beginning of the path of return. However, it is the foundation.

As teshuvah is a genuine homecoming, the route taken is singular and inimitable, according to the uniqueness of every individual. Since no two people are alike, the return to self is a one-of-a-kind experience, tailored according to each person's deepest needs. Teshuvah inspires a coming to life from a place of integration and purpose — *our* purpose.

On our journey through life we may look to other travelers for assistance, advice, encouragement or inspiration, but ultimately we must follow our own road. We may observe the accomplishments and setbacks of others, but we can only grow according to our own range of comfort and challenge. Blazing our own trail might be more difficult than imitating another's, but it is ultimately the only way to be true to ourselves. This is the 'longer, shorter' way: it is 'longer' in that on it we may encounter more tests and doubts and times of loneliness, but it shorter in that it is the only route leading all the way to our destination.

There is also a 'shorter, longer' road. Riding someone else's wave might seem shorter in that it seems easier and more known, but it is actually 'longer' since it won't take us all the way to our destination. We will eventually have to change direction and take our own road, anyway.

When Avraham first heard the Divine call telling him to embark upon his journey, *Lech Lecha*, "Go (for/to/by) yourself" (Bereishis, 12:1), he understood that going "for" himself was for his own benefit, and going "to" himself and "by" himself was to be a lonely journey to self-discovery. No two souls' purposes are identical, and each of us needs to find our own optimal path.

Your journey of teshuvah is yours alone. You do not need to compare your journey to another's. Of course, it is vital to find a solid community of like-minded people, a spiritual home where you feel welcomed and recognized for who you are. When you are surrounded by people who value the journey of teshuvah, you will be encouraged to pursue this path. Still, you will need to own your distinct life journey and purpose, and face your own challenges. Do not measure your growth in comparison to others, even within community. Measure your growth in terms of your own life.

Teshuvah is coming home to our real home, and in truth we are always coming home even when we feel that we are leaving. When you leave your home, no matter how far you are traveling, you are still moving toward home. Life is not only linear but also cyclical. In a circle, any movement away from a starting point is, despite appearances, also a movement toward the point of origin. In teshuvah we access this 'circle' reality and therefore teshuvah can repair the past, as will be explained later on. From the 'circle' perspective, we are always moving toward home.

Teshuvah, translated as 'return', can imply a return to a state we inhabited previously, perhaps when we were younger. It can also imply a process of returning to the cultural practices of our collective heritage. Despite lacking a Torah upbringing, one can reconnect to his spiritual roots, to a place he never consciously knew, but always belonged.

To return to your Jewishness means returning to your natural, perhaps even genetically patterned, spiritual self-expression. Many who have embarked upon a path of teshuvah attest to the feeling of rediscovering something they were always looking for. Often one has a sense of homecoming through a certain place, community, practice, or spiritual understanding of life. In any case, through this innate path, you can return to your deeper soul uniqueness, and reattach to your quintessential self.

Such a personal transformation has cosmic repercussions, generating a positive effect in the world at large, and contributing to the healing of the world's ailments and fragmentation.

As explored earlier, the word *teshuv-ah* is a *tashuv* or 'return' of, or to, the *hei*, the Divine Presence. Through an *aveira* or 'transgression' we *aver* or 'cross over' our own inner *hei*, diminishing and eclipsing our inner core and divine self, and as a result we diminish the revealed presence of Hashem in the world at large. When we embark on the path of teshuvah, by reclaiming our inner *hei*, we restore authenticity and integrity within. Then, there is an analogous elevation of the fallen, eclipsed *hei* throughout the world.

Our sages tell us that the ingathering of the scattered parts of our self inspires an ingathering of a fragmented world, bringing creation closer to a state of unification and perfection (Yumah, 86a-b). A chaotic condition of the external world is a mirror image of the disunity of the internal world. Through unifying the internal dynamic, the world at large will also be healed. Our thoughts, words and actions add to the revelation of Divine Presence throughout space and time.

SYNOPSIS: CHAPTER 6
Retain Individuality in Your Return

Teshuvah means to return to who we really are, to the purity residing within. The teshuvah journey we take is personal and one-of-
a-kind, a result of the uniqueness of our soul. The process of
teshuvah is customized according to each person's deepest needs.

PRACTICE

PRACTICE EQUANIMITY

Often times, people are overly affected by the opinions of the society in
which they are surrounded, basing their sense of self-worth and value on
second-hand observations. Sadly, many people are merely a collection of
the impressions they have made on others. This is living from the outside
in.

*In order to maintain the individuality and composure of your essential
self, to follow your own journey, you must practice* hishtavus *or 'equanimity'.* Hishtavus *is a state in which everything is equal, and you are
unaffected by praise or scorn.*

Begin now to live from a place of hishtavus. Take a few moments for introspection and ask yourself: do I need others' praise to feel good? Without praise, do I feel insignificant? From where do I gain my sense of
worth? Take a few moments to imagine yourself doing something truly
noble. While entertaining an image of yourself at your finest, ask yourself: Am I looking to see if someone else is observing me? When others
shower me with compliments, how do I feel about myself? When no one
is observing me, how do I feel about myself? When nobody knows of the
good deeds I do, how do I do them? Do I value these deeds?

CHAPTER SEVEN

QUESTIONS & ANSWERS:
Striking a Balance

Another definition of the word *teshuvah* is 'response' or 'answer'.
This implies that there is first a question or a need in one's life, and
then an answer, which is teshuvah. The questions that call forth teshuvah
are the deepest questions of life. For example, what is the meaning and
purpose of my existence? Why is life so difficult? Why does suffering
exist? Am I alone? Who am I? Such questions have always vexed human
beings, causing them to turn inward in hopes of finding solace.

The optimum response to suffering is teshuvah's movement toward
wholeness, equanimity and spiritual self-sufficiency. There are many for
whom turning to Hashem is an act of desperation. Pain, depression, loneliness or alienation cause many to search for something larger than themselves for meaning, direction, purpose, and peace. Suffering can break
down the ego's resistance to the experience of the Transcendent. Tragedy,
even more than joy, seems to bring people closer to spirituality, introspection and self-evaluation. Oftentimes, happy experiences reinforce arrogance. How many people trace their discovery of Hashem to a tragedy or
time of need? How many can trace their downfall to 'high times'?

The process of teshuvah is often ignited because one's desire for renovation is in accordance with the measure of his devastation. Slowly, however, teshuvah becomes more than a knee-jerk reaction. On a deeper level, teshuvah is not a derivative of desperation, rather it is an expression of our underlying self-worth. Teshuvah is a healthy response to life, a full acceptance of self-accountability.

On the other hand, before every stage of spiritual growth, there is a void, a need. This is because every *yesh* or 'phenomenon' is preceded by *ayin*, a state of 'emptiness'. For something truly new to appear there must be a moment when 'what is' ceases to be — there must be a shedding of the old. Just as a seed rots in the earth before it can produce new life, our old, stagnant, detrimental self-image must dissolve before our new image can emerge. Even if this dissolution is not brought about by intense suffering, the emptiness can seem uncomfortable or disorienting.

Ultimately, when a new, higher self emerges, there is another stage in which we must reintegrate the past within this higher level. The new yesh is thus fully unified with one's entire being. On the other hand, the process of teshuvah does not usually progress in a smooth, linear fashion. At some points, it may seem easier to simply let go and forget about the old. Yet, unification and integration of the old is ultimately what we desire. We need to repeatedly upgrade our aspiration in order to pass through ups and downs and finally reach the state of true wholeness within which all aspects of our life are integrated.

Responding to life positively does not translate to possessing all the answers to life's tricky or troubling questions. A popular misconception is that for 'non-believers' there are only questions and for 'true believers', only answers. The serenity of someone who has faith does not indicate the end of questioning. Once meaning and higher purpose are found, life may become more serene or energized, but by no means do seeming challenges or obstacles disappear. On the contrary, once a sense of wholeness is found, the need for inquiry can become even more acute, and personal involvement with the world can become even more compelling.

Even if spiritual belief makes life seem more challenging, it is also more stimulating, both intellectually and emotionally. This is because when there is an outlet or an address to which doubts and uncertainties can be directed, questions may arise more frequently and intensely. The spiritual impulse towards teshuvah is such that the more we know, the more we acknowledge what is still beyond knowing. Each time a peak is scaled, the horizon is expanded. The hunger to know and draw closer to Hashem blossoms precisely within this new open space of unknowing.

Within the realm of answers, we find our own distinct comfort zone, according to our physical, intellectual, and spiritual constitution. We set our own organizing principles for life and discover answers within that context. For example, some people are comfortable viewing death as a positive transformation from a state of body into a state of soul. Others say that death is to be accepted as a part of the cycle of life, which includes death and suffering. Still others view death as a goad that drives them to inquire into the nature and purpose of life. Regardless of their answers, everyone is to some degree troubled by the question 'why do we die?'

It is the misalignment in which we live; it is our spiritual *galus* or exile, that puts us in a constant quandary, writes Rabbi Tzvi Elimelech of Dinov. Questions, dilemmas, and enigmas are endemic to the human condition. When we are not grounded in a commitment to a higher power, insecurity, fear and disorientation result. Under such circumstances, the quest for answers may become futile or even meaningless. Teshuvah, however, is the 'answer' that can break through the most opaque questions and dilemmas.

Teshuvah includes both answers and questions as valuable ingredients. Living in the answer, while forgetting the question that gave birth to it, will cause the answer to become mechanical, habitual, or dispirited. Conversely, living only in the question can lead to confusing or debilitating uncertainty and ambiguity. We need both.

Every answer leads to a deeper question; each peak that we scale opens a wider panorama. Every thesis carries with it an antithesis, which calls forth a greater synthesis, until that synthesis leads to a new thesis, *ad infinitum*. Such is the course of human, intellectual and spiritual development: tension and resolve. On a personal level, what may satisfy our intellect today may not and should not satisfy us tomorrow.

To live creatively and skillfully, this dialectical tension between answers and questions must be continuous. Furthermore, answers and questions must be authentic. An integral part of a deeply authentic answer is the recognition that not all questions can be answered; the intellect will not always be appeased. An authentic answer also welcomes further questions.

There are authentic and inauthentic questions. An authentic question is one asked for the purpose of delving into the unknown and procuring clarity. In contrast, an inauthentic question is asked just for the sake of asking; the answer is already formulated in the asker's mind as a rationale for whatever he finds preferable.

"Any argument for the sake of Heaven *sofah l'hiskayam* (in the end will be established)," teaches the Mishnah, "while any argument that is not for the sake of Heaven, *ein sofah l'hiskayam* (in the end will not be established)" (Avos, 5:20). Here, "to be established" means to yield lasting fruits. How do we know if a question is authentic — for the sake of Heaven — or not? If 'in the end', the question is 'established', it will yield the fruit of an answer. A question is fruitful when it contains the seed of the answer. Exile can be fruitful when it calls forth teshuvah.

A question "for the sake of Heaven" also yields the fruit of unity between the questioner and answerer. For example, a human questioner and the Divine answerer will be drawn into a greater unity through the dialectic tension itself. A question "not for the sake of Heaven", on the other hand, is fundamentally divisive. Such a question does not deserve to be answered, because the asker is not truly seeking new understanding. This question should be ignored or overcome, but not with an answer because an authentic answer will not satisfy the questioner. Answering such a question will only yield a deeper state of exile.

Authentic questions and arguments that are aimed at reaching a deeper understanding, writes the Chasam Sofer, are the root of true peace. The word *machlokes*, 'argument', has a numerical value of 578, which is the same value as the phrase *shalom rav*, 'great peace'.

On the deepest level of unity, all the answers we so direly seek are contained within us from the very beginning. When we are out-of-touch with 'who we are', we cannot find our inner answers, and we are plagued by doubt, worry and uncertainty. Teshuvah is to return to who we are in the most profound way, to the essence of our soul. From there, we reach a space where paradox is tolerable; where anomaly is mysteriously reasonable. This is a place of *Keser*, the 'crown', or *ayin*, the Divine 'non-being', the origin in which all opposites are unified and everything is possible. In this realm of paradoxes, questions flourish, yet there is an inner pleasure, a blissful sense of being in love with it all.

It may be difficult to live comfortably in this realm of paradoxes, except though brief peak experiences. Most people settle for a few moments of the tension of paradox, and then quickly return to the comfort of resolution. To maintain the state of paradox takes great equanimity. The symbol of this is a circle, where all points are equidistant from the center; exile and redemption are essentially of equal value. The more common path is of a linear paradigm: we move from questions to answers, and from exile to redemption. The circular perspective and the linear perspective are both true and valid expressions of teshuvah.

From the vantage point of paradox, however, a person functions from a wonderful place of freedom, of teshuvah, of Divine purpose and meaning. Even if one feels stuck, one has access to the tools to get unstuck, and one feels empowered and able. In this state of teshuvah, the dark cloud of personal exile has parted and there is an opening up of tremendous potential, an ability to take charge of life and live fully, with mindfulness and purpose. The question is transparent to the answer; exile is transparent to redemption.

SYNOPSIS: CHAPTER 7
Grow Constantly

There is constant oscillation in the world as we know it. We should never feel as if we have arrived at our final destination. We should continue to pose challenging questions. Such questions are invaluable because they move us forward. If we are not moving forward, we are falling backwards. An answer on one level will lead to a question on a higher level, which will demand the discovery of a new answer.

Do not feel bad for having questions; on the contrary, let your questions open you up to deeper answers. Even if you have had setbacks on your journey, recognize that these can also propel you forward. Challenge yourself to continuously learn more and grow in understanding. The Chidushei Harim says, that when he first came to study with the Kotzker Rebbe, the Kotzker told him, "Come, and I will tell you what a *chassid* is. A chassid is someone who asks himself "Why?"

We should never ever stop asking questions. The moment you stop asking you are no longer being honest with yourself, and you are not truly alive.

PRACTICE
ASK QUESTIONS

Whenever you feel jaded, bored or uninspired, challenge yourself. Ask the deepest question that you can conceive. If an answer comes, question further and further, until your consciousness shifts and your understanding expands.

CHAPTER EIGHT

Hope
IN THE PLACE
of Emptiness

T eshuvah demands letting go of the old and a taking on of the new; it is a journey of shedding and discarding the past, and opening up to the present. It is like changing out of old clothes and putting on fresh ones. In order for a seed to sprout and 'reveal' itself as a fruit-bearing tree, the seed must first shed its original form. All growth comes from a state of decomposition. As long as we maintain our fixed self-images and negative habits, we can never truly grow.

It is common for people to feel an initial high after ridding themselves of outdated, decomposing states, but then a paradoxical sense of uncertainty or darkness can set in. Even when teshuvah is well underway, one may experience a gloomy sense of impasse, with no exit or clarity in sight. In order to grow, we may first need to descend into a darker place, a place of emptiness, confusion or seeming gridlock, and only then may we ascend into a new place of fulfillment, clarity and freedom.

For example, one may have a feeling of being trapped in a wasteland where the old self no longer exists, but there is not yet the comfort of a newly revealed self. This is because in between every *yesh* state of 'being' there is an *ayin* state of 'non-being'. In the *ayin* state, there is no going back to the previous *yesh* which is already dismantled, but neither is there moving forward, since the new *yesh* has not yet fully emerged. One must not despair during this temporary stage of 'nothingness'. We need to pass through this darkness to attain new light. Indeed, there is no brilliance like that which comes out of darkness.

In the beginning and lower stages of teshuvah there can be strong elements of confusion. The word *teshuvah* includes the letters that spell the words *tohu u'vohu*, 'chaos and emptiness' or void and confusion. The letter shin in *teshuvah* conceptually stands for *choshech*, 'darkness', a state in which one cannot find himself. The pain of letting go of the old may intensify this state of disorientation. Many times, the path to our inner Heaven, our inner bliss, leads through our inner *Gehinnom*, or torment. And yet, it is through this place of *ayin*, this womb of darkness and contraction, that light is birthed.

Furthermore, it is often precisely when we are immersed in a state of *ayin* that the realization occurs that we *can* actually transform. The desire to transform may emerge in a state of light and clarity, or when we are taking an honest look at ourselves, and deciding that we want to change. The realization, however, that it is possible to change frequently occurs within the place of ayin.

To discuss the reality of *ayin* we will employ the image of a *mikvah*, or 'ritual bath' of living water. A person immerses in a mikvah to re-attain ritual purity, or to attain a higher level of purity. For example, some have the custom to immerse before Shabbos, in between shedding the garments of the weekday and donning the garments of Shabbos.

It is the desire to transform and become pure that brings us to a mikvah in the first place. Then, when immersed and nullified within the waters, we have a glimpse of infinite potentiality. The word *mikvah* can also be translated as a place of *kaveh*, 'hope'. Within the womb or *ayin* of the mikvah, we have hope that we will emerge transformed, as a new *yesh*.

While 'day' represents the natural, normal and predictable, the dark-

ness and uncertainty of 'night' represents the dream of unlimited potential. In the darkness of night, a time of 'not knowing', we can believe in
the 'impossible' and hope for the miraculous. Paradoxically, when our life
is crystal clear and we feel we know the future, there is no room left for
imagination and dreaming, and thus there is no real possibility for genuine growth. Only in the complete darkness of *ayin* do all possibilities
exist.

If we ever feel rejected and alone, confused or empty, we can intentionally tap into the dark 'mikvah' of *ayin*. In this place we may be able to
hear the question that Hashem asked Adam: *Ayeka*, "Where are you"
(Bereishis, 3:9)? Where are you — what are you doing with your life? If
you are feeling down, hear this call to move upward, to transform.

Earlier, we translated *teshuvah* as 'answer'. This 'answer' is not about
having an answer *for* God, or claiming to understand the Creator's actions or apparent inaction in this world. Nor is it finding intellectual answers to life's vexing questions. Teshuvah, rather, is about responding *to*
God regarding the gift of life that was given to us. We must respond to
the inner call, the essential question that challenges us and invites us to
truly come alive: *Ayeka?*

The proper response to the question *ayeka*, as demonstrated numerous times in the Torah, is *Hineini*, "I am here" — I am present and fully
aware. I am all here. *Ayeka* is thus to be answered with our entire being
— with the way we choose to live and interpret life spiritually, emotionally and physically. The 'I' who answers the question *Ayeka* is the deeper
'I', for that is the one to whom the question is posed. Our answer, our
teshuvah, is to uncover the *hineini* of this deeper 'I' within — to make
manifest the transcendent aspect of our Divine image that was issued to
us at birth.

The Midrash Rabba teaches, "A heavenly voice rings forth each day
to awaken mankind to teshuvah." This Divine voice is a spiritual cen-
tripetal force attracting human beings to release the fragmentation and
splintering of their selves, to enter their core, and to reintegrate and
awaken. Whether this voice of inspiration comes directly from a realm
beyond our normal self-experience, or through psychophysical experi-

ences and life situations, or from our own deeper sense of knowing, the call of teshuvah invites us to respond with zest and strength.

Teshuvah is a dynamic state of being in which we are always becoming. It is a never-ending journey. We are not meant to arrive at a destination and settle into complacent comfort or smug satisfaction. We are meant to constantly move, stretch and mature. The term *taharah*, 'purity', is associated with movement, fluidity, and thus evolution. *Tumah* — usually translated as 'impurity', but really meaning 'blocked' — alludes to living in a fixed state of bondage, stagnation and conditionality. This is why a mikvah must be a gathering of flowing, moving, 'living' water. When we 'purify' ourselves by immersing in a mikvah, we take on the spiritual counterparts of those flowing qualities. There is always movement in 'purity'; there is always hope in evolving, advancing and becoming.

In the daily order of prayers there is a prayer that is traditionally translated as follows: "Pardon us, our Father, for we have sinned; forgive us, our King, for we have transgressed." This prayer for forgiveness follows a prayer for wisdom, knowledge and understanding. The meaning of this sequence is that whenever we achieve a new level of wisdom and understanding, we are able to see our past behavior from a higher, more expansive perspective. We are then able to notice subtle inconsistencies even in thoughts, words and actions that we previously considered 'pure'. We naturally respond by shedding the previous level of behavior. With greater awareness comes greater understanding of our true potential.

This perpetual evolution and refinement of consciousness keeps us from falling into the trap of stagnant self-satisfaction. With every new day lived, we can have greater expansion of awareness and understanding, and we can grasp greater opportunities for evolution. Every step we take upwards and inwards gives us more hope that we can continue reaching toward our higher potential. We gain hope in making a brighter future, not only for ourselves, but for the whole world as well.

In the broadest definition, there are two types of people: those who are full of hope and optimism, and those who lack hope and optimism. Someone who expresses the belief that what has been done is done and nothing can or will ever change, is in that moment a *rasha*, a 'conduit of negativity'. Torah says, "Distant from the *rasha* is salvation" (Tehillim, 119:155). Such a person has distanced himself from salvation in that moment of pessimism. By contrast, someone who expresses hope, even when there were or are negative occurrences, is in that moment a *tzadik*, a 'conduit of righteousness'. With reference to the tzadik, Torah says, "My salvation is soon to come" (Yeshaya, 56:1). This person recognizes the always-present opportunity to redirect his life, grow, and bring salvation near.

We can make a brighter future for ourselves and for the world when we distinguish *taharah*, 'purity' from *tumah*, 'impurity', and the *tzadik*, 'righteous one' from the *rasha* 'evil one'.

SYNOPSIS: CHAPTER 8
Be Hopeful

Moving forward and growing is preceded by a stage of letting go of the old. When you let go, there is a moment when you seem to have nothing. Every new *yesh* or level of 'existence' is preceded by a stage of *ayin*, 'nothingness' and emptiness. We should recognize this stage as part of a process of growth, otherwise we may become disempowered, or worse, feel as if we are hopelessly regressing. On the contrary: it is often precisely in this place of ayin where we realize that we *can* transform.

PRACTICE

READ

Reading stories about the tzadikim can be extremely helpful when you are feeling lost or lacking inspiration. It is also important to read accounts of people who have overcome difficult life challenges, such as baalei teshuvah, *or stories of people who overcame illness, war, or poverty.*

These stories will give you optimism in a graspable form. Although your journey is deeply unique, reading others' journeys of overcoming darkness with purity and joy may help you glimpse higher levels of human potential. This simple practice can have tremendous benefit, inspiring you within your own challenges and helping you to move forward.

CHAPTER
NINE

A Quest for
WHOLENESS

*T*eshuvah, 'answer' or 'response', is to be fully responsive to life. This
requires living from a place of wholeness, and being fully functioning, sensitive and open-minded. Wholeness is utilizing all of our capabilities and potentialities in serving our Creator, our higher self and the
greater good.

The Torah offers a pattern for a fully optimized and integrated way
of life, aligning the *human* with the *being*. This life-pattern is designed to
make complementary what would appear to be divergent energies, so that
we can harmonize our inner conflicts and fuel our actions with complete
authenticity. Torah does not ask us to deny our 'animal' aspect for the
sake of the more spiritual aspects of life. The quest of a Torah life is to
unify the two, the animal with the spiritual, in such a way that each complements the other in a context of growth. Our desires for physical pleasure are to be channeled into a desire to be close to Hashem.

Often incorrectly translated as 'sacrifice', the term *korban* means to
'draw close', and it comes from the root word *kiruv*, 'to bring closer'
(Sefer HaBahir, 109). This implies that our task is not to annihilate the
animal within and offer it up as a 'sacrifice', but rather to bring it closer to

Hashem by utilizing its vast energy for noble causes. What we should be ready to 'sacrifice' or offer up, are the *objects* of our physical desires, while we harness the primal energy of desire itself for spiritual growth.

"An abundance of wheat comes through the power of the ox" (Mishlei, 14:4). Teshuvah is in full force once we are able to mobilize the strength and vibrancy of the "ox", the animal soul, and harness it toward increasing "wheat" or spiritual nourishment. We become whole by coming full circle to our physical drives and integrating all of our past experiences into the present. By thus completing an ingathering of our own small universe, with all of its details, we become an expression of a worldwide ingathering and redemption.

Teshuvah also means 'turning', as in 'turning the page'. We must turn over a new leaf and create a fresh paradigm from which to operate. It is not sufficient, however, to simply create a new standard in our minds, though this is an essential start, since we can't 'turn' without a definite internal shift. Complete teshuvah is a redefinition of self in all aspects, internal and external.

> A young man once complained to his master, the Early Nineteenth Century Chassidic Rebbe, Reb Simcha Bunim of Pshischah, saying that he had read in the holy books that if a person refrains from eating during the day for forty days, Eliyahu ha-Navi, Elijah the Prophet, would reveal himself. "Rebbe, It has already been forty days and the Prophet has not shown up!" The Rebbe looked at him deeply and began to tell him the following story:
>
> > The Baal Shem Tov, as is well known, would travel with *kefitzas ha-derech*, a 'mysterious power that quickens one's path'. A journey that should have taken days would take him but a few hours. Once, the need for a lengthy journey arose. The Baal Shem borrowed strong horses and a wagon and began his miraculous journey. From previous experience, the horses knew that there were many resting areas along the road and they would be fed at each stop.

In amazement, they found themselves traveling on with no need for rest, passing the usual stops. They wondered why they had not been fed. Perhaps, they theorized, they were to be fed at the station where the humans eat; surely they must have become humans! As they also passed by the rest stops for humans, they began to think that perhaps they were not humans either, but angels who have no need to eat at all! At last, the Baal Shem Tov arrived at his destination. The horses were led to the stable where bundles of chaff were laid in front of them. Sure enough, they began to devour their food as any horse would do. By merely refraining from food for a while, concluded Reb Simcha Bunim, one may begin to imagine himself an angel worthy of visitation from the Prophet Eliyahu. The yardstick of spiritual attainment, however, is at the conclusion of the fast, when one is again confronted with food. If one still devours his food uncontrollably or unconsciously, it is proof that at his core he has remained the same horse.

Surface changes affect the external layers of the psyche. An action taken mindlessly and without heart will remain superficial and shallow. Acts of real consequence are expressions of a deeper mode of being. Refraining from over-consumption, or from eating at all, can only refine a person if it is a conscious expression of a deeper purpose. Refraining from food as an end in itself has no value, and a mindless robot can accomplish the same.

Once a young man came to the Magid of Mezritch, Reb DovBer, and began boasting of his piety and the great spiritual heights he had attained. He reported that in the winter, he wore only one thin coat. Additionally, to mortify his body, he would roll in the snow and fast at least three days a week. Hearing this, the Magid walked over to the window and pointed to a horse nearby and said, "That horse too wore only

one thin blanket this winter, it too rolled in the snow, and due
to his poor owner, it too fasted at least three times a week."

"Mankind was created to toil" (Iyov, 5:7). It is imperative for human
beings to work and grow continuously lest they become complacent and
static. There is a force of entropy within our inner spiritual universe,
which draws us toward self-satisfaction. The toil of prayer, self-evaluation, meditation, and a rigorous commitment to growth, reconnect a person to the state of teshuvah. However, "created to toil" does not refer only
to goal-oriented work, for the toil itself is part of the goal. In fact, since
we were "created" for it, our deepest sense of fulfillment comes from the
process of *tzemach* or 'growth' itself. Despite the discomfort of growing,
we are created to be most happy and satisfied when striving and working
on ourselves. We are created to make teshuvah with *simcha*, great 'joy'.

Although we were created with an inherent yearning for perfection,
the deepest part of the self is already perfect. Therefore, our practice of
teshuvah must reflect a balance between our insatiable desire for perfection and the underlying satisfaction we have in the essential perfection of
'what is'. 'Wholeness' integrates states of toil, yearning, joy and unconditional satisfaction.

In a certain way, the *shlemus* or 'perfection' and the *shalom* or 'wholeness' that we so desire are achieved by the very desire to reach them. In
the yearning to be whole, wholeness is found. A part of self is always
shalem, lacking nothing that cannot be found within. Another part of self
is imperfect, yearning for perfection and *tikkun*, 'correction' and repair.
However, this desperate longing for perfection is part of its process of attaining perfection. Teshuvah is more than the power to reach and surpass
our perceived limits. Teshuvah is also the invincible power within our
longing to move toward perfect wholeness.

Throughout the ages, philosophers have debated as to what is more
important: the achievement of desires or the desires themselves. Which is
more significant in creating a healthy and fulfilling life — having ambi-
tions or actualizing them? Could passionate striving to attain goals be an
end in itself? Is the purpose in the journey or the destination?

The difference between human beings and angels is that humans have an ability to desire and possess, says Reb Tzadok of Lublin. Having a desire and inclinations defines us, distinguishing us from the angels. Striving, ambition, passion, urges and cravings, are all parts of the human condition, and desire animates a person throughout his life.

We may focus our desires upon different objects, for better or for worse, but we can never truly free ourselves from desire. We may choose what we want, but we can never truly free ourselves from the necessity to want. The truth is, we would not want to be free from it, because in itself, desire is a divine energy. Even the desire to extinguish desire is itself a desire.

Every movement, whether upward or downward, generative or de-generative, begins with a desire. The forerunner of change is the desire and passion for change. It is the foundation of the journey towards wholeness; without desire, there is no journey.

Often, a strong desire to do a mitzvah evolves into a mitzvah itself. The means become an end. In the words of our Sages, "The reward of the mitzvah is the mitzvah itself" (Avos, 4:2). The Gemarah suggests that a student's yearning to be close to his teacher and assist him is even more powerful than the intellectual study with the teacher (Berachos, 7a). The anticipation is often more potent than the actual deed. Reb Mordechai Yosef of Izhbitz says that the act of study is finite — learning a specific text in a specific period of time, but the *teshuka* or 'striving' to connect with Hashem and Torah expands infinitely in all dimensions.

Seeking truth is itself a form or function of truth. When someone seeks truth, it indicates that the ground in which he is rooted is itself truth. Reb Mendel of Kotzk interprets the verse, "And you shall seek Hashem *from there*, and you shall find Him" (Devarim, 4:29): "the seeking is the finding." Similarly, the verse "One thing I ask, that I shall seek" (Tehilim, 27:4), suggests that King David is asking for just that — to seek; 'Please Hashem, strengthen and inspire me to always seek You in every time and place, and in every face!"

There appear to be two avenues in teshuvah, the quest to reach *shlemus* or 'perfection'. One is the 'retail' approach, in which a person accu-

mulates countless good deeds and accomplishments, which create a critical mass of positive energy, finally establishing a state of shlemus. He has
paid the price and completed all the purchase transactions, so to speak.
However, given the shifting nature of life, this avenue is highly difficult
to achieve, if not unattainable, for most people. It seems as though there
is always another detail to complete.

The other avenue is perhaps more within a person's ability. It is to
sincerely and whole-heartedly declare, 'I am already whole and complete.'
Operating from this perspective, we still have to deal with life's vicissi-
tudes, and there is still much room for growth and maturation. The difference is, here one is not dependent on or defined by any ideal outcome.
Life becomes a joyous adventure, not motivated by fixed goals. This way,
you empower yourself to make a difference, gradually and continuously,
within yourself and within the world.

SYNOPSIS: CHAPTER 9
Recognize Your Perfection & Imperfection

Reb Avraham Abulafiah speaks about the 'perfect self' and the 'imperfect self'. Part of us is always whole and perfect. At our deepest
root, the *shoresh ha-neshamah*, the 'source of soul', we are all *tzadikim*
in a constant state of unity with the Creator. Another part of us,
the revealed self, appears fragmented and imperfect. This part of us
relentlessly seeks the seemingly unattainable goal of wholeness. Yet,
this desire and striving for wholeness is in itself an indication of the
deeper wholeness of our soul root.

We need to learn how to maintain a delicate balance between our
inner perfection, which is always content, and our imperfection,
which is never satisfied. We also have to hold onto a certain measure
of satisfaction in what we have already achieved.

PRACTICE

BE HONEST

Honesty with oneself is of the greatest importance. We should learn to be clear regarding the level on which we are functioning: the perfection of the deeper self, or the yearning of the imperfect surface identity.

For example, say you have already eaten dinner, and you feel full, but yet you desire dessert. While there may be nothing inherently 'wrong' with eating dessert, from the point of view of your deeper self, you realize that you do not really need the object of this *ta'ava*, or 'desire'. You see how this is simply the energy of addictive attachment to physical pleasure. Yet your fragmented surface self demands that you eat it, regardless of the consequences.

The truth is, the answer to this particular dilemma may not be about whether to eat the dessert or to refrain. The answer is to become aware and honest about your motives: is this the urging of my surface self? What is it that I really desire?

Choose a period of time to practice honesty in this way. Maybe you won't have the strength to win every battle, but make sure to give your deeper self a voice. If you do give into the urgings of your lower self, and eat the dessert, be honest with yourself about the loss. Own it and do not make excuses that 'it doesn't matter.' Even casual denial can become a slippery slope — but so can self-blame. Don't make this practice an all-or-nothing situation. Simply recognize that the battle does matter, but you may not have the spiritual strength to overcome each challenge completely.

This practice can be done with any *mutar* or 'permitted' desire that we might entertain, even when we know better than to pursue it unchecked. In life you win some and lose some, but with practice you gradually lose less and less. Success breeds success. Start with the small stuff, small challenges that you know your deeper self can overcome, and build from there. When you feel successful in what you are doing, empowered and honest with yourself, you will have the strength and courage to continue on. The Yid ha-Kodesh once asked Reb Simcha Bunim to tell him what kinds of things he heard people saying in the marketplace. Reb Simcha Bunim said, "I heard them saying, 'To lose money is not so terrible, but when you lose courage, you lose everything.'"

CHAPTER TEN

The Nature of DESIRE

T eshuvah is a reorientation and redirection of our awareness, a shift of being that brings a new way of perceiving ourselves and the world. For some, teshuvah is a complete metamorphosis of identity, while for others it is simply a new ability to be conscious, focused and equanimous.

As with all other matters of life, the motivation to do teshuvah can come from either a positive or a negative source. If one has not committed any serious misdeeds, one may feel a positive urge to grow as a person, and to live a more refined, introspective, joyful life. In this case, to increase the desire for teshuvah, one might look into the mirror and say, "I would like more for myself; I expect more of myself."

Frustration and unease with oneself and one's splintered and stagnant life can also prompt an urgent desire to change. When a person becomes aware of his discombobulated state, he naturally yearns to untangle and straighten himself out. This is the positive function of feelings of emptiness, shame and alienation from one's authentic self and from society. When these sentiments come up, they are meant to impel us to correct our behavior. In such a case, one can increase the desire to do teshuvah by acknowledging his chaotic state, looking into the mirror and saying, "This is not the self I know, nor is this the way I want people to perceive me."

Many people walk around sensing a devastating emptiness, a gaping hole at the center of their being, and they tirelessly seek to fill that hole with all types of things. The problem is, attempting to fill an internal emptiness with materialism will ultimately leave one feeling even more disillusioned and unsatisfied. Some people try to fill the hole with power and money, addictively sacrificing their lives for their career. Others try to fill the void with food, addictively obsessing over what to eat and when. And still, the emptiness prevails. Not only does the problem not disappear, it becomes increasingly exacerbated.

The more we attempt to fill ourselves, the emptier we feel. That is because through the fulfillment of desire, one's vessel of desire expands. As the vessel expands, so does the feeling of need or yearning, along with the sense that one's appetite is never quite quenched or pacified.

It is important for us to understand the nature of need and fulfillment in a spiritual context. The paradox is that if we attempt to solve a sense of lack by any means other than personal transformation, the solution will be temporary. Furthermore, it will ultimately create a bigger void, which will beg to be filled at a later time. Only uncovering and revealing our *shlemus*, the 'completeness' that already always exists within us, can we truly meet our needs.

Spiritual needs are natural, but they cannot be filled with things. The yearning to return to our inner wholeness can never be satiated by objects. This would be similar to the Midrashic tale (on Koheles, 6: 7), in which a poor farmer tries to satisfy a princess' taste for luxury by offering her the best straw bed available. Filling an existential emptiness with material things is not satisfying, because they are simply two different categories. It would be like attempting to patch a broken relationship with a band-aid.

We often chase goals in anticipation of what they will deliver us: happiness, wholeness, or peace. When we finally attain our goal, not only do we still feel incomplete, but we come to the realization that what we have been chasing is nothing more than a phantom. It is like being a spectator at an illusionist's performance. The illusionist walks around with a closed hand, asking the gathered on-lookers to guess at the amazing wish-fulfilling object inside. Each person imagines the closed hand to contain that which he most desires. Some think it must be money, others think it must be some means of satisfying lust, others feel it must be a pill that grants youthful energy or blissful peace. When the prankster finally opens his hand, to the surprise of all, it holds nothing but emptiness.

"A lover of money will never be appeased by money" (Koheles, 5: 9). The Hebrew word for money is *mamon*. The Kli Yakar, points out that each of the four Hebrew letters that spell *mamon* are themselves spelled with the repetition of the same letter. In other words, the first and second letter of *mamon*, mem, is spelled *mem-mem*. The third letter, vav, is spelled *vav-vav*. The last letter, nun, is spelled *nun-vav-nun*. This demonstrates the truth about money and all things money can buy, and also concepts such as power and honor. All these things lead back to themselves, to more of the same, in an endless loop of craving. Having a desire fulfilled only creates more lust for the same object, it is a self-fulfilling prophecy of ever more craving for that which you have accumulated. Chasing these wants places you on a hamster wheel — you feel as though you keep moving, but in reality you get nowhere.

If you desire to find satisfaction through external stimulation or accumulation, your quest is doomed from the outset. There is no guarantee that what you secure for yourself today will suffice for tomorrow. There is no limit to appetite, and gratifying it can exaggerate and distort your sense of reality, creating an ever-greater sense of urgency and demand for accessibility.

Even our seemingly benign chasing after the latest trends, and our desire to acquire all the new gadgets as soon as they are available, are dead ends. Often it is only later on in life, after we have spent many years in pursuit of such external things, that we realize the emptiness we felt was not materially based. It was actually a dire wish to find spiritual wholeness. It was actually a call to teshuvah.

When we can hear the call to teshuvah within the noise of our cravings, we can choose to become more inner-directed and to seek fullness from within. Joy is then readily attainable. As we become relaxed and present, we reveal our inherent wholeness and integrity. A genuine sense of satisfaction flourishes in simply knowing who we are. We are no longer addicted to somehow possessing wholeness in the elusive future.

Body and soul are designed to work in unison. Since the soul energizes the body, the body may experience a spiritual energy-surge in the form of strong physical sensations. When a soul is awakened and feels the need to reveal itself and fill the temporal life with transcendence and meaning, the physical body may also feel an urgency to fill a need. It may happen that the spirit within us is aroused in such a way that the body becomes overwhelmed or disconcerted. Many seek, unwittingly, to drown out the energy of this spiritual inspiration with, for example, alcohol or other dissociating substances. This temporarily mutes the spiritual surge by redirecting the energy into an object. The object and the dissociated state are fed by this energy, and soon they grow to become ends in themselves.

If channeled appropriately, however, the body synchronizes with the soul's energy, and together they each draw closer to the Source as one. When you do this, you experience a sense of intrinsic alignment because your desire is transparent to its true purpose, and you are attuned to who you truly are. The choice is in your hands to utilize moments of strong desire and inspiration for spiritual matters, or to misdirect the energy of desire toward bodily cravings. What will you choose: transcendence and its true happiness, or selfish indulgence and its disappointments?

SYNOPSIS: CHAPTER 10
Refocus Your Desires

Upon sensing emptiness in their lives, most people urgently seek to fill the seeming void with all kinds of things. Yet attempting to fill an internal vacuum with materialism ultimately leaves them with much greater dissatisfaction. Even a moment of selfish satisfaction aggravates and expands the vessel of desire, which then demands to be refilled. In actuality, every desire is divine in its root; it is a natural spiritual impulse to connect, to create *yichud* or 'unification' in life. We need not eradicate desire or completely detach ourselves from it, although detachment may be an important temporary stage in teshuvah. Teshuvah allows us to re-contextualize desire, by redirecting it to its Source.

PRACTICE

MEDITATE ON DESIRE

In order to bring desire back to its positive, non-destructive purpose, first become aware of your desire for material things. Say you have a strong desire to acquire a new pair of shoes, even though you have more shoes than you really need. Realize that this desire is merely a shadow of a deeper urge, perhaps for connection to the Source through an experience of beauty and newness. Ask yourself: 'Can I find a sense of beauty or newness deep within myself? Will another pair of shoes, another drink, book, car, bring me lasting satisfaction?'

On a deeper level, if you are in a strong spiritual place, you can meditatively trace your desire back to its root. To do this, first awaken a physical desire for someone or something. Then swiftly move the energy of the desire away from that object, channeling it into the pure, objectless, core desire for the Infinite One. Doing this, you move from the physical desire for a particular form to a spiritual, formless desire. If you desire to pray with fiery passion, for example, you can contemplate important, physically real parts of your life that you long for, be it your spouse, success or even possessions, and recognize the root of these earthly desires, a desire to connect with your Creator.

CHAPTER
ELEVEN

The Inner Call
TO TESHUVAH

A divine voice rings continuously, calling us to teshuvah and spiritual awakening. Inaudible to worldly ears, it is nonetheless a voice that our souls can hear clearly. To those who have opened their inner ear to this voice, echoes can be heard in the abysmal caverns of existential emptiness, wherein linger feelings of loneliness, a brewing disquiet or sense of disappointment with how we are living. When this voice is honored, it can sometimes grow into a tremendous cry of yearning to be free, or a powerful, confident roar of liberation.

There are various life situations that can catalyze teshuvah. A desire for change often emerges when someone has a moving experience, such as a near-tragedy, or an encounter with a deeply inspirational book, teaching or person. When contemplated and internalized, these experiences can be pivotal, shifting our being, and influencing our action.

A person who does not enjoy science fiction will not be able to appreciate even the finest masterpiece of the genre. Similarly, if our external self is distant from goodness and spirituality, words of wisdom may fall on deaf ears. Sadly, some of us are so far removed from spirituality or meaning that even inspirational words will seem meaningless. The question is, how does an individual in such a difficult spiritual situation find the impetus to transform? Granted, the choice to make teshuvah is available to all people at all times, but we still have to know where the motivation to make that choice comes from.

If inspiration cannot be received from a revealed, conscious source, it must emerge from a place deeper within. Reb DovBer of Chabad says the desire for teshuvah arises from an inner space beyond everyday consciousness: from the ever-pure essence of self. This undiluted intensity of soul is called *yechidah*, 'uniqueness' or 'oneness', for it is eternally one with the One. It is also one in the sense that it transcends all forms of duality, separation, fragmentation and misalignment. Because the yechidah is untouched by any state of disconnection, it can draw the manifest personality out of a place of extreme disconnection and toward an integrated, virtuous life. Thus, sometimes a person who has no interest in spirituality suddenly becomes inspired to pursue a spiritual life. Also, if a person has not been able to actualize his purpose in life by a certain point in his development, his yechidah can take over and shift his path.

The will of the yechidah is synonymous with the will of the Infinite One. A feeling of diminishment arises when we are out of alignment with the Divine will. This feeling is the soul's way to inspire us to seek a life in sync with the Master Plan for our life and for all of Creation. The more dishonest a person is, the more opaque and confused his sense of will becomes. Sometimes an individual experiences an overwhelming sense of anxiety goading him towards teshuvah. The soul's intense thirst to return and be one with its Source will ultimately disallow unfitting materialistic substitutes. Only a return to the Master Plan will suffice.

This role of the yechidah is more important and pivotal than we can imagine. Throughout our journey, there may be times when it seems that a higher force is guiding us to do something, to be at a certain place, or to meet certain people. It may be clear that a power beyond intellect or emotion is leading us in a certain direction. We may meet someone for the first time and feel an instant kinship with them, or we might make a certain choice without knowing why, but it simply feels right. This kind of intuition or hunch is indeed caused by a force beyond rationality — it is the 'voice' of the soul.

There is a life-sustaining energy within Creation — a divine spark within every created thing that gives it life and being. Our collective *tikkun* or 'fixing', our life's purpose and responsibility, is to acknowledge the divine sparks throughout creation and elevate those sparks to their original source in the Divine. Also, each individual soul has a distinct tikkun-mission to locate and elevate the particular sparks with which he feels most connected.

All attractions, proclivities, premonitions and hunches are a result of the soul's yearning to elevate the sparks contained within the objects involved. Even physical cravings emanate from the core within, guiding us to locate the sparks within particular objects and to elevate them. Although the way to elevate the sparks in an object of craving may be to abstain from it, our attraction is still an authentic sign that we are called to elevate sparks there. We may also feel an inexorable attraction and pull toward certain people or a soul mate, and by interacting with them we can elevate their sparks and they can elevate ours.

While teshuvah can be stirred from the essential self beyond our normative consciousness, it is still incumbent upon the conscious self to evoke teshuvah whenever possible. An ancient Midrash reveals a dialogue between the Creator of the Universe and the People of Israel. Israel says, "Master of the Universe, it is incumbent upon You to awaken us to teshuvah." "Return to Me," responds the Creator, "and I will return to you." Hearing this, the People reassert, "No, it is up to You; return us, O Master of Deliverance!" In conclusion, it is written, "Bring us back to You, Hashem, and we shall return to You" (Eichah, 5: 21). Even though we human beings must make the first move, we can only do so when Hashem first empowers us to do so.

For some, teshuvah seems to be a calculated project, an end result of painstaking self-examination and inner reflection. For others, teshuvah seems to awaken unexpectedly, even when they have disengaged themselves from the will to improve their lives. In both cases, teshuvah stems from Hashem's empowerment.

When teshuvah awakens unexpectedly as a revelation from a place 'above' transgression, the challenge becomes putting that otherworldly inspiration to use in the world. Teshuvah can be successful if one sees that this spontaneous empowerment does not fade away, and that the energy is used to light the path to wholeness.

King David sings, "Hashem is my light and my salvation; Whom shall I fear? Hashem is the strength of my life; Whom shall I dread" (Tehillim, 27:1)? These references to Hashem as the 'Source of Light' and the 'Strength of Life' refer to two manifestations of the Divine. One is Hashem as revealed before one transgresses; the second is Hashem revealed after one transgresses (Rosh Hashanah, 17b).

Prior to transgressing, negative and destructive temptation is but a distant fear, and the condition in which one lives is one of light, clarity and certainty. Only upon an intimate encounter with negativity — when the light of life appears to dim — do fear, uncertainty, anxiety and 'dread' become one's condition. Then a person needs the Strength of Life, the One who reaches out and guides him to the path of teshuvah. Even after one has succumbed to character weaknesses and is immersed in negative activities, the power to reorient life is forever available, and Hashem is always there to give him strength.

King Solomon sings, "May His left hand be under my head, and His right hand embrace me" (Shir ha-Shari, 8:3). When embarking on the path of teshuvah we feel as if Hashem's "right" or loving hand is embracing us. When we have lost our way, Hashem extends a hand, as it were, lifts us up, holds, cradles and nurtures us. Aware of this awesome fact, we feel protected like an infant whose parents will hold her tight and not let her go. A deeper realization can then set in: every time we do fall, every time we do jump out of the arms of Hashem, as it were, we are actually falling right back into the Divine embrace. Hashem is still there surrounding us and catching us as we are falling. This "right arm" is equated with the attribute of *chesed* or Divine loving kindness.

The left arm is equated with the attribute of *gevurah* or 'strength'. This is the strength Hashem gives us when we fall. In human terms, it takes a real inner strength to hold our heads up when we have fallen or are falling. This too is Hashem's empowerment.

At times, in the path of self-elevation, the ego presents itself as a real obstacle. Therefore, the breakdown or nullification of the ego, rendering it more transparent, may be a prerequisite for the awakening of teshuvah and an intimate experience of spiritual light. A person who has difficulty being or staying inspired can contemplate the following metaphor: a wooden beam catches fire more readily when splintered. Similarly, the opaque ego requires deconstruction in order to catch fire spiritually (Zohar, 3:168a). When the ego is humbled, the light of teshuvah permeates and illumines all levels of our consciousness.

Tragedy, distress, loneliness and alienation may give rise to a state of disempowerment and humility. At that point a person may be open to entering the path of return. The Torah predicts this response in the verse, "When you are in distress...you will return unto Hashem your God" (Devarim, 4:30). When the ego collapses under a distressing experience, its resistance to transcendent power is removed. The person realizes he is not in control of his reality, and he might feel lost and perplexed, leading to the possibility that he will come to embrace the transcendent Source of Power. Positive experiences, however, often enhance and reaffirm the un-rectified ego. When human beings are self-satisfied and in control, life makes sense and there seems to be no need to take into account the existence of a higher order.

It appears that the resolve to believe in something more, something beyond occurs when the belief in one's own omnipotence begins to dwindle. The nature of the human being is to turn to a Higher Force when he, as a lower force feels most threatened, beaten or defeated. "Our vision comes not from the white of the eye, but rather from the part that is black", the Midrash says. The darkest hours of despair and hopelessness tend to awaken the most influential states of hope and vision. If one realizes that he is responsible for darkening his life and the lives of others, his pain can arouse a tremendous desire to open his eyes, and draw near to the Source of Life and Light.

On the other hand, the efficacy and sustainability of teshuvah whose motivation is generated from a place of disempowerment is tenuous. When the condition of distress or darkness passes, often so does one's resolve. This form of teshuvah is reactive in nature. A more profound form of teshuvah comes from a place of love. The teshuvah of love is positively charged and life- affirming, allowing a sustainable commitment to the maximization of life. It enables the healing and integration process to accelerate without the distraction of dramatic stress and suffering.

There are many levels to the teshuvah of love. In the most elementary level, where teshuvah is a form of repentance and expiation, it begins with awareness. Becoming aware and sensitive to his situation, the person enters into a state of teshuvah with an enthusiasm and energy matching that which he previously channeled into the misdeed. Where he passionately transgressed, now he passionately clings to Hashem. We will continue to discuss the teshuvah of love in future chapters.

According to the Midrash, Reuben, the eldest son of the patriarch Yaakov, was the first person ever to undertake teshuvah. Though, as we mentioned, Cain did teshuvah many years prior, nevertheless, this occurred only after he was rebuked and informed of his impending punishment. It was the harsh reality of his predicament that propelled him to do teshuvah. Reuben however, declared teshuvah simply upon sensing that he had done something wrong; it was not a rebuke or a humbling experience that moved him, but sensitivity to the subtle spiritual implications of the act itself. He made a choice, based on his introspection, to return to his true self. For this reason, Reuben is considered to have opened the doors of teshuvah for all future generations.

At this juncture it should be asserted that the laws of spiritual reality are diametrically opposed to the laws of the physical world — at least as most people understand physical laws. Almost universally, people see through a Cartesian lens, obsessed with measurability, location and linear time. If a person living in New York wishes to be in California, he knows that if he travels 3,000 miles westward, he will find it. Getting there is a matter of trudging through fixed amounts of time and space. In the spiritual realm, there is no separate location to reach. We are always potentially 'there' — we can instantaneously transform 'there' to 'here', depending on our point of view.

Changing a point of view is in no way similar to traveling from New York to California. In fact, we all change points of view constantly and effortlessly. However, we can also hold onto certain limiting beliefs, judgments and reactions that we made in the past, and so we can make ourselves appear to be separate from 'here', calling it 'there'.

When we act on the basis of unconscious or limiting points of view, we further concretize our projected Cartesian view of spiritual reality. When we embark upon the path of teshuvah, however, a new point of view opens to us. The elevated spiritual level we longed for is acknowledged as the very context and space of our life. Ironically, after years of searching everywhere else, we find that this lofty state has always been right here, deep within our being, waiting to be unveiled and integrated.

SYNOPSIS: CHAPTER 11
Be Open

Teshuvah can awaken through a conscious decision to change, through a deep, subconscious calling of the soul, or from a completely unexpected direction. We need to be open and listen for the voice of Hashem calling us to teshuvah. This call might come through an epiphany, through the words of other people, or even through the seemingly mundane events of our lives. The Creator is always speaking to us. Normally, we just tune into the outer *kelipa* or 'shell' of life. We can also listen to the inner rhythms of our life and ask: 'What is Hashem telling me right now?' We have to be careful not to impede our ability to listen by filling up our sense of emptiness with busy-ness or material things.

PRACTICE
LISTEN DEEPLY

For at least one week, before going to bed each night, meditate on the events of your day.

Remember some of the words you heard people say, and some of the things you saw.

Open yourself to understanding the Divine messages hidden in these events — spoken softly, but directly relevant to your soul's journey. Soon, you will become attuned to the guidance being transmitted to you at all times.

CHAPTER
TWELVE

RETROACTIVELY
Transforming Ourselves

H aving imperfections is part of being human. Anyone can slip spiritually, ethically or morally. These imperfections, however, do not negate our yearning and striving towards an actualization of our deeper perfection. When we stumble and fall, our inner self demands that we do teshuvah, and that we live continuously in the present, untangled from the difficulties and distortions of the past.

Living in the present is one of the most powerful secrets of teshuvah. The Midrash says that the Torah's word for 'now', *ve-atah*, is a direct reference to teshuvah. We need to view everything and everyone through the clear lens of the now. In Torah law, once a person embarks on the path of teshuvah, it is forbidden to remind him of his shameful past (Baba Metzia, 58b). This law also applies to the individual himself. Once you have authentically declared teshuvah, you must evaluate yourself as you are now, without taking the negative past into consideration. Not only would it be inappropriate to define yourself according to the past, it would be inaccurate. Once the path of teshuvah has been undertaken, the person you once were no longer exists.

Teshuvah brings us into the present, but it extends its influence into the past as well. It has the capacity to retroactively transform past mistakes. There are no irredeemable misdeeds. Fear-motivated teshuvah reduces past *mayzid* or 'intentional' acts into *shogeg*, acts of 'negligence'. Love-based teshuvah is even more powerful, as it can convert malice into actual merit (Yumah, 86b). But how is it possible to go back in time? What was done in the past has passed; it is forever gone. How can an act in the present remedy or redeem an act performed in the past? These are deep questions and we will explore them in this chapter as well as in later chapters.

Every action that a person takes throughout his life creates an energy that clings to him, the doer. This energy stays with him for all eternity. Since the action is an outer expression of an internal state of being, the individual must transform his inner being, or the misdirected energies will serve as chains, binding him to an errant path. Although changing the outer behavioral patterns is important, transforming the doer himself is paramount. Tapping into teshuvah, and transforming ourselves we can make a reassessment of past behavior with compassion and understanding, viewing errors compassionately from within the context wherein they occurred, specifically the spiritual eclipse that prevailed at the time. This shift in perspective influences our present, and future, for now, the energy of the negative past is flowing positively towards us.

The authority of teshuvah is such that not only does it disassociate the doer from the doing, and thus the negative energy released from past negative actions has no affect on the doer, but rather, a total revolution occurs. Looking back at the previously committed actions, writes R. Yosef Albo, they seem to have surely been done in error and unintentionally. The person on the path of teshuvah now becomes the observer of his past and is thus no longer burdened by those errors. For this reason, the Torah opposes the stigmatization of any wrong doer.

Throughout history, most societies have stigmatized their wrongdoers. Often, past sins could never be erased, even if the individual had later reformed his ways. In ancient Babylon, a person who was found to have stolen would have his hands cut off. In other cultures, one who went to prison would be tattooed so that he would forever bear the status of criminal. A person who transgressed once was stigmatized and disgraced for life.

The Torah's approach to reform is quite the opposite: it is not assumed that 'once a thief always a thief'. A scarlet letter is not affixed to an individual who committed a wrongful act. Rather than stigmatizing the wrongdoer, the Torah invites him to teshuvah.

The Torah also attempts to ease the emotional trauma of a person attempting to undergo real change. An example of this is a certain written law regarding thieves. If someone stole a brick and used it to build his home, and later on he desired to do teshuvah, he need not destroy the building in order to return the original stolen brick. Instead, he can compensate the rightful owner with the monetary value of the brick (Gittin, 55a).

Our sages tell a story of a thief who wished to relinquish his destructive ways and decided to return everything he had ever stolen. Upon hearing of his new resolution, the man's wife said that if he were to return everything he had ever stolen, he would quite literally be left without the shirt on his back. Realizing the predicament, the man opted to continue living as a thief. Upon hearing of this incident, the sages announced that in order to facilitate the path of teshuvah we should not accept stolen goods returned from a thief (Baba Kama 94b). The ruling was an attempt to make the path of return accessible, so that no one would be discouraged from elevating his life, due to an impossibly steep incline.

No one is beyond hope or redemption, and the option of teshuvah is always open before us. We have the potential to transform ourselves into anything we so desire. One prominent example of this potential is the celebrated Talmudic sage, Reish Lakish. Though once an infamous bandit, his radical teshuvah allowed him to become one of the most sharp-minded sages of the Talmudic period (Baba Metzia, 84a). The power of teshuvah encompasses past, present and future, allowing one to transform the impact of his entire life, from beginning to end. Teshuvah can convert malice into merit, and liabilities into assets.

We perceive time as rigidly causal and linear: yesterday is always in the past and tomorrow is always in the future. This unidirectional flow naturally seems non-reversible. But this is precisely the claim of teshuvah — we can revise the past, we can reverse the causal progression of time. How is this possible? It is easy to understand that we ourselves can change, but how can we honestly change the nature of a historical event?

To begin to answer that question, we have to back up. What *is* teshuvah? The Torah says, "This mitzvah that I command you today is not hidden from you and is not distant" (Devarim, 30:11). According to Nachmanides, the Thirteenth Century mystic and codifier of Jewish law also known as 'the Ramban', this mitzvah alludes to teshuvah. Many commentaries align themselves with this interpretation.

Other interpreters maintain that the phrase 'this mitzvah' is a general reference to all the mitzvos. In fact, Maimonides, 'the Rambam', does not see this verse as an allusion to the mitzvah of teshuvah at all. Some maintain that according to the Rambam there is no Biblical directive for teshuvah; if one desires to do teshuvah, he should follow the procedure prescribed in the Torah, but the act itself is not a commandment. This seems puzzling at best. Teshuvah appears to be a fundamental principle of Torah, so how then can it not be a commandment?

We could answer that teshuvah is a state of being, rather than a state of doing. It is not just an act, and therefore it transcends the category of mitzvos, which are prescribed acts. Teshuvah, rather, connects us to the very Source of the mitzvos, explains Reb Schneur Zalman of Liadi. While doing a mitzvah, we perform the Divine will, thereby connecting with the Divine through the intermediary of 'will'. Teshuvah connects directly with the *Baal ha-Ratzon*, the 'One who wills', the Essence beyond the attribute of 'will'.

The nature of connecting to the *Baal ha-Ratzon*, rather than just to the *ratzon*, can be illustrated by the metaphor of a relationship between a parent and her child. The parent instructs the child to clean his room. The instruction is for the child's own benefit — to teach responsibility — but for whatever reason the child does not listen, the room is not cleaned, and the parent's will has been disobeyed. The initial reaction of the parent is frustration. She punishes the child, again intended for the child's own benefit, seeking to teach him that his actions or non-actions are significant and are attached to consequences. Although tearful and hurt, the child instinctually turns to the parent and reaches out for a comforting embrace. Suddenly, the parent is in touch with a place deep within herself where her love for her child is more powerful than her desire to be obeyed, or even to teach her child a lesson. This natural, instinctive love is the true essence of the relationship. The child is now connected to the 'one who wills'.

If the child had cleaned the room, his act would have satisfied the parent's will. When the child, however, reached tearfully for an embrace, his 'state of being' triggered a reconnection that was much deeper than will —beyond the causality of reward and punishment and even the sequential flow of time. The parent, holding the child tight, now sees his essential beauty, and is even endeared by his rebelliousness. The past offense is now a merit.

We too can access this deeper connection with our Creator, even after we have severed our connection with His will. Divine love runs deeper than a contractual, reciprocal relationship. The Creator is not like an overbearing parent who demands, 'What have you done for me lately?' Rather, Hashem calls to us, 'You are my child and I love you!' When we do teshuvah, we awaken the true nature of our relationship with the *Baal ha-Ratzon*, the Source of all will, and revise history.

Nevertheless, like the child in the allegory, we may need to experience tears and the 'punishment' or consequence of our actions. That is because we experience our Source and Ground of Being as a wellspring of life. When we stray from our internal path, we impede the flow of this wellspring. If we fill our lives with nonsensical thinking, trivial self-expression, and actions that are inconsistent with who we truly are, the resulting blockage will intensify until our wellspring runs dry. Having exhausted our energy-flow on foolish pursuits, we must recover our deeper resources of inspiration. At this point, rigorous excavation is required in order to restore the flow of the pure, living waters of our being.

Now that we appreciate the power of teshuvah to transcend time and will, we can begin to decipher the inner workings of this power. There is a Midrashic tale in which 'Wisdom', 'Prophecy', 'Torah' and the Creator are gathered in discussion. The question is raised: 'What is to be done with a person who has transgressed?' Wisdom offers a wise text, saying, "To one who has transgressed, evil shall pursue him" (Mishlei, 13: 21). Prophecy replies with a prophetic text, saying, "The soul who has transgressed shall perish" (Yechezkel, 18: 4). Torah suggests a principle of the Torah, saying, "Let he who has transgressed bring an offering and thereby be absolved." Finally, the Creator rules, "If a person has transgressed, let him embrace teshuvah and return to Me; he shall be forgiven" (Yalkut Shimoni).

Let us analyze these four perspectives. In the world of intellectual wisdom everything is governed by cause and effect. Anything that exists was caused by some other force; in turn, it will cause something else to come into existence. This is a rigidly objective, logical cosmology. When a person does something negative there must be a particular effect; evil always begets evil. When we inject negativity into this universe of cause and effect, it rebounds upon us. Therefore, Wisdom maintains that one who has done evil shall be pursued by evil. In the realm of intellect and judgment, writes Rabbi Moshe Metrani, there is no room for teshuvah.

Prophetic consciousness, operating from a place beyond human comprehension and logic, argues that one who commits a vice must perish. Prophecy is a highly expansive state of consciousness connected with angelic beings. A prophet enters loftier realms of reality and mystic states undefined by time and space. In these realms or states, past, present and future merge as one. In a prophet's world of undiluted spirituality, the existence of evil has even less legitimacy than in the world of the intellectual. In fact, evil simply does not exist — everything is only good.

In the angelic realm, beings have no free will to do evil. Therefore, if a person commits a negative act, be it by omission or commission, Prophecy maintains that there is no place for him in existence; one who entertains negativity must vanish and cease to exist. From the perspective of Prophecy there is no alternative to goodness, and no opposite.

The Torah was given to this world for our refinement and renewal.

From the Torah's viewpoint, humans must live within this world while aspiring to stand above it. The overwhelming temptations and negativity of this world are thus understandable, and deviation from goodness is a legitimate possibility. Anticipating this predicament, Torah contains 'remedies' — when something negative is done, something positive must then be brought into the picture to rectify it and balance it out.

According to this view, there is a cosmic equilibrium that must always be maintained. When the scales are tilted to the negative, we must increase positive deeds to correct the imbalance. If one does not fulfill the desire of the Creator, he must fill that space by performing a mitzvah to counteract the loss. 'Torah' therefore suggests that one who transgressed should bring a *korban*, an offering, in order to re-establish spiritual equilibrium and be absolved. A positive act; a mitzvah/sacrifice/connection must be offered in the place of an *aveirah*/ transgression/disconnection.

From the perspective of Torah, every negative action obscures the Divine light that radiates into existence, diminishing the energy that is imminent within creation. The *ohr memale*, 'permeating light' that illuminates all Creation from within, is reduced with every spiritually destructive action. To replenish that light, one must connect with the *ohr ha-sovev*, the 'surrounding light' that transcends and envelops creation. The korban offering was a way to connect with the *ohr ha-sovev* and replenish the diminished *ohr memale*, correcting the imbalance. Today, we accomplish this through prayer, generosity, and other methods.

After the assembled had each given their advice, the Creator ruled that one who transgresses should declare a state of teshuvah and be forgiven and reunited. The Creator thus allows negativity to be transformed and included within *achdus*, Divine Unity. In this context, transgression becomes an opportunity for growth and development. Teshuvah thus transcends conventional cause and effect and posits the seemingly miraculous: the effect of negativity can be positive. In fact, not just its effect, but, the negativity itself can be positive; the transgression itself can be a merit.

Let us explore this radical concept further. The relationship between servant and master is a traditional illustration of our relationship with the

Creator. Such an alliance revolves around the fulfillment of the master's desires through service. It is not necessarily a love connection, although it can develop into that as well; the relationship is founded on the quality of the servant's deeds and his ability to actively please his master. When a servant disobeys, he severs his connection. In order to recreate the relationship he would need to make an appeal for forgiveness and then extend himself to prove his sincerity. To demonstrate his change of heart, he would execute his master's desires with greater care as well as try to make up for lost opportunities to do so.

All relationships, including deeply loving ones, suggest duality. Our essential unity with Hashem, however, is absolute and non-dualistic. Through teshuvah, we can reveal this unconditional achdus or unity that Hashem eternally has with us, and with all Creation.

As we journey to the center of the human soul, we pass beyond all views and opinions, beyond even the spiritual realms, until we reveal the transcendent purity that has always been the backdrop and essence of our existence. Our essence is innocent and pristine, untainted and unaffected by the seemingly aggressive nature of the universe. Even briefly glimpsing this unified field, we can acknowledge a deeper identity that is totally free of negativity, where negative forces do not and cannot exist.

When we live the life of teshuvah, we demonstrate that the negative actions in our history are not indicative of who we are. We are really beyond the modes of relationship that are dependent upon deeds. When we discover the intrinsic bond between our essence and the essence of our Creator, the Baal ha-Razton, then our actions truly have positive effects. Then we have the capacity to retroactively transform demerit into merit. The remainder of this chapter will be a summary of a rare and advanced teaching that illustrates this point.

This teaching is drawn from a verse in the Book of Shmu'el: ...*Ki E-l de'os Hashem, v'lo nisk'nu alilos*, "...For a God of *de'os*, 'knowledge' is Hashem, and [man's] deeds are *lo*, 'not' accounted for'" (Shmuel I, 2:3). In this verse the word *lo* has a difference between its *kesiv*, the way it is 'written', and its *kri*, the way it is 'read' or pronounced according to oral tradition. As it is written, *lo* has an *aleph*, meaning "not", as in 'man's deeds are nothing.' This suggests that our deeds have no effect Above; they only matter in their own context, namely our world of linear causality. However, *lo* is traditionally read as if it has a *vav* instead of an *aleph*. This changes the meaning to "to Him". Then the verse means, "And [man's] deeds are *lo* ('to Him')," suggesting that our actions below are potent and do have an influence — even on the Divine realm, Above.

Which of these two contradictory messages does the verse intend to convey? The truth is, both interpretations are correct. The verse itself admits that there are two levels of knowledge: "For a God of *de'os* is Hashem" — the word *de'os* is plural. In other words, there are higher and lower forms of *de'ah* (or *da'as*), 'knowing'.

These two levels of knowing are different perspectives. They are different ways of seeing what is 'Above' and what is 'below'. Higher *da'as*, also called 'higher unity', sees what is Above as *yesh*, 'existence' — the True Existence or Divine Being. It sees what is below as *ayin*, 'nothingness', the fundamentally non-existent world of action. Lower *da'as*, also called 'lower unity', sees the world of action below as *yesh*, concretely 'existing'. It sees Divinity above as ayin, 'no-thing-ness' — an imperceptible Source.

According to the perspective of higher unity, our actions have no effect, as in *lo* with an aleph, 'not accounted for', since the world of action below is 'nothing'. According to the perspective of lower unity, action alone is real and so it has a tremendous effect. *Lo* with a vav means 'to Him'; our actions are real and reach the domain of the Creator, so-to-speak. Since both perspectives are equally true, our deeds simultaneously do and do not have an effect. The universe of action is both *yesh* and *ayin*.

"To Him" indicates the system of *sechar v'onesh*, 'reward and punishment', cause and effect, action and reaction. Since our actions are real and mean something 'to Him', Hashem responds in kind. "Not accounted for", on the other hand, implies that *sechar v'onesh* is merely a natural consequence of action in the human realm below. From this perspective, there is no sin that reaches Above, thus there is no punishment that comes from Above.

The *Atzmus* or 'Essence' of Hashem is paradoxically beyond both yesh and ayin. It is the context that includes both *de'os*. Hashem is 'not affected by action', and yet He chooses to include the *lo* of 'to Him' and be affected by action. Hashem chooses, as it were, to care about us and our deeds. From a place of infallible, transcendent non-duality, there is a deliberate choice to lovingly respond to human fallibility and duality. Therefore, there is *onesh*, 'punishment', but it is only an expression of loving concern, and it is always for the good.

In conclusion, the life of teshuvah is the life of essence. Here, misaligned actions still trigger 'punishments' or natural consequences, and yet, these are recognized to be only Divine goodness. An act that results in goodness is by definition a meritorious deed. Thus, in the state of teshuvah, where all acts result in goodness, transgressions become merits. We see that everything is good, and yet with great care we deliberately embody goodness in our every deed.

SYNOPSIS: CHAPTER 12
Acknowledge Your Good Points

Instead of paying attention to the negative things that you have done, and allowing that awareness of negativity to fill you until you identify as a bad person, focus on your good points. Negativity is not who you are, it is only what you perhaps did. Your misdeeds are not your being. Negativity is external to your ever-pure essential soul.

PRACTICE

FOCUS ON THE GOOD
WITHIN YOU

Right now, focus on at least one good point within yourself, even if you judge it as insignificant.

The truth is, a good deed, word or thought is never insignificant, no matter how small in appearance. The more points of goodness you find within yourself, the more you will also find in others. Now, turn your focus to who you really are, your inner being apart from all of your actions or inactions. Recognize that your soul is one with the Source of All Goodness; in essence, you are a single ray of this splendorous Infinite Goodness.

DECONSTRUCTING DUALITY:
Operating from the Point of Unity

"The soul that You have given me is pure" (Berachos, 60b). Purity is our real condition. A negative action is like a stain on a fine garment. Sometimes even after washing it, the stain remains *nichtam*, 'apparent' (Yirmiyahu, 2:22), yet it is still only a stain upon the garment of the soul, not upon the soul itself. Negativity, teaches Reb Shalom DovBer of Chabad, is a superficial accumulation, 'external' to our pure essence. It is contradictory to the nature of who we really are.

If our soul were like the axis of a rapidly spinning wheel, our actions would be located at the outer rim of the wheel. Because of the centrifugal force, no action would ever approach the axis. The axis or core around which our lives revolve is permanently immune to outside influences.

> Our sages tell of a young man who vowed not to marry a certain eligible young woman, thinking her unattractive. When Rabbi Yishmael heard of this vow, he took the young woman into his home and had her beautified. Then, he called the young man into his home and asked, "Did you make a vow regarding this woman"? "No, certainly not", the boy re-

sponded, not recognizing her. At that moment Rabbi Yishmael rendered his vow null and void. Then Rabbi Yishmael
wept and lamented, declaring, "The daughters of Israel are so
beautiful; it is only the harshness of poverty that makes them
seem unattractive" (Nedarim, 66a).

Our innate spiritual beauty is so magnificent and brilliant that no
outer representation or appearance can fully reflect it. Occasionally,
poverty of spirit may obscure our true beauty. Still, with the power of
teshuvah, we can shake off the dust, cleanse ourselves of obscuring grime,
and reveal a ray of our inner light.

Our soul is like a perpetually burning ember. Although it is occasionally covered by dirty ash, we can blow away the ash with the bellows
of *ru'ach* or 'spirituality', and uncover our *aish tamid*, our 'eternal flame'.

Teshuvah is like working on a spiritual excavation. When we care-
fully dig below the build-up of debris and brush off the sand, we uncover
the contours of our original, authentic self. While performing a self-evaluation, we may come to realize that some layers of our past were inappropriate and must be discarded. We must, however, not throw out pieces of
the precious artifact that we are uncovering. If we say, 'Something was (or
is) wrong with *me*,' we are discarding the wrong element, cutting ourselves off from life and fostering low self-esteem. If we say, rather, "I *did*
something wrong," we can separate the action from the person and recover the treasure of our pure self.

When we desire to shed negativity and discover our quintessential
purity, we can do so with relative ease by declaring who we truly are, and
then living our life from that context. Living from our essential purity is
not about continuously experiencing 'peak moments'. The term 'peak' itself suggests the fact that we will also experience valleys, plains, slopes
and plateaus — all of which have their own type of majesty and beauty.
Yet, if we are living from our essence, we can perform good deeds and
mitzvos with *simcha*, 'joy', no matter if we are experiencing a high or a
low or something in between.

When we can do mitzvos with passionate joy and love, rather than as weighty burdens or obligations to be reluctantly performed, this is an indication that our teshuvah is genuine. We come to see doing a mitzvah as shooting an arrow of love into the infinite sky. The arrow trails a cord that connects us and unifies us ever more intimately with the Infinite One. Through this loving connection, our deeds can elevate us into harmony with the spirit of Divine law, to the extent that our desires are completely in sync with what our Beloved desires for us.

Before the ideas of quantum physics became known, the scientific consensus was that nature operates within a continuum of absolute time and space. Conventional Western society has continued to affirm this rigid, linear perception of time: what is done in the past creates the present and impregnates the future — there is no exception to the rule that every action brings about a reaction. One's negative actions of the past inevitably create negative conditions in the present or future. At best, perhaps one can act in such a way that negative effects are mitigated or counterbalanced, but in no way can one change the nature of the original cause. In an ideology such as this, the universe becomes a closed system and there is no possibility for qualitative change.

In truth, however, causality only exists in a world where the past, present and future are seen as separate in nature. There is a truth deeper than separation: the world of *yichud* or 'oneness'. Newer scientific insights hint to the fact that the basic state of all reality is unity, and from this perspective, the linear, separate appearance of time is not absolute. According to these insights, all of time and space can be seen as simultaneously present, unified in an infinitely simple oneness.

Teshuvah preceded the creation of the universe. It is of a higher order than what is immediately perceived with our five senses. Teshuvah propels us into the orbit of the world of yichud, bringing us beyond perceptual separations in time and fragmentations of space. We gain the ability to break free from separation and causality.

This brings us back to our discussion of the mysterious power of teshuvah to go back in time and recreate our past. Within every one of us resides a part of the Infinite, the *yechidah*, or 'oneness' in the inner core of our soul. Connecting with this divine oneness within allows us to move

beyond definition and limitation, to a presence that surpasses and encompasses all dimensions of time and space. In this state of teshuvah, this
non-linear state of conscious infinity, the past is no longer past; the past,
present and future are simultaneously present and unified. Therefore,
through teshuvah, we can rectify *in the present* whatever actions are con-
ventionally projected as 'past'. Being in the oneness of the eternal here-
and-now gives us the power to reconstruct our personal history.

Again, the above paradigm should not puzzle the modern, scientifi-
cally minded person, for the paradox of Schrödinger's Cat can be used as
an appropriate metaphor. Schrödinger imagined a box containing a cat
that was hidden from view. An electron would be shot at the box in such
a way that it would go through one of two slits. If it were to go through
the right slit, a trigger in the box would release poison and the cat would
be killed. If the electron passed through the left slit, the cat would live.
However, in reality, there would be no way to know for certain which slit
the electron entered until the observer looked to see the results. Until an
observer views the place and time of the electron's path, the event is not
defined. It is not simply that we do not know what happened until we
look. In a sense, right now the cat is both alive and dead — both results
are equally real, and the electron has 'chosen' both slits equally. Once we
look, our observation determines the past event. The past is just as we see
it.

Teshuvah includes a radical change in the way we see our past. This
ability to change our perspective is our access into non-linear, multi-di-
rectional time. Teshuvah reaches beyond linear time, dissipating the destructive energies stored in our psyche from past negative actions, and
replacing them with healthy and constructive energies. We thereby reconnect to our timeless wholeness, and reinvigorate our lives.

Our perception of time expands and contracts with the expansion
and contraction of our consciousness. The more expansive we are, the
faster time seems to move; the more restricted we are within, the slower
time seems to move. Imagine, for example, sitting on a bench, having a
delightful conversation with someone whom you deeply love. You feel
free to express yourself, and your joy expands. Now exchange this person

with someone that you dislike. You feel constriction and unease with the awkward conversation. If both conversations took exactly ten minutes, the first scenario may have nonetheless felt like a fleeting moment, whereas the second may have felt like hours. When we are in a state of love, joy or unity, time evaporates.

Through teshuvah, we reveal our innermost desire to unite with the Source of Love. This desire draws us progressively into *harchavas ha-da'as*, or 'expanded consciousness'. In this state, the separations between past and present begin to evaporate. Without rigid boundaries of separation, the harsh pressure that the past had been placing on the present is reduced. All negative energy from the past gradually conforms to, and then is converted into, positive energy.

When we hear the teaching of our sages that teshuvah can transform transgressions into merits, we may think it means that the one who declares teshuvah is elevated, but not the actual transgressions. However, we can now understand that negative energy becomes positively charged, applying new significance to the transgression. On one level, the negativity becomes positive by serving as a motivation to do teshuvah and draw closer to Divine Unity. Every past failure can then be viewed as an invitation for greater success in the present. Every trial can be seen as a lesson, every missed opportunity an open door. Every mistake can serve as a beacon of light illuminating the way to making better and wiser choices.

Despite what we have done, we begin anew, right now. Precisely because of our negative past, we are propelled toward goodness, and toward reorienting, rebuilding and redefining our character. In this way, past transgressions are the kernels of present and future virtues, and our fall allows us to experience a greater rebound. Not only can we heal the pain of the past, we have the ability to transform pain into a redemptive force. Our transgressions no longer cause us to fall further; they encourage us to arise.

On a deeper level, the transgression actually becomes a mitzvah. Nested within every possible action is a seed of goodness. Teshuvah is of the world of yichud and inclusion, and from here we are able to include, reveal and expand that seed of goodness. One who seeks to do teshuvah belongs to the *dorshei yechudecha*, the 'seekers of Your unity'. He seeks to expose Hashem's unity and goodness hidden within Creation.

As teshuvah preceded Creation, it is the very foundation of Creation. Therefore, its embrace must envelop all aspects of Creation — the positive as well as the seemingly negative. Leaving behind the universe of *pirud*, 'separation', we enter the world of yichud, where everything is included. The actions and attitudes that alienated us from our deeper Divine self are included among our good deeds. Just as a good deed brings goodness and blessing, now the negative deed also brings goodness and blessing.

Practically speaking, in order to turn a fault into an asset, or an obstacle into a rung on your spiritual ladder, you must first recognize and acknowledge your innate connection with the Infinite One. Miraculously, the obstacles and feelings of estrangement themselves can promote this recognition. If you have descended and degraded yourself, you can allow your natural feelings of grief to shift into the intense desire to ascend. Then you can allow your brokenness and chaos to reveal the utterly wonderful connection you have with the Infinite One. This connectivity may not have been revealed without your descent. When a layer of the soul descends for the sake of an ascent, the descent is in actuality *part of the ascent*.

Now we can appreciate the fact that teshuvah is a crucible in which pure gold is distilled from the dross and silt of misdeeds. Within the lack, within the transgression itself, is the spiritual quality that we need to access and manifest. When we access this quality, we can reach our very best and achieve personal redemption. For example, Adam and Chava's spiritual downfall was triggered by their eating from a fig tree (according to Sanhedrin 70b). Yet later, they sewed garments for themselves out of fig leaves from the very same tree, and covered their nakedness. The medicine was in the poison, the light was in the darkness. As our sages say, 'There is no light like that which comes out of darkness.' There is no goodness like reconfigured negativity.

Following are three basic terms that the Torah employs for 'transgression': *cheit*, referring specifically to unintentional misdeeds; *avon*, referring to intentional transgressions; and *pesha*, sins done in spite. It is interesting to note that these three terms can be translated in such a way that suggest directly opposite meanings. For example, the root of the word *cheit* is also used in a context of cleansing and purification, as in the verse, *Va-yis'chatu ha-Levi'im*, "The Levites *purified* themselves."

Avon, when pronounced slightly differently, takes on an entirely different meaning. The three Hebrew letters that make up this word, aleph-vav-nun, can also be pronounced as *ohn*, meaning 'strength' and empowerment, as in *matzasi ohn li*, "I have found power for myself" (Hoshea, 12:8). When we rearrange the first two letters of the word *pesha*, we reveal the word *shefa*, 'abundance' or a flow and influx of blessings.

These are not merely etymological tricks; they are signs and confirmations of the truth that we can extract gold from the dross of our lives. When we redirect the energy of transgression, we trigger a cleansing process, and eventually we discover that a source of power and blessing was there all along. *Cheit* actually becomes a purifying experience; *avon* transforms into to a source of strength; *pesha*, the harshest of transgressions, becomes a flow of abundant blessings.

The device, action or situation, that is used in the performance of a mitzvah, called a *hechsher mitzvah*, can sometimes be considered as part of the mitzvah itself. This includes a preparatory action that was necessary in order to perform a particular mitzvah. For example, building a sukkah is a hechsher mitzvah for 'dwelling in the sukkah'. As an extension of this teaching, we could say that a past negative deed can serve as a preparation or precursor to teshuvah. Disconnection can thus become part of the act of connection.

Every experience, every object and subject, contains sparks of the Infinite Light of the Creator. From a kernel of grain to the majestic heavenly spheres, everything houses traces of that primordial light. To employ an analogy, we could say that the light or energy has traveled a long way from the Original Source, and having passed through many filters, has been transmuted from an abstract spiritual energy into a physical substance. Within this physical substance, the light is dimmed to the extent of being camouflaged from view. The challenge of our lives is to transform ourselves in order that we will be sensitive enough to recognize and reveal that light. Then we can reconnect those sparks to their source in the Infinite One.

Tikkun, 'repair', is the word that describes this self-transformation and subsequent reconnection of sparks to their Source. This entire process is activated through the performance of mitzvos and good deeds. When we do mitzvos, whether they are mitzvos consisting of actions or refraining from actions, our awareness is expanded and we begin to locate the Divine sparks within Creation. Withholding ourselves from inappropriate behaviors protects our inner clarity and sensitivity, which is necessary for the subtle perception of Divine sparks. Conversely, inappropriate behaviors reinforce our myopia and distorted interpretation of experience, which in turn perpetuate the concealment, exile and imprisonment of the sparks.

When a person who has engaged in negativity makes changes and begins to function as a more integrated, healthy person, he often does so with fervor and intensity — in the language of the Zohar, "with increased vigor" (1:129b). As with all new things, when one begins to experience the state of teshuvah, there is excitement and passion. In fact, the greater the alienation or distance from his Source, the greater is a person's yearning, excitement and vigor in returning.

One who has strayed from who he is and then wishes to re-align does so with greater zest. The thirst for life is greater in those who have passed through a dry, deadly wasteland. The yearning and enthusiasm of the returnee helps him rouse the powerful strength he needs in order to pull away from his previous mode of conduct and consciousness. This enthusiasm, strength and courage may not have manifested if not for his desiccating, deadening deeds. The numerical value of *cheit*, 'misdeed', is 18, the same value as the word *chai*, 'life'. The intense energy that was channeled toward spiritual death is now channeled into the affirmation of life and enthusiastic performance of mitzvos. Every good deed builds the momentum of tikkun and the passion for Divine aliveness.

Awakening this aliveness, the returnee generates more spiritual momentum than the *tzadik*, the righteous one who has always been on the right and proper course. According to the prevailing opinion of the Gemarah, the *baal teshuvah*, the one who declares teshuvah, stands on a spiritual rung unattainable by even the greatest among the tzadikim (Berachos, 34b). The tzadik operates with calm, steady love; his spiritual service and goals are achieved in a relatively smooth and stable fashion. The path of teshuvah, on the other hand, can be treacherous and fraught with extreme states, and thus the energy that is harnessed is more powerful. Only with such extreme energy can darkness be transformed into light, and death into life.

In the larger scheme, however, both the tzadik and the baal teshuvah need and complement each other. The baal teshuvah, filled with questions and uncertainties, looks to the tzadik as the embodiment of answers and certainty. When the tzadik encounters such an individual, he is touched and subtly destabilized by the questions, and compelled to look deeply into his own heart. When he merits to reveal innovative answers, the tzadik is allowed to experience a measure of excitement, passion and yearning normally known only to the baal teshuvah.

Tangentially, let us keep in mind that these two perspectives and personae are also two dimensions within each individual. We all have an inner questioner and an inner answerer, an inner baal teshuvah and an inner tzadik, and an interplay between uncertainty and certainty.

Like a bow and arrow, the further the questions pull, the more powerful is the force of return, and the greater the flight of the answer. The baal teshuvah is propelled by a previously untapped resource of soul (Tikunei Zohar). The Gemarah says that one who is tempted and overcomes temptation demonstrates a profound measure of self-control; a beautiful light shines above his head, and his face glows with a special radiance (Rashi Sanhedrin, 31a).

With the discovery of this profound light of the soul, the baal teshuvah is empowered to transform in such a way that he becomes a much better person than he would have been, had he not fallen. This internal, personal transformation seeds a reintegration of the world at large, where even the most 'negative' elements of Creation are sweetened, their goodness revealed, and their wholeness ultimately redeemed.

SYNOPSIS: CHAPTER 13
Seek Unity

Realize that a negative past can be a kernel of virtue for the present. From the point of view of absolute *yichud*, 'unity' and inclusion, the total redemption of your past is already accomplished. On the relative level, all actions or attitudes that alienated us from our deeper self need to become the source of a passionate desire for reintegration. When we consciously acknowledge our connection with the Infinite, our faults can be converted into merits, our obstacles into stepping-stones, and our sources of chaos into sources of goodness and blessing.

PRACTICE

TRACE PATTERNS

List some of the blessings in your life.

Maybe you are blessed with a beneficial relationship, job or talent. Begin to trace the events that led up to the manifestation of these blessings. If you are in a loving relationship, how did you meet your partner? Who introduced you? Try to trace the causes as far back as you can. You may notice that some trivial event, chance occurrence or uneventful encounter ended up being the pivotal moment that opened the door to this blessing. You may even notice that events that seemed totally negative or challenging at the time, such as feeling very low, became the kernels of the positive elements in your life today.

CHAPTER
FOURTEEN

Reifying
THROUGH SPEAKING

T eshuvah requires that the returnee articulate through speech the relinquishing of his negative past, as well as his positive commitment
for the future. This verbalization of regret is known as *viddui*, 'confession'.

There are codifiers who are of the opinion that the verbalized confession is a culmination of teshuvah (e.g. Rambam): confession follows
the process of return. According to this school of thought, viddui is the
returnee's reification or concretization of his new intentions in life, and
the beginning of his new reality.

Another school of thought (including the Chinuch) suggests that
through verbalization one will be inspired to commence teshuvah. Here,
viddui initiates the process of return — the confessing of misdeeds stim-
ulates the yearning to change.

Both of these schools agree that teshuvah is a positive mitzvah. Yet,
there are also other schools that maintain that teshuvah is not a precept
or mitzvah, but rather an inevitability of life. When teshuvah awakens
within a person, it will be manifest spontaneously through a sincere verbal confession.

There is one point upon which all these schools of thought do agree:
teshuvah requires viddui. Why is this? What is the great importance of

making a verbal confession or commitment, especially as it is done not in front of a person but in front of Hashem alone? Doesn't Hashem already know our thoughts and intentions? How does verbalization facilitate, stimulate or cement the life-changing process of teshuvah?

There is no unanimous opinion as to why verbalization is essential for teshuvah. The reasons given vary from analytical and psychological to purely mystical. Each explanation offers another insight into the efficacy of confession.

On the most elementary level, speaking gives a physical voice and vibration to our thoughts, rendering them more clear and intelligible. This helps us crystallize and structure our inner thoughts, feelings, and sense of intention. The narrative of our life becomes more coherent when spoken aloud. By articulating our thoughts, we unveil deeper insight and understanding into the matters at hand. For that reason, even while we are alone, mulling over an issue, we might speak our thoughts out loud to get a better grasp of what we are perceiving. Thoughts, as they exist in the mind, can remain elusive, evasive and unstructured. Once they descend into the 'vessels' of language, they become more tangible.

Upon the passing of the sage Rabbi Yehudah, his students declared, "Whoever says that Rabbi Yehudah has passed away shall be pierced with a sword" (Kesuvos, 104a)! Although they knew intellectually that he had passed away, they could not bring themselves to verbalize it. They felt that until the moment someone announced that he had died, he would still be alive. Similarly, when we hear bad news, our first response is often disbelief and denial, sometimes we may even say, 'don't say it.' It is as if what is not verbalized does not exist. Similarly, as long as an unresolved spiritual issue remains unspoken, we can ignore it and feel as if it does not exist. Therefore, we need to make verbal confessions of our unresolved spiritual issues.

We are creatures of speech, and we are strongly affected by all we say and hear. Ancient thinkers defined the human being as a *homo sapiens*, a 'rational animal', while others called him a 'tool-making animal', a 'social animal' or a 'worshiping animal'. Classical Jewish thinkers, such as Rabbi Yehudah ha-Levi, author of the Kuzari, define the human being as a *medaber*, a 'speaking being'. Language is essential to the human condition. Not only is verbal language the main mode of our communication with others, it is the tool we use to decipher, interpret and contemplate our own external and internal worlds. There is linguistic determinism, as it were, as language influences the way we think. Words create our reality — when we verbalize something, it becomes more real to us.

Universes are created through speech. The world, as alluded to in the Torah, was brought into being through the Ten Utterances of the Creator: "And Hashem said 'let there be light', and there was light." When Hashem speaks, the world responds and things come into being. It is the same with our utterances, for we are created in the 'image and likeness' of the Creator.

The medium of speech is not only essential for creation but for taking responsibility for what we create. A small child who spills milk will say, "Mommy, Daddy, the milk spilled!" A more mature child will say, "Mommy, Daddy, *I* spilled the milk." In the context of teshuvah, we must say, "I did it. I spilled the milk, and therefore, it is I who must clean it up." We can only clean up our lives when we claim responsibility for the action in question. Speaking the truth breaks us out of denial and out of the stance of an aloof and passive witness who implies that the spill occurred on its own.

Through speaking honestly about ourselves we can come face-to-face with our own truth, painful as it may be. Putting our inner thoughts out in the open may render us more vulnerable, but this is the only effective way of breaking our complacency. By putting aside any foolish pride, honest confession gives us the ability to make real changes in our lives.

An element of maturity coincides with the ability to verbalize shortcomings. This is because verbalizing brings subjective shortcomings into the light of objectivity, enabling us to evaluate them and respond to them responsibly. Once we bring an issue into the open, we can trace it back to its source, namely, the spiritual deficiency that gave rise to it.

"The voice arouses intention" (Taz). Through verbalization, we expose our inner desire and intention to return. The more we speak of feelings of the heart, the more real they become. When we speak of teshuvah, our intention of teshuvah is enhanced. Even when one has not made an intention to undertake this journey of change, the verbal articulation of what needs to change will eventually bring the person closer to intending teshuvah.

We all long for connection with the Source and other people, often not realizing how much we need it until we lose it. One of the most demoralizing feelings that one can have is the sense of loneliness that comes from social and spiritual disconnection. We can, however, begin to overcome this most unsettling sense of isolation through articulating our feelings, our present condition, and our deep desire to reconnect.

Speech is comprised of sound vibrations as well as intentionality and meaning, and even the sound of our verbal confession can bring us closer to wholeness. When we hear our own words, we are both listening and speaking. It is as if there are two people present, a speaker and a listener. As the 'speaker', you are in the presence of a compassionate, nonjudgmental 'friend' who is silently listening.

As the compassionate, silent 'listener', you can heal the 'speaker' of the extreme loneliness that arose from his or her misaligned desires, and offer awareness of 'the other'. Our sages advise one who is troubled to speak his heart to a friend (Sotah, 42b). A person may feel cured of his troubles merely by opening up to someone who will listen. It gives us courage to know that we are never 'alone'.

An even greater level of healing, of course, is realizing that the greatest listener of all, the Compassionate One, is present. By opening up and communicating freely with Hashem we create new channels of Divine love and acceptance within our being, until we are permeated with them.

Philosophers, mystics and codifiers of law throughout the ages have advocated openly and spontaneously speaking to the Creator. They saw the tremendous value of speaking to Hashem as a child speaks unselfconsciously and honestly to his parent, or as one confides in a loving friend. Through venting our thoughts before our Creator, new horizons and life-opportunities can present themselves. We gain strength to overcome our daily challenges. This organic, candid speech is particularly encouraged in an individual who is on a quest for teshuvah and higher states of spiritual integrity.

Reb Nachman of Breslov revealed an entire spiritual path and prac-

tice based on free dialogue between creature and Creator. He called this
form of informal prayer *hisbodedus*, 'being alone' with Hashem. It is a
simple verbal form of meditation, often performed in nature, or at least in
a private room or on a solitary walk. During *hisbodedus*, one should open
his heart to Hashem and speak in his own native tongue, freely expressing anything and everything that comes to mind. Nothing is too trifling
or insignificant to bring into the flow of connection with the Divine
Friend.

Rebbe Nachman once counseled a follower to pray to Hashem even
for a lost button. When you are free to speak to Hashem even about superficial, mundane issues, you will be surprised by the deeper issues that
emerge from the subconscious mind, arising in order to be resolved. This
practice of holistic connection with the Creator is not meant to supplant
the formal prayers, but rather to achieve a more comprehensive relationship with your deeper self and with the Creator. It is the epitome of personal prayer.

"Return, O Israel, to Hashem your God", thunders the Prophet
Hoshea (2:14). One meaning of this verse is 'Do teshuvah until you can
call Hashem *your* God.' The Magid of Koznitz explains: "Return until
you are able to relate to Hashem as one friend confiding in another."
Spontaneous communication can pave the way for future encounters.
Communication that is grounded in honesty with oneself, and honesty
with another person, promotes greater closeness. Spiritual intimacy with
our Source is greatly enhanced when we speak with selfless authenticity.
We begin to feel free to share all our worries, troubles, doubts and frus-
trations in the Divine Presence. Only with such openness can we feel
completely at ease with our Creator.

When we verbally acknowledge the areas that keep us entrapped,
their energy is diffused. Beliefs and actions that prohibited our full self-
integration diminish and dissolve.

Verbalizing thought is a means of acknowledging who we are and
what we think. It is not an act of conjuring up experiences, but rather an
act of reifying experiences or giving them 'vessels'. A 'vessel' allows the
speaker to realize his actual hegemony or ownership over the object. By
owning it he can navigate and negotiate his situation. The problem be-

comes manageable. Before giving a name to a strong energy pattern, it can appear overwhelming or even threatening. By speaking in this way, we are not actually subduing something outside of ourselves, but calming the mind in order to respond effectively to the tumult within.

Unfulfilled fantasies can perpetually haunt us and grip us. Desires lodged in the subconscious mind are hard to forget. Confessing them makes them concrete, and once they are concrete, they can be released and forgotten. We cannot forget something that we hardly remember. Until a desire is clothed in objectivity, it remains a fixation or a latent tendency and cannot be deliberately released. When this desire is garbed in words, it can then be properly addressed and subsequently dismissed.

There is a psycho-spiritual principle that if you tell the truth about something with proper intent, you dissipate the energy around it. In terms of teshuvah, you can use this principle to liberate yourself from the prison of guilt and shame. If you experience guilt and speak of it honestly, the speaking itself can help dissolve the guilt. Clearly, the articulation must be done in such a way that it sheds light on the guilt, and releases you from the hold of reactivity.

There are various methods for releasing old, deeply entrenched negative energies, but the most powerful way is simply to cease denying that they exist. Acknowledge your feelings, confess that your transgressions are real, and then declare teshuvah.

When energy is denied or repressed, or when faults and imperfections are swept under the rug, they will reappear and manifest themselves, possibly with a force greater than the original. Hiding from something does not remove it. By allowing negative memories to surface into consciousness, we also allow them to become diluted. Confession decisively delivers imperfections into the compassionate hands of the Master of the Universe. In this way, we enable ourselves to be forgiven, and to forgive others, to heal the past, and finally to move on with our lives.

SYNOPSIS: CHAPTER 14
Confess

Our inner thoughts may be elusive, but speaking about them makes them more concrete. Once they are concrete, we can change them. If you feel a desire to change your life for the good, verbalize your feelings. Tell them to the Ever-present Divine Friend.

PRACTICE
AFFIRM

Repeat these words from the morning prayers: "My G-d, the soul You have given me is pure."
If ever you want to empty your mind of inappropriate thoughts, recite this formula three times: "Create in me a pure heart, O G-d, and renew within me an upright spirit" (Tehillim 51:12). Accustom yourself to repeating positive affirmations as you go through your day. This will give you strength to confess your shortcomings.

We need to be mindful of how we use our words, whether in communication with others or in communication with our own self. If you find that you keep on knocking yourself down, saying, "I am not a good person," or "I am lazy and incompetent," exchange these words for, "I *did* something that was not good," "I have been *acting* lazy, *as if* I were incompetent." This can be a first step in teshuvah: confessing and defining your actions, without depreciating yourself in the act. Then, you can strengthen the trajectory of your teshuvah by creating positive 'confessions', such as, "I *am* essentially a good person," "I am essentially a committed, competent person," or "I have the inner resources to change the direction of my life."

CHAPTER
FIFTEEN

Elevating Our Three Garments:
THOUGHT, SPEECH & ACTION

W e matter, and our actions matter. Our individual actions determine
the rise or fall of the collective spiritual energy in the universe. We
have tremendous value, and we exert a powerful influence on the world
around us. Every action or inaction creates ripple effects throughout the
cosmos. When a person commits a negative act, destructive vibrations are
released into the 'ether' — the spiritual and psychic atmosphere — rendering an imbalance in the very fabric of the universe. To counterbalance
and rectify these effects, one needs to release vibrations of wholeness and
goodness.

Verbally articulating teshuvah atones for negativity and rebalances
the energy field of the universe. Every good deed we do creates positive
vibrations or 'pure angels', perpetuating healthy energies throughout the
world. Indulging inappropriate thoughts creates 'impure angels', who in
turn create vehicles for increased impurity and impure deeds. Teshuvah is
the process of dismantling these vehicles, dissipating the pollution of
negativity, and generating positive, balanced energies instead.

Angelic energies born from human thoughts and deeds are named according to the activity that created them. If a person lies, for example, the angel created is called *Shakran*, 'Liar', and its life-force emanates from the combination of the letters that spell *sheker*, 'falsehood'. In order to diffuse these forces, the person needs to uproot them at their source. This can be accomplished by verbally declaring regret and the desire to stop lying. Then, the letters of the word sheker are disassembled and the life-force that emanated from them disintegrates.

The soul possesses three powers, or instruments, of expression: thought, speech and action. These are referred to as the 'garments' of the soul, meaning interfaces between the soul and the world. The way we use these interfaces can elevate us or bring us down. We need to cleanse our garments for genuine elevation to occur. Thinking about positive change cleanses our thoughts; speaking about positive change cleanses us of negative speech; resolving to change helps to cleanse our actual deeds.

Everything is multi-dimensional; every object and subject is comprised of a physical and a spiritual dimension, a body and a soul. Even a misdeed has a body and a soul: the 'body' is the misdeed itself, and the 'soul' is and the pleasure enjoyed in the act. Reb Schneur Zalman of Liadi says that the yearning for teshuvah, felt deep within the heart, diffuses the soul of the action. The verbalization of teshuvah, which is a minor form of action, erases the misdeed's body.

The Torah is the blueprint and the spiritual backdrop of Creation. When a person commits a negative act, whether by omission or commission, he causes a defect in the letters of the Torah in the verses where that particular action is mentioned. For example, as Reb Nachum of Chernobyl teaches, when someone steals, the letters of the Torah that state, "You shall not steal" become smudged. Only when the person sincerely declares, "I will not steal," are these letters restored to their clear, original condition.

Our body is a physical reflection of the soul, while the soul is an individualized reflection of the Torah. The Torah reveals 248 positive mitzvos, which correspond to the 248 positive energies of the soul, which correspond to the 248 'limbs' of the body and their positive states of health. Likewise, the 365 prohibitions of the Torah are the 365 protective functions of our soul's immune system, and the 365 main 'veins' that channel life-force and manage the immunity in our body.

In other words, the Torah is written within our souls and bodies. "You shall not steal" is part of who we are. Therefore, the protective power of one's inner Torah becomes lessened with every breach of this prohibition. The more accustomed to lying he becomes, the easier it is for him to continue lying, and he compromises his spiritual immunity. If the letters of his soul are heavily damaged, they may no longer spell "You shall not steal," but instead, 'You *shall* steal.' It becomes almost impossible for the habitual thief to even entertain the thought of stopping. In extreme cases, the internal psycho-spiritual damage can result in physical maladies as well.

This underscores the importance of verbalizing teshuvah. If we have lied in the past, when we then assert, "I will stay away from lies," or "I want to speak the truth", we begin to repair our inner letters of Torah that spell, "Stay away from lying." We thus recreate the harmony between our outer self and our inner Torah soul-vibration. When we thus fix the immune system of our souls, our bodies will respond with increased health and energy. Not only can we heal ourselves through teshuvah, we can create a level of spiritual clarity and resiliency that we never had before.

As we discussed in the previous chapter, *viddui* or 'verbal confession' plays an immensely important role in the process of teshuvah. It benefits us on every level, from psychological to mystical. Yet it should be understood that the key to this effectiveness, the secret ingredient that allows viddui to eradicate spiritual blemishes, is *simcha*, 'joy'. Viddui is not a solemn, gloomy task requiring much weeping and bitterness of heart. As with all mitzvos, when viddui is performed with healthy, balanced, and sincere joy, it ennobles and glorifies the doer. Cleansing the self of impurities is actually a happy undertaking.

Once, the Baal Shem Tov visited a small town on the days of *Selichos* or 'Forgiveness', the days of intense teshuvah leading up to Rosh Hashanah. Joining the service, he observed the cantor reciting the prayers of repentance with joy, singing them with upbeat and even jubilant melodies. After the service, the Baal Shem approached the cantor and asked about his peculiar behavior. The cantor replied, "Rebbe, just as when a mortal king is about to return from a long vacation and his servants are cleaning the palace, they work with great happiness and excitement. Should it not be the same when a man is cleaning and opening his heart so that the King of All Kings, the Master of the Universe, can enter?" When the Baal Shem heard this interpretation, his face lit up with a smile, and he kissed the cantor on the forehead.

The Talmudic sages debate whether confession must include specific details or not. Should one recount all of his wrongdoings and mistakes, or simply speak of a general resolve? Rabbi Yehudah asserted that one should elaborate the details, while Rabbi Akiva maintained that one should not. Their arguments stem from their opinions regarding the primary motivator for teshuvah: is it fear or is it love? Rabbi Yehudah says teshuvah essentially comes from a fear of reprimand or of not being rewarded. Therefore, one must specify the commissions or omissions for which one experiences contrition. This is because the specific transgression determines the exact negative consequences; since the objective of viddui is to nullify all of the negative consequences, the precise details are important in allowing viddui to have its full effect.

Rabbi Akiva believed that one who comes to teshuvah is stirred by an emotion more elevated than fear: love and deep yearning for unity within himself and with the Source of all Life. An almost supernatural love beats within our hearts waiting to be revealed and manifested. Recounting the details is beside the point; the messy specifics of sin are not necessary in the revelation of love. For Rabbi Akiva, what is most important is to unleash the deep human yearning for reconnection and return.

Post-Talmudic scholars and codifiers of Jewish law, such as the Rambam and the Rif, continue this debate on whether one must confess the details or not. Despite Rabbi Akiva's high regard for humanity, the sad reality is that most people operate on a much lower grade, where teshuvah is more a matter of fear than of love. Most people need to be shaken out of their spiritual complacency to come to the realization that change and growth is an imperative. Indeed, for most people to awaken to teshuvah, they need to recount the details, implications and ramifications of their status. This is a sort of 'shock treatment'. Still, our deeper aspiration, whether we are conscious of it or not, is to be guided by love. Our soul desires that we come to teshuvah from a sense of self-acceptance and wholeness of heart, rather than from a sense of fear, alienation or shock.

When fear of consequences is our main motivating factor, the atmosphere in which we live is saturated with anxiety. When teshuvah, is based in love, relationship and connection, our atmosphere is imbued with joy, harmony and forgiveness. The choice is ours.

Up to this point, we have been exploring action and speech, our outer and middle soul-garments. Now we will turn to the innermost garment, *mach'shavah* or 'thought'. The progression of our discussion — from action, to speech, to thought — reflects the fact that our good deeds affect our speech, and our positive speech affects our inner thoughts and intentions. On a global, historical level also, as we evolve toward universal redemption, the refinement of humanity progresses inward from actions, to speech, to thought. Today, we need to begin focusing on refining the inner garments of the collective spirit.

In the era of the Holy Temple, if one committed an action that transgressed spiritual law, he could attain teshuvah by means of another action: bringing an animal sacrifice to the Temple. Of course, he would also offer speech in the form of verbal confession, and thoughts in the form of *kavanah* or 'intention'. However, the main focus of the atonement process at that time was the physical act of animal sacrifice. After the destruction of the Temple, we shifted into a state of *v'nishalma parim sifaseinu*, "Our words take the place of sacrificial offerings" (Hoshea, 14:3). The Gemarah states that when we study the sections of the Torah that discuss sacrificial offerings, particularly when we verbalize the words of these verses, it is as if we are bringing actual sacrificial offerings (Menachos, 110a). Thus, the essential element of teshuvah changed from action to speech.

As always, to insure that our speech will create change, our intentionality is vital. Now, as we approach the Final Redemption, our task is to elevate our intentionality. Teshuvah on the level of thought includes optimizing the 'hard-drive' of the subconscious mind in order that our conscious reflexes will be pure and noble. The *shaar* or 'gate' of holiness is the power of imagination through which we *m'shaer b'libo*, or 'conjure things in the depths of our heart'.

Fantasy and false imagination are the roots of negative speech and action. Therefore, when we do teshuvah on the level of action by stopping an outward behavior, it may not be complete teshuvah. Complete teshuvah includes transforming our inner world, our thoughts and attitude. Refining this inner garment is especially important after many years of being bombarded with unhealthy images and messages from the culture and media surrounding us, whether through explicit or subliminal imagery. Over time, this imagery accumulates in the storehouse of our subconscious mind, and certain experiences can trigger this imagery and bring it up into conscious awareness like a belch. To transform ourselves completely we need to work from the inside out. We need to learn how to perform the teshuvah of *mach'shavah*, refining and reprogramming our powers of thought and imagination.

It is said that *hirhur* or 'fantasizing' about misdeeds is worse than the physical deeds themselves (Yumah, 29a). Imagination runs deeper than action, and therefore it can be more damaging to our psyche and inner heart. One reason for this is that mental transgressions are almost always more elaborate then the actions they represent. Since imagination is outwardly invisible, an apparently healthy person can walk around for a long time concealing a perverse and tangled fantasy world. The secret to rectifying the imagination is to vividly and persistently imagine yourself as who you really are: a tzadik, and an ever-pure soul radiating light and goodness. When you imagine that the inner attributes you are working on are already perfect, you begin to turn destructive fantasy into holy imagination. Holy imagination helps transform transgressions at their root, converting them into merits or even mitzvos.

When enough of us have transformed ourselves at our core and are actively involved in envisioning a redeemed world, we can begin to usher in a collective redemption, with the revealing of Mashiach, may it come speedily, in our days.

SYNOPSIS:CHAPTER 15
Recognize the Power of Your Thoughts, Words and Actions

The soul has three garments or instruments of expression: thought, speech and action. Every thought, word or deed either elevates these three powers or degrades them. They have cosmic effects as well, determining the expansion or contraction of the collective spiritual energy of the universe. For teshuvah to be fully transformative, it is not sufficient to merely change our objective actions and words. We must also have our subjective thought and imagination in our conscious control — luminous and directed toward the Source of Light.

PRACTICE

TAANIS DIBBUR
'FASTING FROM SPEECH'

When we fast from the act of eating, we can become less dependent on food and enter a more spiritual state.

Similarly, the practice of fasting from speech can allow us to become less dependent on mundane speech, and to enter a more silent state. When we are quiet, we slow down, and later when we do speak, it is with more *kavanah*, 'focus' or intention.

Before you go to sleep, give yourself a period of time to practice *taanis dibbur*. Resolve that at some time each night you won't speak for at least fifteen minutes. Later, you might extend this to an hour. The amount of time should be challenging, but not oppressive to yourself or others. This practice will enable you to bring more consciousness and choice to the times that you are speaking.

An even deeper practice is *taanis mach'shavah*, 'fasting from thought' — meaning from certain forms of thought. Take it upon yourself each day, for an amount of time that goes a little beyond what you think you can handle, to think only positive thoughts and intentions, while ignoring negative or mundane imaginings. It might initially be difficult to push aside unwanted thoughts. If lower thoughts arise, tell yourself, "Okay, give me a few minutes and then I will think about this, but right now I'm busy being positive." Continue delaying them at their onset, if and when they reappear.

An *avodah* or 'spiritual discipline' that is even greater than formal fasting is to interrupt a habit mid-stream. Here, in the very moment one feels the intensity of his desire or habit-energy, he chooses to take control and refrain. In relation to food, it takes a higher spiritual level to cease eating in the middle of a meal, than it does to fast completely. Similarly, it takes more mastery to refrain from un-mindful speech when you are engaged in conversation, than when you are not speaking at all.

In regular 'fasting', there is less temptation since there is a distance between the person and the object of desire. In relation to imagination and thought, which can be extremely subtle, there may always be less distance between the person and the habitual pattern. It is important to appreciate this challenge when taking on a *taanis mach'shavah*.

The key to any spiritual discipline is to integrate the transcendence that one has cultivated in a formal practice or a peak experience into the normal flow of everyday life. One should avoid swinging between self-denial and indulgence. Teshuvah is a balanced approach to life.

EXPIATION
vs.
DRAWING CLOSER

As we said earlier, some translate the word *teshuvah* as 'repentance' or 'rectifying past misdeeds', and some more accurately as 'response' or 'return'. However, the common denominator between all these interpretations is that teshuvah is an effective remedy for a fragmented or negative state, a poor choice or transgression — and it is a return to wholeness and happiness. Yet the essential quality of teshuvah reaches far beyond this paradigm.

In general, there are two states of teshuvah: *teshuvah tata'a*, 'lower teshuvah' and *teshuvah ila'a*, 'higher teshuvah'. Teshuvah tata'a deals with contrition and regret over actions taken or not taken. The remorseful returnee decides to change his ways through contemplating his state of estrangement, how he has 'bound the King in the gutters' (Shir ha-Shirim, 7:6), and how he has dragged his deepest Divine self into degradation and deceit.

Teshuvah *ila'a* is based on *deveikus*, 'cleaving to the Source'. It is a spiritual awakening triggered not by a sense of moral disgust, but rather by a yearning for life, aligning oneself with Hashem, and healing the world. Ever since one's expulsion from his mother's womb, where his soul was enveloped in the warmth of Torah, one's soul hungers for reconnection and wholeness.

As we have learned, teshuvah is comprised of two Hebrew words: *tashuv*, 'return', and *hei*, a letter that symbolizes the Divine Presence. In the Four-Letter name of Hashem, *yud – hei – vav – hei*, the letter hei is repeated. The latter or 'lower' hei represents Divinity within the realm of *Malchus*, the world of action. The first or 'higher' hei represents Divinity within *Binah*, the inner world of higher understanding. Teshuvah on the level of the lower hei is *teshuvah tata'a*, where one repairs his marred actions or inactions. Teshuvah on the level of the higher hei represents *teshuvah ila'a*, which is not about rectifying doings or non-doings, but rather reorienting the doer himself.

Teshuvah tata'a expiates for the individual's past, expunging the damaging consequences or resonance of a wrongful action. Teshuvah ila'a, however, draws the individual closer to Divinity, expunging negativity in its very root, and retroactively re-creating the past. This is the form of teshuvah that transforms damage into virtue.

In the 'Divine absence' or personal incompleteness that we may sometimes sense, our insatiable pining for wholeness reveals the ever-present essence of wholeness. When we engage in teshuvah ila'a and become deeply aware of the Divine Presence in our lives, there is a radical transcendence of all desire for things outside of self. This heralds transformation of all negativity, since negativity is rooted in the desire to receive wholeness from external or limited objects or subjects.

The Days of Awe are perhaps the most observed of all holidays. It is interesting to note that the sequence of these holy days seems to be reversed. First comes Rosh ha-Shanah, "the Day of Judgment", followed by Yom Kippur, the day dedicated to teshuvah. How is it that we are first 'judged' for what we have done, and then afterward given an open portal to atonement? Wouldn't a more logical order be to start with a day of teshuvah and cleansing, and conclude with a day of judgment or vindication? Upon closer scrutiny, the sequence of the Days of Awe and their season makes perfect sense and reveals a deeper understanding of teshuvah.

Preceding Rosh ha-Shanah is the month of Elul, an entire month dedicated to honest introspection, self-evaluation and renewal. Therefore, before Rosh ha-Shanah, we have already immersed ourselves in unwavering soul-searching and returning to our spiritual compass from which we may have strayed. The astrological influence of the month of Elul is the sign of *Besula*, 'virgin' or Virgo (Sefer Yetzirah, 5:8). During the course of this thirty-day period of cleansing and expiating our negativity, we attain a virginal purity of spirit. Having undergone this arduous clean up, our ballot is completely spotless, and we are ready for a positive judgment on Rosh ha-Shanah.

The Midrash recounts that we go into Rosh ha-Shanah dressed in our finest, most elegant attire, trimmed, showered and prepared to be judged. We come with confidence and certainty, for we firmly trust that the coming year will unfold in the most favorable ways possible. Rosh ha-Shanah is the confirmation and culmination of the process of teshuvah tata'a.

Following Rosh ha-Shanah are the "Ten Days of Teshuvah", ending with Yom Kippur. On these most auspicious days, as Reb DovBer of Chabad writes, "the Source of Light is drawn to its sparks," and we are given the opportunity to attain the greatest heights available. This is an amazing reversal of the normal trajectory: sparks are usually 'drawn back to their Source'. However, in this case, the Infinite One is lovingly drawn down to the finite — to us and our own unique shards and glimmers of Divine Light. The Ten Days of Teshuvah are on the level of teshuvah ila'a, the all-transforming teshuvah of love.

When Yom Kippur comes, it reveals the essence of who we truly are: children of Hashem, sourced in Hashem, reuniting with Hashem, and ultimately a "part of Hashem, in the literal sense". Yom Kippur is the culmination of the process of teshuvah ila'a and at-one-ment. It is not merely a day of expiation, it is a day of absolute Divine love, nearness and identification with the One.

In the daily prayers between Rosh Hashanah and Yom Kippur, there is an ancient custom (since Talmudic times) of replacing the words *Melech ohev tzadakah u'mishpat*, "King who loves righteousness and justice", with the words *ha-Melech ha-Mishpat*, "King of Judgment". This practice, while on the surface a mere linguistic trick to signal a heightened time of reflection and judgment, transmits to us a deeper message. Following the month of Elul, we can afford, as it were, to be judged by the 'King of Judgment'. In other words, to gain a favorable judgment, we do not have to resort to activating the elements of "love" or mercy, as in the qualities of the "King who *loves* righteousness and judgment". Entering Rosh ha-Shanah with a clear slate, we are already so empowered that we no longer have to plead for loving kindness; we can 'demand' a good year. We come before the Master of the Universe and declare with self-confidence, "I have mended my ways, and I deserve to be given a good year!"

Our relationship with our Ultimate Source is mirrored in our human relationships. Human relationships are often founded on what each participant can obtain from the other; one gives in order to get. This is a conditional love (if it can even be called that), and the relationship lasts as long as both parties are getting what they want. For example, an employer may appreciate, or even 'love' an employee for what he or she does for the company. The moment, however, the employee ceases to produce desired results, the employer ceases to experience warm feelings for the employee.

Other human relationships are rooted in a higher reality. For example, many spousal couples that stay connected across many seasons and through many ups and downs are not limited to the give-and-take modality. Their interactions express a measure of unconditional love. They may never even consider the question, 'What has s/he done for me lately,' and both partners might be focused only on fulfilling the other person's desire or will. Yet most spousal relationships also begin with a conditional love — their origin and foundation being initially contingent on physical, emotional or intellectual attractions.

There is a love that is even higher than spousal love, one that is intrinsic and unconditional and is not founded in physical sensations, emotions or intellect. One example of this is parents' love for their children. Regardless of their children's behavior or capabilities, parents continue to nurture, protect and love them. As long as the parent does not inhibit this natural flow of love, the mere 'being' of their child arouses a loving response.

There are three valid 'frequency ranges' of loving another person:
•*Doing*: Loving *what* the other does for us — loving their actions.
•*Expressing*: Loving *how* the other is — how they look, think, or speak — loving their self-expression.
•*Being*: Loving *who* the other is — regardless of their actions or appearance — loving their essence.

While these three ranges may be simultaneously in play, the third and highest level of love is not contingent on how smart, beautiful or generous the other person is. The love of parents for their children is naturally uninhibited because their children share their very essence. Parents and children are not inherently separate. Unwavering, ever-present and uninhibited love flows naturally from the recognition of oneness.

As our Divine Parent, Hashem's love for us is similarly unconditional and ever-present. It is we ourselves who occasionally distance ourselves, strain the relationship or render our connection conditional. That is, if we deviate from our authentic self, the relationship appears *to us* to be conditional. Teshuvah ila'a is looking deeper within to unveil our unconditional and uninterrupted oneness with our Creator. This reveals the love that transcends cause and effect. We are loved — regardless of our behavior or appearance — simply because we exist.

Even if we are grappling with darkness, there is an inner space deep within us that remains pure, luminous, and one with the Source at all times. Our own inner light is an extension of the *Ohr Ein Sof*, the 'Endless Infinite Light' of Hashem. Yom Kippur reveals this oneness, which is the essence of who we are.

One of the oldest and most mysterious of all Jewish texts is *Sefer Yetzirah*, the 'Book of Formation'. This text states that Creation consists of three primary elements: 1) *olam*, 'universe' or space, 2) *shanah*, 'year' or time, and 3) *nefesh*, 'soul' or consciousness. We are always in some location, at a certain time, and in a particular state of consciousness. These three planes are so intricately linked that one cannot exist without the others.

Space, time and consciousness each expand out of a central point of oneness. Just as there is a point of oneness within the perspective of 'soul' or consciousness, namely the level of *yechidah*, there is also a point of oneness at the center of time, namely Yom Kippur. This day is the pinnacle and essence of *shanah*, from which the oneness of the Infinite One begins to stream outward into finite time. It is an open opportunity to experience and express the yechida, the oneness of soul that is one with the Divine.

On Yom Kippur, we aspire to function from a transcendent, angelic reality. The Rambam writes that on this day we "cease" from eating and drinking. This is not merely about afflicting the body, since if we wished to do that, there would be many other effective ways of doing so. Rather, we cease to operate according to normative physical causes and effects. In doing so, we dedicate ourselves to our soul's transcendence — our liberation from materialism, the ego and all of its derivatives. We extinguish all negativity that may arise from separation.

In Hebrew, the word most commonly employed to describe negativity and its parent power is *ha-satan*. We traditionally translate this word as 'Satan' or the evil inclination and its harshest levels of narcissism and selfishness. However, the word is better understood as 'the adversary', that which seems to stand in the way of you being your best, most loving, and most conscious self.

The numerical value of the word *ha-satan* is 364 (hei=5, shi¬n=300, tes=9, and nun=50). A solar year cycle is comprised of 365 days. Most days of the year we may struggle with our own inner adversary, but on the day of Yom Kippur we transcend such negativity and reactive self-deprecation altogether (Yumah, 20a). Yom Kippur is not a day dedicated to remembering the sordid details of our past misdeeds, mishaps and failures. On this day, there exists no transgressor or un-holiness; there is only absolute freedom.

The reality of Yom Kippur alludes to a level of teshuvah that we can engage every day of the year. This is the teshuvah of *yechidah*, 'unity' beyond any trace of negativity, and the recognition that everything is part of Divine Unity. Reb Naftali of Ropshitz would say that throughout his life he never once 'returned in teshuvah' — meaning that he never regretted his past deeds, whereas regret is usually part of the course of teshuvah. The deeper message of this enigmatic statement is that he recognized, from a place of yechidah, that everything that he experienced came from Hashem.

Reb Naphtali's insight was retrospective, in looking back on his life. This helps explain the paradox in one of Rabbi Akiva's teachings in Pirkei Avos: "Everything is foreseen, and yet, (free) choice is given." Everything in the past was Hashem's will and was meant to be, and yet with regard to the present and future we must act from a place of choice; we are empowered to make decisions and co-create our reality.

"The essence of the day of Yom Kippur atones" (Shevuos, 13a). In other words, the day itself has powers through which all of a person's transgressions are eliminated. After the ensuing debate in the Gemarah, all the sages agree that the essence of the day does bring atonement. However, the question arises: do we need to activate this atonement through participation and desire for change, or does the day itself atone without any human involvement or declaration of teshuvah?

Clearly, even if we say that the day itself atones without active teshuvah, we must concede that a minimum participation on the part of the person is required. What sense would it make to forgive someone for something if he does not even desire to be forgiven? Thus, a bare minimum is needed: the person must at least be passive and not interfere with the healing and unifying powers of Yom Kippur. For these reasons, all of the sages finally agree that in order to achieve a complete and total teshuvah, one must partake in the process.

Genuine growth can happen when we are able to fuse the 'inspiration' from above with the 'perspiration' of spiritual work below. Our active participation allows the Divine revelation of total forgiveness to permeate our consciousness, embedding itself deeply within our psyche. Then this revelation can become part of our every day reality, giving us the ability to live an inspired and inspiring life.

SYNOPSIS:CHAPTER 16
Remember, You are Loved

Deep in our souls, we know that Hashem's love for us is constant, unconditional and ever-present. We are loved not because of our deeds or attributes, but because of the essence of who we are. If we actively alienate ourselves, we will perceive Hashem's love as ephemeral, conditional and distant. Teshuvah allows us to reconnect with our own depths, to remember the radical truth: the perpetual presence and accessibility of Divine love.

PRACTICE
AWAKEN

Meditating on unconditional love can bring on spiritual awakening.

Dwell for a minute on how an excellent parent loves his or her children. The potential for such unobstructed love exists within each of us. How much greater than human parental love is the Divine love, which transcends nature and any sense of limitation.

Now, contemplate the spark of Divine love that Hashem has placed within your own being. Awaken this spark and nurture it throughout the day.

CHAPTER
SEVENTEEN

Inspiration
&
INTERNALIZATION

F or some people, the state of teshuvah begins with a sudden inspiration that shifts their life trajectory, or a moment of recognition that
spurs radical change. For others, attaining the state of teshuvah is a gradual and more challenging process. The illustrious sage Rabbi Yehudah
once wept, "Some acquire eternal life...*b'sha'ah achas*, 'in one hour'" (Avodah Zarah, 17a). *B'sha'ah achas*, 'in one hour', can be read to mean 'in one
fell swoop', or in one moment. The Zohar concurs: teshuvah can be attained instantaneously (1:129a).

Rav Kook writes that the reason some people continue down their
path of destruction and do not do teshuvah is that they do not know how
easy it is to initiate teshuvah. In order to begin awakening your deepest
self, all you have to do is turn around and face the other direction. Of
course in order for teshuvah to be real and integrated, it must be lived
over the course of time. Once you turn yourself around, you must move
forward with all of the strength of your being and never give up. However, taking the first step gives you the strength you need.

Often, those who have radically changed over the course of their lives cannot point to a single event or day when they were compelled to redirect their lives. For most of us, change comes about slowly, through progressive stages of learning and enlightenment that gradually build a critical mass of change. Teshuvah is cyclical and continuous. Like a circle without a fixed beginning or ending point, in the state of teshuvah any moment can be a new start. Every day brings with it new challenges and new opportunities. New levels of spirituality and growth become available to us with every life experience.

As we mentioned earlier, teshuvah transcends the constrictions of time. Since it actually precedes the creation of time, teshuvah has retroactive effects. It is, in a sense, capable of manifesting change simultaneously in the present and past. For this reason, spiritual transformation can manifest instantaneously. Yet instantaneous and drastic overnight conversions are not the only kind of teshuvah available. Some people assume that their teshuvah is diluted or disingenuous if it does not bring a fantastic or cataclysmic change or an instantaneous illumination.

There are many pitfalls with the 'instantaneous transformation' model. If one expects that stepping into teshuvah should cause an immediate and total change, he may be disappointed. When he honestly declares a state of teshuvah, he may feel hypocritical if he suffers setbacks in certain areas. He may decide that he has not yet attained genuine teshuvah, or else he would not have fallen again. Desiring authenticity and freedom from hypocrisy, he might give up and revert to his old ways of misconduct. This subtle excuse of 'authenticity' allows a person to continue living as they always had until they passively experience some earth-shattering inner transformation or enlightenment. This is an error.

Teshuvah is much more than a sudden burst of light that wonderfully illuminates all of life's darkness. Although in a few cases teshuvah begins this way, genuine transformation and illumination necessitates intensive inner work. Real transformation takes a lifetime, and that is why we have a lifetime.

Children naturally rebel when they feel their parents are overbearing. Many adolescents seek to change their labels or self-images, such as rejecting a conservative, traditional identity and embracing a more liberal or unconventional identity. This kind of change is, of course, superficial. They exchange the pre-programmed responses instilled by their parents or educators, for another set of pre-programmed responses — those of their peers. Nothing has internally changed, certainly not in terms of true inner freedom and autonomy. Most often, when such young people outgrow their rebellious stages, they revert back to their original patterns. Similarly, if our teshuvah consists of accepting one set of responses over another, without real work, integral change does not occur. Over time, excitement fades, and one regresses, at least inwardly.

If you find yourself regressing into negative behavior, the following is one way to reset and reprogram your actions on a deeper level. Reb Mendel of Rimanov teaches, in the name of the Arizal, that in order to undo negative patterns of behavior, a person should assert a positive pattern for forty consecutive days, corresponding to the time of *yetziras havelad*, the formation of a viable fetus. When you change your behavior for forty days, it will become easier, and the 'gestation' of teshuvah will continue to develop. Refraining from the old habit and pursuing the new habit will become more like second nature, until the day you find you have birthed a new spiritual status.

Initially, in order for one to wake up from spiritual torpor and complacency, his early steps must be taken quickly, with vigor and force, creating a powerful 'about-face'. Then, once the journey is well underway, the process can be lived more deliberately. The young and immature nation of Israel left Egypt — representing a spiritual state of constriction and confinement — in haste. They were instructed to eat their meal with their belts pulled tight and their staffs in hand, ready to leave at a moment's notice.

In the preliminary stages of the journey of teshuvah, we have to be ready to move with alacrity and decisiveness. Later on, when we have achieved a measure of freedom, we need to internalize the change and let it soak fully into our consciousness and behavior. In later stages, teshuvah is no longer separate from who we are, it is the very context in which our life occurs.

There is a story in the Gemarah of a man named Eliezer Ben Durdayah who, upon realizing his lowly spiritual state, began to feel an over-whelming and passionate desire for teshuvah. He was not properly pre-pared for the force of this existential crisis, nor was he equipped to integrate his feelings in a sustainable manner. His *chapel perilous* or 'dark night of the soul' propelled him into a deep rapture, his soul lifted from his body, and he died in ecstasy.

This extreme case demonstrates the fact that when a spiritual awak-ening happens too quickly, it can be psychologically and even physically harmful. Elevating consciousness too suddenly can cause a *ratzo b'li shuv*, 'transcendence without return'. Our task and challenge is to respond to our need for change and growth each and every day, while not allowing ourselves to become too overwhelmed by spiritual urgency.

Even when our path of teshuvah is balanced, the first steps may be strenuous or painful: "All beginnings are difficult" (Mechiltah). Shifting from one path to another, from one state of being to another, is a radical act. By choosing teshuvah, we are committing not only to an internal shift, and a change in our outer behavior, but also a shift of identity. In our becoming present we may need to dramatically cut ourselves off from certain elements of who we were in the past. Later, when the journey is well under way, we can settle down and perhaps re-incorporate the many positive elements of our past identity.

This stabilization occurs when we take the inspiration that prompted teshuvah and bring it into the minutiae of day-to-day life. There are often two stages in teshuvah: the stage of passionate desire for transformation, and the stage of returning to normal life, where we meet the real challenges. In this latter stage, we have to filter and internalize our consuming passion in such a way that it integrates with the sensitive ebb and flow of everyday life. Then we can find the Creator within the Creation, the peak within the valley, and 'the universe in a grain of sand'.

Countless people who have resolved to enter the path of teshuvah say that in the beginning, implementing their resolution came relatively easily. However, after a time of smooth sailing, they began to encounter frightening setbacks. The excitement and invigoration they had felt dissi-pated. They experienced even greater uncertainty than they did before they began to move toward teshuvah. Chaos and ambiguity once again became the backdrop of their lives. Their spiritual practice even began to appear as a wasteland fraught with boring and tedious routine.

When you begin living a life anchored in teshuvah, the exciting closeness you initially felt to your true self and to Hashem may seem to diminish. Echoes of your estrangement from life may begin to resurface. According to the Arizal's terms, your *gadlus* or 'expansiveness' and open-ness of mind and heart, may be replaced by an ominous *katnus* or 'con-striction' of spirit. You may sense that the Divine Presence has departed, and that you are back in exile.

It is important to understand this phenomenon so that you can suc-cessfully integrate teshuvah into your day-to-day life. Reb Simcha Bunim of Pshischah offers an analogy. When a person enters a candy store, the owner may draw him into making a purchase by giving him tastes of var-ious samples of the sweets. However, once he has tasted the samples and is ready to buy something, nothing more is given for free.

When we enter the doors of teshuvah, everything seems to be free. Anyone with a desire to taste the sweetness of truth, meaning and pur-pose, is offered free samples. All that is required is that one take the first step by entering the store and showing interest. The sampling is referred to as gadlus rishon, 'initial expansion' or an introductory sense of great-ness. Once we decide to make a purchase and bring the sweetness home into our day-to-day lives, we have to pay for it with work and exertion. The reward of teshuvah is revealed through the work itself. We must commit to the way of closeness to Hashem with the same intensity as one might 'commit' to self-centered and destructive desires.

When teshuvah becomes our way of life, although the initial highs may fade, the wholeness that we experience is more real and more re-warding, since it is the fruit of our own labor, not just a 'sample' or free-bie. Similarly, the love that has grown and matured with time and hard work is of an incomparably greater quality than the 'free' introductory high of falling in love.

The beginning of teshuvah is like a child's first steps, says Reb Moshe Chaim of Sudylkov. When a child is learning how to stand and walk on his own, the parent at first lifts the child to his feet, holds his hands, and walks with him. Then, once the child is more confident, the parent lets go, and runs to the other side of the room to welcome the child with open arms. This motivates the child to do the actual work of walking.

In the beginning of a spiritual journey, we may experience feelings of closeness, as though someone is holding our hand, walking us through the process. Once we are on our own feet, and more established in the state of teshuvah, we may feel a strange distance. This is only because now our Parent in Heaven is able to let go — motivating us to go further — and take pleasure in seeing us walk independently. We have grown up and we are now capable of continuing on the path of teshuvah.

Ironically, self-righteous and judgmental attitudes are often found in those who have radically transformed their lives through teshuvah. At times, these attitudes are coupled with feelings of holiness and saintliness. For some people, these sentiments are genuine and valid, indicative of real progress, but for the majority, these holy feelings are bestowed upon them in the form of a test. Will these feelings lead the person deeper into transcendence or into enslavement to a spiritualized ego? Such a person is challenged: can he begin to walk with humility, or will he slip into self-pride?

A parent may wish to assess his child's sense of responsibility in taking care of a precious gift. If he wants to give his child precious jewelry, he may first give the child cheap costume jewelry and observe how she cares for it. According to the child's responses, the parent can choose whether to give the child the real gift, or to withhold it.

In the initial stages of teshuvah we may feel that we have attained expansiveness of mind, clarity of vision and an open heart. We may think that from now on, we will always be able to express our deepest self and serve Hashem with diligence and rapture. Yet, we need to keep in mind that this expansiveness may be like the cheap costume jewelry, given to us as a trial to see how well we handle our spiritual emotions. Do we allow them to augment and inflame the ego, or do we allow them to lead us into balance and wholeness? Do these feelings give birth to a sense of 'arrival' and complacency, or do they inspire a desire for even further growth?

To make teshuvah real, we need to learn how to function with wisdom and understanding in all our ups and downs. During our ups, we need to know that there is still more room for growth, and that arrogance, entitlement and complacency are to be vigorously avoided. In our downs, we need to realize that ascents are sometimes reached through descending drastically. Occasionally, we need to crouch down in order to leap even higher.

SYNOPSIS:CHAPTER 17
Be Patient; Real Change Takes Time

Your initial movement into teshuvah may have been filled with excitement, vigor and a sense of nearness to Hashem. It is normal for these feelings to change. Patience is needed, for real change in life comes about gradually. Spectacular or sudden changes are often superficial and temporary. Real change takes a lifetime, and that is why we *have* a lifetime.

It is also important to recognize that part of spiritual maturity is ceasing to beat yourself up when you slip. Forgiving yourself and others will help you to understand that everything that has happened in your life was meant to be. Acceptance will also give you the strength to make changes that last.

PRACTICE
JOURNAL

On the path of teshuvah, once the initial flashes of inspiration have faded, it might feel like you have hit a spiritual plateau.

It will help to take some time each day to observe your successes, no matter how small, and to write them down.

Celebrate these successes. Think of how you can build upon them and write down your ideas. You can note your setbacks as well, and record what thoughts or reactions led you to these experiences. From time to time, reread your journal entries. Then, write about how you are progressing and how you are going to sustain your progress over time.

CHAPTER EIGHTEEN

FORGIVENESS

T eshuvah completes our past, creates our future, and connects our consciousness to the Creator in the eternal now. When a person steals, for example, teshuvah includes returning the stolen objects. His making amends in this way helps him complete his past, but it also helps to create a better future and reestablish his lost connection with Hashem's ever-present forgiveness.

When one inflicts harm on another human being he is actually transgressing three different forms of connection to wholeness: 1) he separates himself from the conscious awareness of Hashem, 2) he places a false separation between himself and the other person, and 3) he internally separates himself from his own higher potential and self-acceptance. To fully experience forgiveness and the power of teshuvah, this person needs to reestablish and repair all three of these ravaged connections.

Let us begin with the third category, repairing your relationship with yourself. In order to be able to move on with your life, you need to learn to stop condemning yourself and learn to cultivate forgiveness and unconditional positive self-regard. Only when you learn this is your teshuvah complete and empowering. Forgiving yourself is a crucial component in this process, doing so helps complete your past so that it does not invade and crowd out the present.

This state of teshuvah gives us the freedom to be in the present without feeling imprisoned by the past. We feel forgiven and healed when we wholeheartedly surrender our foolish hope, our 'if only' daydream. The past is done and was meant to be. What we can do is redeem our past through present actions and higher consciousness.

We need to attribute all that has already transpired to Divine Providence, but with regards to the present and future, everything is dependent on our free will and our right to choose. This is a psychologically liberating and energizing perspective: let the past be, and at the same time take up the responsibility of free choice for the present and future.

Upon committing an offence against another human being, one must first ask forgiveness from them. Until forgiveness is granted, teshuvah remains incomplete. For example, even if a thief returns what he had stolen, his teshuvah is incomplete until he has been forgiven by the other, or until he has made a sincere effort and requested forgiveness at least three times (Baba Kama, 60b).

When on the receiving-end of a negative act, we need to learn the art of forgiveness and letting go. If someone has wronged you, although the ramifications of their actions may still stimulate pain, once they have asked for your forgiveness it is up to you whether to open up the channels of healing or not. Closing your heart and carrying a grudge can be quite exhausting, and even worse than the original wound.

If you go through your life feeding your anger toward the offender, you end up carrying the negativity with you wherever you go. You thereby place your power of choice and moving forward in the hands of the very person who hurt you. Holding onto anger is more harmful and has more power over you than the offense itself. Forgiveness is the way to release your involvement with the offender and the offense — you have a choice to expunge their influences from your system. Forgiveness does not mean forgetting. In fact, it is often beyond our control whether we forget or not. We cannot demand of ourselves that we forget, yet we can certainly choose to forgive.

The truth is, forgetting is usually based in selfishness while forgiving is based in selflessness. It is empowering to work on forgiveness and not to focus on forgetting. When you say to someone, "Forget about it," or "Don't worry, I already forgot about it," you are essentially saying that their actions do not matter to you, and that is why you were able to move on. There is hidden but disempowering self-importance and anger in this attitude. To forgive is to selflessly move on with your life even if their actions did matter to you, and even when it still hurts.

Forgetting is usually 'for-getting', for the purpose of getting something from the other person — namely a false sense of power. Forgiving, on the other hand, is 'for-giving', for the purpose of giving something. When you forgive, you may still be very much aware of the other, their actions, and your own feeling of loss, yet you give the person a free gift: an increased power to do teshuvah.

When forgiveness is given not for any personal, financial, physical, or psychological benefit, it is pure unconditional love. This highest level of forgiveness is not a logical calculation, as in, 'I might as well forgive that person so that I can feel better / be a better person / encourage him to do teshuvah.' Rather it is an act of pure selfless giving.

The issue of forgiveness and the need to forgive is complex, and it would behoove us to explore it in greater detail. To simplify, there are three types of wrongdoing:

• Wrongs committed against you, which can be, or have been, compensated
• Wrongs committed against you that are irrevocable by nature
• Wrongs committed against another person, wherein it is irrelevant whether or not compensation is possible

There are some circumstances in which the past wrong can be repaired and offering forgiveness is then obligatory. For example, say 'Person A' steals money from 'Person B', but then he repays the full amount and asks for forgiveness. As long as 'A' is asking forgiveness with seriousness, 'B' is required to forgive him. 'B' is allowed to test the sincerity of

'A's remorse by making him ask for forgiveness on three separate instances. But once he has requested forgiveness three times, there is a
Torah obligation to forgive.

There are other circumstances in which the damage done is irre-
versible, and the victim has the right to forgive or not forgive. For example, 'A' has spoken slander against 'B' in front of others, and now feels
remorseful and asks 'B' for forgiveness. Since the words spoken against 'B'
are irretractable, forgiveness is optional. If 'B' does not forgive, however,
he will end up clinging to the hurt and walking around with anger.

Finally, there are some circumstances in which granting forgiveness
is forbidden. We cannot forgive someone for a wrong they have inflicted
upon another; we are not allowed because it is not our place. The only
person who can grant forgiveness is the one who was hurt, and only for
the deed that was directed at him. There are instances when someone
acts negatively in a way that on the surface it seems to be directed at you,
but it is really directed toward your family, your larger community, or to
someone else for whom you were mistaken. In these cases, it is forbidden
and impossible for you to forgive.

Rabbi Chaim of Brisk, the celebrated Nineteenth Century
Talmudist, was once traveling alone on a train when two well-
dressed young men approached him. Thinking he was a poor
beggar, they began to poke fun at him. When the train arrived
in Brisk, they realized to their dismay that the person they
had been harassing was none other than the famed Rabbi of
Brisk. In great haste and contrition they approached the
Rabbi and pleaded for his forgiveness. Reb Chaim, however,
refused to forgive them. He said that his refusal stemmed not
from a desire to cling to the negative experience, but rather
from his lack of authority to forgive. He explained that it was
forbidden for him to forgive, since the person they had ha-
rassed was not the same person who was asked for forgiveness. They had offended a poor beggar, and now they would
have to find such a man and seek *his* forgiveness.

Upon being forgiven by others, a person soon finds himself more apt to flourish as a healthy member of society, unencumbered by looming guilt or the weight of a negative past. Simultaneously, the individual turns to the Master of the Universe and asks for forgiveness and empowerment to repair his relationship with the Creator.

Of course, the very notion of a severed relationship is only valid from the perspective of a physical person; for it is only we who function from a binary condition of an up and down, near and far, one and many. From the perspective of Infinite Unity, there is no such thing as severance or any form of separation. Yet, within our reality of duality, the beginning of teshuvah is a movement, a reaching out for reconnection, a repairing of a damaged relationship.

Hundreds of years ago, some thinkers suggested that a person who transgressed and deviated from his inner balance had to re-focus himself through bitter remedies and sacrifices. Paining or even beating the body was believed to help one achieve a complete teshuvah. Fasting and physical mortification were seen as effective ways of cleansing the body of the spiritual effects of physical misdeeds. Basically, the philosophy was that negativity should be combated with another form of negativity. There is a grain of truth in this approach, since in order to counter over-indulgence in bodily pleasures, a certain degree of renunciation of indulgences is helpful. However, harsh austerities are effective for a very small group of people who have a certain character type and psychological persuasion. Today, austerities are definitely not the right path for most of us.

Early Jewish ethical teachers, such as the pious Rabbi Eliezer of Worms, and texts, such as the *Orchos Tzadikim*, speak of four categories of teshuvah: *teshuvas ha-ba'ah*, *teshuvas ha-geder*, *teshuvas ha-mishkol* and *teshuvas ha-kasuv*.

Teshuvas ha-ba'ah is teshuvah for a misdeed that 'comes into your hand'. This is when you refrain from repeating a certain transgression when you encounter the same conditions or environment that originally engendered that initial transgression. The temptation may be the same as before, but you decisively avoid repeating the act. Such restraint indicates that you have expunged that behavior from your system. You have tangibly transformed your life as well as the ripple effects created by your life.

Teshuvas ha-geder is a teshuvah of 'boundaries' or refraining. This is when you accept upon yourself extra precautions, barriers and restrictions, so as not to be tempted in problematic areas. Here, you can guard yourself even from that which is permitted yet not beneficial. For example, if you desire to avoid speaking slander, you may refrain from speaking about other people altogether, even when your speech would have been neutral. You might choose to communicate by speaking about abstract 'ideas' rather than about specific people.

Teshuvas ha-mishkol is a teshuvah of 'measurement', or penance commensurate to the transgression. The penitent punishes and pains himself equivalent to the measure of pleasure he had enjoyed when committing the misdeed. For example, one might roll in snow for wrongdoings performed with passion. A deeper model, more relevant to today, is that one might devote himself to the attainment of pleasures through matters of the spirit and Torah — through song, study, or service — equivalent to the pleasure received through performing the damaging act.

Teshuvas ha-kasuv is a teshuvah 'of the verse', where one accepts upon himself the likeness of the judgments written and detailed in the Torah. For example, if the Torah's punishment for a particular offense is *malkus*, 'lashes', the transgressor will actually whip himself. Of course, there may be more appropriate applications for this practice today, as well. For example, if the Torah says that a certain deed results in the consequence of being 'banished from the camp', one might separate himself from the community and spend some time alone in reflection. In any case, such practices can only be willfully accepted upon oneself, and their intention is only to positively affect the person in order to stimulate introspection, healing and purification.

Bodily mortification and physical renunciation are not essential ingredients of teshuvah. Integral teshuvah includes *charata* or 'regret', and *kabbalah*, 'receiving' or acceptance of responsibility and a resolve to act differently. Charata is a deep remorse and renunciation of the past deed. This word has the same letters as *charitah*, 'engraving'. Charata is thus understood as a remorse that is deeply engraved within us.

The word *kabbalah* in this context means sincerely reflecting on the past and receiving or accepting it for the sake of a better present and future. In essence, this is to accept 'what is' exactly as it is, making peace with the past, finding the purpose in it, and preparing to move on.

Today, the consensus among the expert *dayanim* or 'judges' of *halachah*, 'law', is to refrain from supererogatory fasting and most other physical afflictions. For most people, fasting only leads to depletion of physical energy, which in turn can easily give rise to impatience and anger. Instead of afflicting or renouncing the body in order to reach the soul, we need to work with the body, using it as a medium to attain a deeper connection with the soul. If you wish to refine yourself, do so through physical deeds such as giving charity, speaking words of Torah, or doing other mitzvos. Our aspiration should be to include and employ the body, not to denigrate or punish it.

Spiritual healing is not brought about by neglecting the body. On the contrary: "A small hole in the body is a colossal cavity in the soul." To attain a sense of inner peace and harmony with life, we must first secure a healthy relationship between body, mind and soul.

> A Chassidic teacher once noticed that his disciple took upon himself to fast for the purpose of atonement. The teacher approached the young man, gave him a pat on the back and said gently but poignantly, "Well done. I see you are completing the job. First you transgressed and destroyed your soul, now you're fasting and destroying your body."

As a body without a soul is lifeless, a soul without a body is useless. They need each other. The soul enlivens the body and the body gives the soul a vehicle by which it can interact with physical existence — the realm in Hashem's Creation where the fullest spiritual realization occurs.

If we want to attain wholeness we need to join soulful inspiration with bodily activity. In terms of practicing teshuvah, this means that we need to utilize the very body parts that were used to perpetuate self-serving and damaging activities to manifest actions of righteousness and holiness. We must use the same physiological pathways but redirect the energy into good deeds. Rabbeinu Yonah writes that if we need to correct the act of lying, we should allow only truth to pass our lips. If we need to mend speaking slander, we should see to it that only words of meaning and benefit are spoken. Of course, we should always speak truth, meaning and benefit, etc., but by correcting and reorienting ourselves, we elevate the body and include it in the wonderful journey of the soul.

Like most spiritual practices emanating from the Torah, teshuvah is not about neglecting or rejecting the physical for the sake of the spiritual. Transcendence is to be found within the physical as well as within the spiritual. Although we may be inclined to view 'God' as synonymous with 'spirit', this is not quite the case. Hashem is Creator of both the spiritual and the physical realms, the dimensional as well as the dimensionless, finite multiplicity as well as Infinite Oneness. Just as a materially-oriented life can be devoid of spirit, so too can a spiritually-oriented life be void of Godliness.

To come closer to Hashem we have to become more Godly, not more 'spiritual', otherworldly or detached. We are to become more involved, present, caring and creative, even as we become more transcendent. This balance is wonderfully accomplished through doing mitzvos, for mitzvos are 'transcendent' deeds performed in the physical here and now. The mitzvos join Heaven with earth and earth with Heaven. The very deed connects the doer with the Creator.

This is the essence of the *Magen David*, or six-pointed star. The symbol is comprised of two triangles — one pointing up, and one pointing down. The triangle with the wide side on top symbolizes the limitless expanse of Heaven, and through *tzimtzum* or constricting and condensing itself, it descends through the proverbial 'glassblower's tube' of the Tree of Life. Like a funnel, this triangle contracts the energy of Heaven until a specific soul-spark manifests in a unique, individual point of projection and presence in the physical plane — a limited body or form results.

The triangle with the wide side on the bottom has its base in the four corners of the finite universe, and wells up like a wave or a mountain. It rises up to the highest crown of Creation, the infinitesimal point of upper Unity. As human beings, we are situated in the middle of the two interpenetrating triangles. We embody a strange mixture of stardust and sand-dune; we elevate flesh to flame, while at the same time we reveal Hashem in this world. We offer earth up to Heaven and we bring Heaven down to earth. We harness physicality in service of the spiritual, while at the same time we experience the spiritual through the physical. Ultimately, we experience the unity and transcendence of all these dichotomies; we are one with the oneness of being itself.

The mitzvah of teshuvah harnesses and integrates all of our innate, natural powers toward the goal of transcendent immanence. We are to become fully expansive and complete human beings, who celebrate life by transforming the mundane moment into a noble eternity. By turning each and every ordinary encounter into an elevated experience, we may live a truly extraordinary life.

After we have done teshuvah with all our strength, we should begin to feel forgiven. Immediately following Yom Kippur, a day dedicated for forgiveness, we begin praying the evening prayers with the words, *V'Hu Rachum…*, "And He, being merciful, will pardon iniquity…" What iniquity are we speaking of? We have just completed Yom Kippur, fasted, prayed, and done powerful teshuvah. What transgression could we have possibly done in that short moment between the conclusion of Yom Kippur and the evening prayers?

In that moment, there is just enough time to entertain the thought: 'Did it really work? Have I really been forgiven?' Having gone through the gut-wrenching, soul-searing, transcendental twenty-five hours of Yom Kippur, the greatest sin would be to believe that Yom Kippur was a waste, or that maybe forgiveness was not granted. And so we say, *V'Hu Rachum*, 'O Merciful One, forgive us — forgive us for thinking that we were not forgiven. Forgive us for doubting ourselves. Forgive us for doubting Your power to forgive.'

Self-confidence and forgiveness are not in contradiction. The illumined King David said, *V'chatasi negdi samid*, "My sin is *before* me constantly" (Tehillim, 51:5). If you transgressed and did teshuvah, but still feel overburdened by the effects of your actions, if you still feel inadequate, unworthy, doubtful or hopeless because of what you have done, then your actions are no longer "before" you, but rather they are *within* you. Even more devastating than that, it is as if your sins *are you*; they are associated with who you are, they appear to define you as a person. When you consciously deal with them and release them, they are 'before' you, they are externalized and separated from your core sense of self. This is similar to the effect of speaking aloud your transgressions: once spoken, they are externalized, they lose their power and hold over you, and you can approach them, deal with them and dissipate them.

The past can sometimes be overwhelmingly heavy, like an anchor or an anvil. By obsessing over the past, you give it permission to keep you from living your life in the present.

There is a point where you must move on. True, you need to deal with the past, but do not let it crowd out the present. There is no question that you need to fix what is wrong, yet it should not take over your life. Sometimes we need to stop focusing on the past altogether and begin focusing on the present and future. We need to let go of the 'imperfect self' and begin focusing on the 'perfect self'. When we fail we should not give up hope or feel that we are a failure. We need to learn to cut our losses, at least for now, and move on.

Following the episode of the Sin of the Golden Calf in the desert, according to Rashi, we were told to erect the *mishkan* or 'tabernacle' as an atonement for that sin. Moshe told the people to bring the materials for building the Mishkan, and we began bringing them. The verse says that the wise elders came to Moshe and said, *Marbim ha-am l'havia*, "The people are bringing more than enough..." (Shemos, 36:5).

Reb Yehoshua of Belz teaches that, aside from the literal meaning that they had brought "enough" physical material, the verse is saying that their *inner* work was "enough". The verse is then reinterpreted as, "The people are bringing; [this is] more than enough." By seeking to do teshuvah, you have done "enough".

To be forgiven means to be unburdened by the weight of your past actions. Then the past no longer blocks your reception of the gift of the present. Not to say that you relinquish ownership of those past actions, or that you glibly discard them, but that you acknowledge those actions as "my sins" that are "in front of me". Through this process of teshuvah, what was once unconscious and toxic has become conscious and purified. Acknowledge the facts: "I did wrong but I am forgiven. I can live freely in the now." Feel empowered, confident and capable.

The saddest and most devastating *kelipa* or 'concealment' in the world, the greatest hindrance to genuine spiritual growth is self-doubt and *yiush* 'giving up hope'. A person cannot move forward with yiush. There are those who doubt their abilities and then there are those who doubt themselves as a person. Sometimes this is because of their past actions and sometimes it could be partly because of their upbringing. To rid ourselves of such self-doubt and lack of belief in ourselves and our future, we have to always remember that if Hashem, the Master of the Universe, thinks we are worthy of being created and sustained at this very moment, then we certainly are worthy.

SYNOPSIS:CHAPTER 18
Let Go

Our teshuvah is only complete when there is full forgiveness flowing from us to others, from others to us, and from Hashem to us. We need to learn to feel forgiven and worthy, as well as to be able to forgive. When someone who has offended you has made compensations and shown true remorse, it is up to you to forgive and let go of that person and that event. If you still withhold forgiveness, you will be letting the other person's negative influence continue to be with you, and to affect you.

PRACTICE
CIRCLE OF LOVE

Take a few minutes each day for the following visualization.

Close your eyes and see yourself walking into an empty room. In the room is one of the most beloved persons in your life — perhaps your spouse or child — sleeping peacefully. Open your heart to feel the tremendous love and acceptance you have for the person laying there, and their love for you. There is no judgment or tension, just love. After a few moments, imagine more people whom you also love walking into the room; feel your love flowing toward them as well. Slowly, allow more people into the room, those with whom you are not so close but still friendly, and expand your feelings of warmth toward them. After a while, begin welcoming someone for whom you feel unresolved tension, and allow your love and acceptance to extend to him or her as well. Continue enlarging your circle of acceptance and love.

CHAPTER
NINETEEN

RESPONSIBILITY:
Owning Life

As a rule, no one is born into an innate condition of sin. Each and every one of us was born clean and unsoiled, neither good nor bad but innocent, with the ability to articulate whatever we so desire. Since we are born uncontaminated it is impossible to suffer or be punished for another's wrongdoings. Each one of us is solely responsible for our own life and how we choose to lead it.

Teshuvah occurs when we rise to life's challenges and take full responsibility for our condition and for the actions we have committed or omitted. Responsibility means that we identify and reclaim ownership of our actions and our life, for better or worse. Responsibility is empowering. Acknowledging and recognizing that we are the director of the orchestra of our lives opens us up to tremendous inner strength.

Regarding teshuvah, the Midrash offers the following metaphor:

> A man was once fording a stream when he realized that the load he carried was weighing him down and causing him to sink. Those who were observing the scene noticed that he hesitated to relinquish his load, and they shouted: "Let go of your load so you don't drown!"

Similarly, one who feels as if he is drowning spiritually may bitterly complain that his iniquities are inundating him — yet, for whatever reason, he may still be holding on to them. The voice of Heaven urges such a person, 'Let go of your load, it is only weighing you down and holding you back.'

Swimming through the currents of life, we have the option to make ourselves heavier by being at odds with ourselves and our world, or we can become lighter through our spiritual attitude, and learn to swim with agility. The very same wave that capsizes one person carries another. While the responsibility to teach a child to swim lies with the parents (Kidushin, 29a), we ultimately have the responsibility to internalize the swimming lessons we have received from life, and to use them. Similarly, in the spiritual realm, mastering the waves of life is our own responsibility. We can choose to ride these waves gracefully and triumphantly.

We live in a culture that attempts to rationalize and make sense of everything and everyone. When something goes wrong, most people immediately shift the blame onto someone or something else. When a person commits an inexcusable crime, psychologists and psychoanalysts are brought in by the defense to offer explanations and pretexts for the deviant behavior: 'He acted the way he did because as a young child he was abused, taunted, abandoned, etc.' The offender's acts are blamed on a parent or acquaintance, or some past incident. The attribution of causality is thus shifted from the individual and placed on an external factor in order to excuse or even justify the offender's actions. There are, of course, times when such arguments are valid. Still, it is ultimately the person himself who is responsible for his actions, assuming he is a sane individual.

It is clearly mentally and spiritually unhealthy and counterproductive to constantly give up your power to circumstances — to your upbringing, environment, education, genetics, etc. But this is precisely what you are doing when you use these excuses to explain away your behaviors and feelings. Feeling sorry for yourself or claiming that you have been cheated by society might in some cases be valid, but it still does not get you anywhere.

You may find that there are problems with society. Do you want to complain about them or solve them? The question is what do you want to emphasize or amplify? Of course it can be beneficial to investigate and critique our upbringing, societal influences and everything outside of ourselves in order to get a clear picture of our environment and its challenges. But often, after this original diagnosis, we get stuck in the blame game. 'Everything is the way it is because of so-and-so.' Put this way, we become entranced by the disempowered voice such thinking creates. Ultimately, the question must become: 'Where am I in all this? Who am I? What did I do?' More importantly, 'What can I do? What can I contribute to my environment, my history, my life?'

When all is said and done, the shape our life takes is entirely contingent on our desire and capacity to choose our responses. Not every wish will be actualized, but we can still choose how we are going to interpret things. What are we going to do with the events and people and conditions that are presented to us? We cannot control what happens to us, but we can respond in a conscious way rather than reactively or by rote.

We are not able to choose into which family, society or era we are born, nonetheless, we can focus on how we will utilize these phenomena and move forward. The idea of responsibility is 'response-ability', meaning the ability to choose what your response will be. To live responsibly means to make your own decisions, to live proactively and mindfully. We can evolve and develop within the limits of our gender, nationality and family. This is analogous to a jazz standard, wherein the chord progressions are the given parameters, while your improvisational solo melody depends only on the free choices that you make within that structure.

The human being is unique among all creatures in that he alone has the power and freedom to make conscious choices. When something unpleasant occurs, we have the ability to respond rationally and appropriately and not allow the predicament to take hold and overwhelm us. Or we can choose not to choose, to remain passive and allow the situation to take us hostage. We may not be able to control what happens to us, but we can contribute consciousness to our response. For example, when something bad happens, the first impulse, certainly for someone who has not worked on his anger is to feel anger. Now, we can either attempt to channel our anger and behave graciously, or we can opt to allow anger to flow out of us in mean-spirited words and hostile actions.

This ability to choose is a God-like power. Possessing a spark of Hashem, we too can create and shape the content of our lives, regardless of the context. Other creatures operate according to their pre-designed or pre-destined disposition. For example, animals, to the best of our knowledge, are integrated creatures; their actions and being are one and the same, they act according to what they are. Their actions are instinctive rather than truly chosen, and their patterns are 'hardwired' into their bodies. On the other hand, only the human being has the potential to be at odds with his nature, for better or worse. In fact, many people find themselves at odds with their own impulses and actions. We may desire something one way, but find internal opposition based on other moral, psychological or physical considerations.

The specifically human dynamic of being at odds with oneself provides the tension and restlessness that catalyzes almost every area of human development, whether spiritual, artistic or technological. To a certain extent, progress depends on this existential dissatisfaction.

Not only do we have traits that allow us to deviate from natural or instinctive behaviors and evolutionary processes, we also have unique abilities to realign ourselves with our Higher Self and tap into the effortless flow of the essence of our being. Humans are cerebral, creating philosophies, choices and forms of communication. In short, we have the ability to fashion our reality. While we are part animal, we are also spiritually creative. In a sense we are quasi-angelic — spiritual like an angel, but physical like an animal.

We humans are able to create abstractions and to choose the philosophies and symbols that will shape our life. We have the power to establish a morality founded on articulated principles. The essential quality and substance of our life is based on how aligned our actions are with our principles. Inner strife and conflict is not universal among human beings; many choose to live from a place of freedom and higher consciousness.

The amazing gift of choice and creativity has an additional benefit. We can recreate our life by declaring teshuvah. We can thus call forth new paradigms and reinvent the philosophies that inform our actions. If we only desire, we can re-contextualize our life to the extent that we transform ourselves into 'another person'. Being formed in the Creator's image implies that no matter how alienated we may have become, we can always return and become whole again.

The Rambam discusses the concept of *bechirah* or 'free choice' in the Mishnah Torah, his comprehensive code of Jewish Law. He juxtaposes this discussion with an elaboration of the laws of teshuvah — similar to the way the Torah itself juxtaposes teshuvah and bechirah (Devarim, 30:11-19). Teshuvah and free choice are interrelated, for transformation cannot exist without the ability to choose it.

Had the human being been created without free choice, the performance of mitzvos would have been largely predetermined and mechanical, but the mitzvos themselves still would have existed. Without free choice, however, there would have been no responsibility — and thus no concept of teshuvah. In a world of pure determinism there would be no reason to re-align ourselves with Hashem, even if we did something wrong. In fact, in the context of determinism there is no right or wrong. Every step in life would be pre-designed and predestined. Life would be beyond our control, thereby obviating the need for the desire and ability to change.

To live in a state of teshuvah, and in particular the higher teshuvah of love, is to live free and empowered. In this deeper state, choices and decisions are genuinely possible. When a person acts responsibly, he moves toward independence and self-mastery, rising to a level of non-conditionality. In contrast, reactive behavior leads toward further depravity, inward slavery, and ultimately, complete dependence upon on externally imposed conditions.

We have the power both to change and to transform. What is the difference between 'change' and 'transformation'? 'Change' occurs when we fix what is broken or flawed, while 'transformation' occurs when we realize that we are already, in potential, whole and perfect.

On the other hand, each act of change contains within it the potential for transformation. In order to change, one must have an awareness of what needs to be changed. Becoming aware of our faults can paradoxically lead toward transformation, because when we become aware, we are able to realize how our self-expression contrasts with our potential wholeness. When we are deeply aware of our imperfections — that we are not living fully in our power, passion or potential, or that that our life is not unfolding as perfectly as we wished it would — we are already beginning to reveal our potential perfection.

Rabbi Avraham, the son of the Rambam, recounts a story that occurred with his father.

> The Rambam once heard one of the important members of the community boast on the Eve of Yom Kippur, "I am so flawlessly righteous that I do not know why I would even need teshuvah!" Hearing this utterly pretentious declaration, the Rambam whispered to his son, "Perhaps he needs teshuvah for the mere fact that he thinks he has no need for it."

Teshuvah is a liberated perspective where we no longer feel the need to blame others for our demeanor or behavior. When we are thus liberated, we are empowered to stand up and say, "This is my life and I take full responsibility." Even if circumstances would seem to warrant the interpretation that we have been cheated or abused, teshuvah gives us the choice to respond positively and proactively. We can harness the power that moves within us, and live life to our maximum potential. Rather than being enslaved by life's predicaments, we can master them and choose our responses.

This is in no way suggesting that the realization of responsibility is easy to come by. Even if we intellectually understand the value of responsibility, it is still not automatically absorbed and digested. Recognizing that we are the creators of our responses to life can be overwhelming and occasionally exhausting, yet it is ultimately energizing. The qualities of free choice and responsibility are God-given; when we activate them, we open up to our divine potential on all levels.

Truly, to be human is to take responsibility. Our collective human birthday is the day of Rosh Hashanah, also the Day of Judgment and accountability. The implication is that the original human condition is to yearn and strive for accountability and ownership of our lives, to be the ones who guide ourselves upon the paths that we choose, and then reap the fruits of our choices. Animals, ruled by instincts and the circumstances of their lives, are not fully accountable for their actions. The impulse to embody responsibility is intrinsic to the human spirit; after all, we were born on the cosmic Day of Responsibility.

When we take responsibility for our reality, we reveal our true potential. The human being is designed for noble self-mastery. When we act thoughtlessly, flouting spiritual responsibility, we alienate the human spirit within us. Owning our actions reintegrates the 'human' with the 'being'.

After Adam ate from the Tree of Knowledge, the Torah says, *Va-yi-garesh es ha-adam*, "And (Hashem) sent the human being out of the Garden of Eden" (Bereishis, 3:24). This, says the Mitteler Rebbe of Chabad, means that the *adam* or *mentsch*, was banished from Eden. When Adam did not heed the voice of responsibility, which told him not to 'eat from' or 'identify with' the Tree of Knowledge and Duality, he immediately deflected responsibility and blamed his wife Chava. At that moment, the *mentsch* or the human spirit within him was lost or self-banished. Our goal in teshuvah is to reclaim that human spirit within our own being, and live as a fully realized and fully responsible *adam*.

SYNOPSIS:CHAPTER 19
Own Your Life; Be Responsible

Often, what life serves up to us is beyond our control. Nonetheless, we do have a choice in how we respond. Some of us go through our lives creating excuses for why we cannot move forward, and perhaps these are very valid-sounding excuses. You can blame your parents, teachers, friends, bosses or culture for your misery, or you can take responsibility for your own life. I, and only I, can determine how I will respond to my challenges.

PRACTICE
MAKE A PROMISE

Whenever you find yourself making an excuse for your behavior, stop for a moment and realize your response-ability, your ability to choose other responses.

One way to cease making excuses is to make a promise or vow to yourself. For instance, you might vow (although you should say *bli neder*, 'without making a Torah binding vow') that for the next two hours, you will not make any excuses for your behavior. When those two hours have passed, promise to yourself again that for the next two hours you will not make excuses. Success breeds success, so make sure that your promises will be sufficiently easy to fulfill. Upon having gained for yourself a few successes, you can begin to extend the time, or the breadth of your goals.

CHAPTER TWENTY

NATURE, NURTURE
& Beyond

The Gemarah relates that Eliezer ben Durdayah was an extremely promiscuous person who visited every courtesan possible. Once he heard of a harlot who lived in a distant land. He decided to go, and took a bundle of coins to pay for her services. Off he went with his money stash, crossing seven rivers to reach her. He finally arrived. During their rendezvous, he accidentally passed wind. She turned to him and said, "The wind does not return to its source and the same is true with Eliezer Ben Durdayah. You have strayed so far you can never return to your Source!" Hearing her ominous prediction, a change of heart overtook him, and he felt an overwhelming desire to return and embark on the path of teshuvah.

In agony and desperation he ran into the wilderness searching for a reprieve for his anguished soul. Finally he settled between two great mountains, and turning to them, he cried, "O mountains, stand before the Master of the Universe and pray for me!" The mountains shrugged him off and ignored his plea. He then turned to the sky and the earth and begged, "O, please pray on my behalf," but their reaction mirrored the mountains' indifference. Desperate, he turned to the celestial beings, the sun, moon and stars and cried, "Please, take my case before the Creator and plead on my behalf!" They too ignored his heart-wrenching pleas. In utter desperation, he placed his head between his knees and began to weep. Reaching deep within, his soul ignited and in a state of deep rapture, his soul departed from his body. At that moment a Heavenly voice was heard: "Rabbi Eliezer Ben Durdayah has secured himself a place in the World to Come" (Avodah Zarah, 17a).

The realization that change is imperative can originate from the strangest and most serendipitous of places. Poignantly, Eliezer ben Durdayah's desire for teshuvah was ignited by the very harlot with whom he wished to transgress. Irrespective of how far astray a person may have wandered, no matter how depraved the level of spiritual deterioration, there always remains the *Eli-ezer*: *Eli*, 'my God', *ezer*, 'helps'. Even amidst our deepest darkness and falsehood there is always a glimmer of light, a still, small voice that challenges us and helps us return to truth.

For this particular person, his *ezer*, his 'help', was imparted through the nexus of his weakness. At the very moment he tried to sin, he was challenged to confront himself at the heart of his darkness. When such a challenge occurs to us, we must look deep within and acknowledge that all of our decisions are ours alone. We are responsible for our actions, and we cannot honestly blame anything or anyone else. At first, Eliezer wished to place the burden of his plea and predicament upon the mountains, the sky, the earth, the sun, the moon — everything in his environment. Only when he realized that he had no other 'help', did he truly enter the state of teshuvah.

There is an ongoing debate in developmental psychology as to whether it is 'nature' or 'nurture' that causes a person to behave in a particular manner. Some assert that a human being is a product of nature and his genetic makeup: genes determine the way we behave, think and feel and cannot be altered or manipulated; your biology dictates your choices and your destiny. Biology is destiny.

Others firmly disagree and hypothesize that the mind begins as sort of a blank paper, and we write our experiences and habits on it: our choices are directed according to the ways we are nurtured and reinforced. According to this opinion, even our instinctive or subconscious behaviors can be drastically altered by the love, attention, information and discipline we receive, and by our culture, environment, education, and the choices we make.

A third faction claims that our destinies are written in the stars. This was a major view hundreds of years ago, although it is not as prevalent today: the heavenly spheres and configurations of the zodiac determine our behavior and personality. This is similar to the 'nature' theory, in which who we become is seen as predetermined and fixed.

These three theories parallel the three objects that Eliezer Ben Durdayah turned to on his path toward teshuvah. The "mountains" allude to ancestry, genetics and nature — they are fixed. "Heaven and earth" are metaphors for nurture — they provide for our physical needs, and are analogous to our mother (earth) and father (sky, Heaven) and our upbringing. The "celestial beings" represent the signs of the zodiac — they are also fixed and impersonal.

According to the theory of 'nature', we are the product of countless layers of ancestral genes, just like a tall Alpine mountain is built upon layers of minerals and matter that have collected over countless years. Formulated over the centuries, these genes have become you. When Eliezer Ben Durdayah's desire for teshuvah was first ignited, he turned to the mountains to plead his case. In other words, he tried to place the blame for his behavior on his faulty genetic ancestral inheritance. When he tried to lean on them, however, they declined. They could not help him or serve as an excuse because they were not the ultimate reason for his choices.

Eliezer then turned to the Heavens and the earth. He thus shifted the blame from 'nature' to 'nurture'. His upbringing, environment, education — these, he thought, must be the real culprits. Had he only been treated well by his mother and father, fed the right foods and counseled to enter a wholesome career, surely he would have turned out differently. There was no response from the Heavens and the earth. They were also not ultimately responsible for his behavior.

Finally, Eliezer turned to his astrological sign to explain his failures, but he couldn't lean on this excuse either. He could only look deep within and depend on himself for teshuvah and liberation.

Traces of truth are found in all three theories; we are a conglomerate of various elements and factors. Our character is indeed influenced by our genes, education and upbringing, and to some degree, as our sages teach, by the astrological configuration at the time of our birth (Shabbos, 156a). In terms of genes, studies have shown that children are born with certain genetic proclivities that are activated by the nurture they receive. Certain environmental triggers can switch genes on, and certain conditions allow them to remain mere dormant potential. All cells carry the same genes, but not all produce the same results. Therefore, the issue is not nature versus nurture, but nature via nurture.

Nature, nurture and astrology are not the whole story, however. There is more to us than what we have inherited or acquired. Part of who we are is lodged in infinity, entirely transcendent of all definitions, confinements or patterns. Deep within, there is a divine core that is beyond the natural realm and can choose freely and unconditionally, without need for nurture or coercion. Because of this, we can be proactive and co-creative in forming our character and our behavior. We can subdue and master any impulse, or enhance and exaggerate it. Eliezer Ben Durdayah finally found this place of transcendence, and took his place above the laws of nature and cause-and effect. He was thus able to achieve genuine transformation during the last minutes of his life.

The Maharal writes that if Eliezer Ben Durdayah's name did not allude to the meaning of the story, perhaps the Gemarah wouldn't mention it at all. Indeed, his name hints at looking deeply inward and disposing of one's superficial self. There are two aspects in his name: *Eliezer*, his personal name, and *Durdayah*, his father's name. These represent his present and his past, respectively. As we mentioned, *Eliezer*, means 'God helps.' *Ben* means 'son of' and *Durdayah*, his father's name, is rooted in a word for the sediment of wine — the leftovers that have spoiled.

Eliezer's past contributed to his troubled present, but it also contained his hidden potential. In powerful self-reflection, he touched the transcendent core of his being, rising above his limitations and the influences of nature, nurture and astrology. His consuming teshuvah reached beyond his present, beyond his character and conduct. He quickly mastered his whole life, retroactively transforming the spoiled dregs of his past, his *Durdayah*.

When you realize that you alone can turn your life around, you too can recreate your past through the process of teshuvah in the present. Converting your negativities into meritorious states is possible because teshuvah transcends the dimensions of nature, time, transgression and separation. Teshuvah connects us to a spiritual realm where the soul is wrapped up in the Infinite Unity of the Divine Essence, untouched by any limitation, negativity or distortion.

SYNOPSIS:CHAPTER 20
Reveal Your Infinity

The way we express our selves in the world is due partly to our natural predisposition and genetic makeup, and partly to the nurture of our life experiences, education and upbringing. Yet this is not the entire story. There is more to us than our biology and conditioning; part of who we are is lodged in Infinity. From the vantage of this unconditioned Higher Self, we have the ability to exercise free choice, to choose response-ability, no matter the circumstances.

PRACTICE
ARGUE FOR YOUR POTENTIAL

At times it may seem that our ability to believe in ourselves is dependent on others' (or our) limited evaluations of who we are. However, if we accept these points of view and go about arguing for our limitations, lacks and difficulties, sure enough, we will conform to those limitations. We become the person we imagine ourselves to be. If we go about arguing our limitations, feeling powerless because of a low IQ, negative upbringing or lack of education, sure enough, we will become that limitation.

Instead of arguing for our limitations, we should begin to argue for our true soul potential. Whenever we are faced with a spiritual or physical challenge, we need to change our response from 'I can't,' to 'How can I make this work?' Hashem does not present us with challenges we cannot overcome — we are also given the inner resources to overcome them. Therefore, when you find yourself challenged and arguing for your limitations, simply stop. Change your response to "I have the ability make this work."

CHAPTER
TWENTY-ONE

Dealing
WITH THE PAST

L ife is lived in the present, although much of our psyche is tied to the past. Past experiences and our reactions to them have formed us into who we are today as well as prologue our future. We simultaneously move forward as we peer over our shoulders at the places from which we came.

Inevitably, included within the prouder moments of our past is some darkness. At times these moments of darkness may threaten to cloud over or infringe upon our present. These murky memories serve as ominous reminders of a past preferably forgotten. These are our mishaps or misdeeds, when the ego or foolish temptation prevailed over our better judgment.

Actions of the past may latch onto our subconscious as unwanted baggage, stubbornly clinging to our memories and conscience for days, months and even years. Sadly, there are those who carry the burden of their past for the rest of their lives. They may temporally live in the present, but parts of their consciousness are trapped and preoccupied in their past.

While traveling back in time can be incredibly painful, the challenge

goes beyond just revisiting an experience of pain and brokenness. Ultimately, the goal is to be able to journey back into the past and then return
to the present cleansed, clarified and empowered.

Most people have done things in their youth that seem incongruous
with their established persona today. Dealing with that past and righting
those wrongs is arduous and tricky.

Ironically, the very nature of dealing with past negative experiences
is negative in itself. "One who works in a perfume factory inevitably
smells sweet", says the Midrash, "while one who spends his day in the
tannery will undoubtedly smell foul" (Pirkei D'Rebbe Eliezer).

When we deal with spiritual pollution, even with the constructive
intention of rectifying or reversing any persistent negative affect, its odor
inevitably tends to rub off on us. In this way, thinking of sin can be a sin
itself. Understandably the opposite also proves true. By concentrating on
transcendence and positivity we become more transcendent and positive.
By simply thinking positive thoughts, our inner point of goodness begins
to strengthen and become manifest.

Remorse for past misdeeds is essential for any real alteration in our
behavior and can serve as a catalyst for change and ultimate transformation. However, our past should neither become our preoccupation nor our
fascination. While it is true that those who cannot remember the past are
condemned to repeat it, a distinction must be made between *remembrance*
and *reliving*, between what we will call memory and regressive projection.

The idea of memory does not eclipse the now. Entertaining events
of the past does not negate the realness of the present. Such ruminations
allow one to conjure up images of the past and then let go of them and
move on with life.

Regressive projection, however, means preoccupation and total reca-
pitulation of the past at every moment. Regressive projection is when the
past relentlessly clings to one's consciousness, overwhelming the present
and stifling any genuine progress into a renewed future.

We need to learn from the past in order to insure that previous mistakes or miscalculations will not be repeated. Subsequently, we also need
to deposit the past to memory — to learn from the past and then to place

it in a mental memory album, as it were, and move on.

Everyone makes mistakes. Most people have done things in the past that are later frowned upon and regretted, whether in the form of chances blown or incorrect paths followed. Despite this, we have the amazing ability to continuously inaugurate new beginnings. We may even use our past as a guiding post for the future. Rabbi Menachem Ben Shlomo, the Meiri, teaches that the awareness that something is negative is in itself half the solution. If we can recognize the past for what it is and the purpose it thus serves, this in itself is a form of redemption of the past. We should strive to view past mishaps as path markers or traffic signals, recognizing each mistake as a signpost placed perfectly so that we can safely advance forward with awareness.

Beyond learning from our mistakes and judging them as destructive, teshuvah gives us the opportunity to ultimately redeem our past. The high point of teshuvah is where we reach a space within that is transcendent of judgment and negativity. At its peak, teshuvah has the power to venture into the past and retroactively illuminate any lingering darkness. As the path of teshuvah leads us into the world of *yichud* or 'unity', we have the ability to reveal the intrinsically positive value imbedded within even a seemingly negative past.

Transformation of this sort occurs when we are able to perceive that residing within everything, whether object or subject, is a spark of the Infinite. In the innermost depth of darkness, there is a positive, Divine and life-affirming light that is the true animating energy of all existence. The process of transformation ensues when we recognize traces of goodness within the apparent negativities of life.

A hint of this kind of non-dual awareness is present within one of the Purim traditions. We are charged with two sayings on Purim: 1) 'blessed is Mordechai' and, 2) 'cursed is Haman'. These two polar opposite sayings, one praising an ancestor and one cursing an enemy, have the exact same *gematria* or 'numeric equivalent'. Revealing that on some level, beneath the surface of appearances, duality and confrontation breaks down revealing the cosmic tapestry of infinite unity. This alludes to the paradoxical perspective that somewhere, even within the curse, there is a blessing waiting to be revealed, reclaimed and re-integrated.

In a world of polarity, everything contains its opposite. There is an indestructible point of light within the darkness and a necessary point of darkness within the light. Schism does not really exist, but is merely the tendency of our dualistic mind to filter the world through binary oppositions.

When we approach teshuvah we realize that beneath the dichotomies of the universe there is a perfect state of *yichud* or 'unified wholeness'. When we become aware of this truth, negativity begins to settle and diffuse.

On a personal level, this awareness translates into our ability to recognize the goodness and blessing that can be retrieved from our very own flaws. Even our so-called destructive traits can be redirected toward positive application. Anger, for example, can be channeled and focused as indignation over the world's injustices and a burning desire for righteousness. Arrogance can be re-directed as intolerance of our own lowly behavior. Once this perspective of yichud and inclusion is established, a genuine healing on all levels of our being can occur.

> A Chassid once inquired of Rabbi Moshe Leib of Sasov: "If within everything there is an element of the positive, tell me then Rebbe, what is so positive about heresy"? "That is simple", the Rebbe replied. "When a poor person comes to your doorstep pleading for assistance, do not tell him, 'God will provide', instead be an atheist and act as if no one else exists to help him but you".

These contrasting notions of unity and duality are the essential paradoxes of creation, though in truth all is non-dual and there is complete and seamless unity. In the face of present and future suffering we need to take a proactive stand and fight against it as if we are the only ones available to help; while with regard to the past, we can and should look for the goodness, blessing and purpose embedded within all circumstance, even suffering.

Cheit is one of the Hebrew words for 'vice' and is comprised of three Hebrew letters: *ches*, *tes* and *aleph*. The word *cheit* is pronounced with the *aleph* remaining a silent letter. This poignantly illustrates, says the Baal Shem Tov, that even within cheit or 'sin'— a negative and destructive act — the Holy One is present. The aleph, which is the first and primal letter of the Hebrew alphabet alludes to Hashem who is present within the cheit, albeit silently. This understanding — that there dwells within everything an element of Divine Goodness — allows us to reclaim that very component of goodness and its power for greater growth and wisdom, even from the wreckage of past mistakes or misdeeds.

Even more empowering than the fact that every trait can be both negative and positive, is the fact that everything of the past has an overarching theme of positivity. This means plainly that there is goodness and blessing within everything of our past. The goodness, in the case of teshuvah, is that the very negative actions of the past are what initially bring one to a desire for teshuvah.

Past misdeeds can often serve as prime motivators that catapult us toward teshuvah. The negative acts themselves are ironically what inspire a more intense and sincere desire to pursue truth. The misdeeds become the initiators and ignite the process. The negative past is what brings one to the point in life where he decides to change and mend his ways.

Failures are often the instigators that arouse re-thinking and re-alignment. In this way, all acts of the past are included within one's present teshuvah, as they comprise the impetus that gave rise to transformation. Our present is the totality of our past, which then becomes the foundation upon which our future is built.

Mistakes can bring us to spiritual heights, or depths, which we would have otherwise not visited. Quite frankly, our past should be honored and valued for the purpose it serves — as a stimulator that inspires us to teshuvah. Armed with this outlook, genuine integration and healing can occur.

Working from this perspective of *yichud*, 'unity' or integrated wholeness, teshuvah does not necessitate a renunciation or estrangement from the past. On the contrary, it affords us the ability to bring all of life's experiences to the table. Teshuvah is most efficient when we can take the past and positively integrate it into the present in a transformed state. Rather than abandoning or forsaking the past, teshuvah allows us to include the past within a much larger context. Practically speaking, we should aspire to reincorporate all past life experiences into the new life that we have birthed for ourselves.

A common sentiment among many who have experienced a total life shift and drastic redirecting of priority is the feeling that all previous life experiences are best if left forgotten. The past seems completely removed, strange and of a different universe. Compared to the state that one is in today, all that was done prior is often viewed as a complete waste of time and energy, and thus best left to dormant memory. This may be valid with regard to certain past experiences which are — for now — entirely unsalvageable. But as a whole, genuine perfection is attained only when one is able to look back at the shadier parts of their life, retrieve something positive and then employ its very energy toward their new positive trajectory.

A complete hiddenness, or eclipsing, of the self is often required for the sake of rebirth. Certainly, when we are talking about an individual who has committed serious atrocities, a radical severance from the past is desperately needed. For such a person it is insufficient to merely mouth a desire to change. Extreme moves are required that allow for the systematic breakdown and deconstruction of their entire past. This can include such decisive actions as relocation, change of name and complete cessation of certain relationships. Ideally, once one has been able to 'put themselves back together' they can attempt to re-integrate — especially in regards to various familial relationships that may have suffered at the expense of their teshuvah.

On a lighter note, the form of teshuvah that is relevant for most people requires merely a hiding away of the old self for a period of time. In order to get a healthy distance from ingrained patterns of behavior one should attempt to separate himself from his old life and habits. But afterwards the inescapable recollection process needs to occur when one retrieves and reexamines all of the lost pieces of his past.

Initially, the process of change commences with a devastating *havdalah* or 'separation' and exclusion. This can manifest as a radical distancing of oneself from their past and resultantly having nothing to do with it for a while. In effect, this is a deadening of the past so a rebirth can occur.

Then comes the real challenge — the idea of *hamtaka* or 'sweetening'. This is the process of including, integrating and bringing together all the past brokenness of life and of self into the renewed present moment.

In English, the word *holy* is derived from the Anglo Saxon term for whole. To be holy is to include and incorporate all of our character traits within a greater spiritual context. The process goes something like this: first we must separate or isolate the wholesome elements within our character structure from the deleterious or damaging ones. This allows us to sift through our psyches and see what is actually there — what is worth keeping and developing as opposed to what is best left behind or thrown away.

This process of separation is essential to the pursuit of holiness, as the Hebrew word *kadosh* subtly suggests. For the word *kadosh* means both 'holy' as well as 'separate'. This illustrates that there is something intrinsic about the stage of separation in the process of establishing integral wholeness. It is only after this initial stage of separation that we are then able to consciously absorb what is deemed appropriate into a positive context and make it "special".

On the two holidays that we celebrate our national and individual freedom, *Pesach* or 'Passover' and *Sukkos*, the 'Festival of Booths', we enact symbolic activities that represent our retrieving and returning what was left behind — the broken pieces of our past — into the fold of the present.

On Pesach, the entire Hagadah is recited over a broken piece of flat bread. The middle matzah is divided in two. One part is hidden away and eaten later as the *afikoman*; the other part remains sandwiched in between two whole matzos. It is customary for the children to go about searching in order to retrieve the broken piece that is hidden, bringing it back for the adults to eat. Children reflect the purity of self before any sense of brokenness or disarray. When children bring back the afikoman, they are bringing back our youth — our innocence and purity. The child within us is bringing back our broken pieces to the adult we are now.

Children also represent the next generation. And this ritual can be a profound reminder that it will be our children and offspring who must deal with all the brokenness and pollution we leave behind. So in effect, this ritual can also be seen as a tangible reminder to act with caring and caution in the present. This is especially pertinent with the acquisition of any new sense of freedom, which Pesach so potently communicates. For it is not uncommon for newfound freedom to be abused, whether personal or even political.

The other half of the broken matzah, the one that remains on the table between the two whole matzos, represents the aspect of our soul that, although damaged or darkened, is still connected to wholeness and unity. This 'sandwich of brokenness' reminds us that although we may at times feel disconnected or deconstructed, it is from a place of wholeness that we come and it is ultimately to a place of wholeness that we return. This broken matzah represents the part of our soul that, although broken, remains pure and connected. It is the part of our self that we merely need to uncover in order to recover — the part that is always there, always perfect, just waiting for us to return.

Similarly, Rosh Hashanah and Sukkos are connected by a practice of casting away and then followed by one of retrieving, like the afikomen which is at first hidden and then returned by the children.

There is a custom on Rosh Hashanah called *tashlich*, 'to throw'. It is a ritual in which we walk to a body of fresh water and then ceremoniously and symbolically throw away our sins into the water. This is a symbolic act of casting away our negativities into the depths of the water and disassociating ourselves from any spiritually destructive past actions. But really, we are not 'throwing them away', so to speak. We throw them into the water in order to be washed clean — to be purified and stripped of their negative energy. For nothing is altogether negative. Every act committed contains some spark of holiness or subtle aspect of our own vital energy.

And so, a short time later during the holiday of Sukkos there is a festive celebration called *Simchas Beis ha-Shoeva*, 'The Joy of the Water Drawing'. This is a ceremony of joyful celebration — of dance, music, acrobatics and performances of various kinds. This ceremony was performed literally during the times of the Holy Temple, and today is performed symbolically.

During the Temple period the ceremony began in the evening with the ritual drawing of water from the deepest wells. The water would eventually be poured over the altar the following day. In contrast to the ritual of Tashlich, where we were throwing away all negativity into the waters, we are now diving deeper into the waters in order to draw forth that which promotes life and growth.

For water is that which cannot be corrupted or contaminated. This is illustrated by the mikvah or 'ritual bath', which was used to purify all that had become unfit for the proceedings of the Holy Temple. For although a mikvah is the repository of all that is unclean or unkosher, never the less, the mikvah remains a source of purity.

And now, instead of casting aside and separating, we extract that which was previously thrown into the water back from the depths and use it to prepare the altar. The joy experienced and expressed is one of re-unification, of finding something that had belonged to us and of brining it back — this is the joy of returning. This is the essence of teshuvah. All the brokenness is restored, all of the past is included and ultimately even malice is transformed into merit.

This two-part water ritual alerts us to water's mysterious and multi-dimensional modus operandi. Water can both take away as well as impart. Water can wash away our impurities and also fill our jugs with life-affirming and transformative energy. And water, as in the case of a mikvah, can absorb untold amounts of toxic energy and still remain pure; always retaining it's cleansing and enlivening affect.

This becomes even more interesting when we consider our sages statement that, 'there is no water but Torah'. Meaning that, like water, Torah can both help to cleanse the stains from our soul's garment, as well as fill our receptive vessels with pure, clean and life affirming energy and spiritual nutrients.

In the initial stages of teshuvah, as noted, there needs to be a radical shift, a total break, a devastating *havdalah* or 'separation' with the past; only then can the *hamtakah* or 'sweetening' be truly effective. But even before the havdalah or temporary severing of ties with the past, before we can throw away our negative habits and relationships into the waters, we need to experience the crucial state of *hachna'ah* or 'submission' — a humbling of the self.

This is the three-part process of teshuvah and transformation: 1) First comes *hachna'ah*, 'submission', 2) then *havdalah*, 'separation' and 3) finally *hamtaka*, 'sweetening'.

Hachna'ah is the humbling stage of submission and acceptance. This is the process of looking honestly at one's life up until and including this present moment, fully acknowledging all past and current mistakes and shortcomings, and humbly accepting them as your own doing. At this stage a person needs to take responsibility for their life and claim, or reclaim their past as their own; only then can the second stage of severing begin.

We cannot forget that which we do not remember. First, there needs to be the hachna'ah — an acceptance of the past, a submission to 'what is'. Then we can experience a real havdalah — the severance and separation from all that is undesirable or contrary to our desired direction.

Ultimately, from that place of separation, we will then be able to enjoy the full *hamtakah* or 'sweetening: the full reclamation and integration of the sliver of light from within all the past darkness, the elevation of the descent — spiritual recycling so to speak. Like the end result of composting, where all the previous waste goes into the bloom of a beautiful flower.

Yichud or 'inclusion' needs to be extended to all levels of self, not only to our past actions, but also to unique personality traits and talents as well. Our aspiration should be to recruit all aspects of our ingenuity and personality to attain teshuvah. What is required to be left behind in the course of teshuvah is the *direction* of life that one was leading, but by no means should there be a relinquishing of *self* in the process.

Hobbies, talents, character traits, or proclivities toward music, for example, or the fine arts, should not be forgotten or left behind. Doing so would only leave one incomplete — like a spiritual amputee.

What we do need, however, is a radical redirecting and re-focusing of those very talents and traits. Instead of a person viewing his entire past existence as a mere waste of time — causing a complete internal demoralization and crippling the process of a healthy and healing teshuvah — one should aspire to take along all of one's self in the journey of teshuvah.

Reish Lakish was one of the preeminent Talmudic sages of his era, yet his rise to prominence had quite humble beginnings. A physically strong man before becoming a sage, he occupied himself with nothing less than thievery.
Once, as Reish Lakish was passing Reb Yochanan bathing in the Jordan, he impulsively jumped into the river. Reb Yochanan, upon seeing the strength of Reish Lakish, said to him, "Your strength should go toward Torah". Hearing this, Reish Lakish replied, "And your beauty should go for women". It was agreed upon that Reb Yochanan would give the hand of his sister — herself equally as beautiful — to Reish Lakish in marriage. In exchange, Reish Lakish would begin to study Torah. In due time, Reish Lakish the bandit became Reish Lakish the Sage (Baba Metzia, 84a).

The stamina, energy and cunning once used for thievery were put to use toward the discipline, ingenuity and creativity necessary for Torah study.

SYNOPSIS:CHAPTER 21
Live Forward & Redeem the Past

In order to move forward into a brighter future, we need to learn how to properly evaluate our past. Even if we have made mistakes, we must be gentle in our self-evaluation. Focusing too much on previously encountered negativity will dull our energies and keep us stuck. What is more, within the negativity of the past there is always a spark of goodness and blessing waiting to be recognized and redeemed. It is important to learn how to retrieve that spark.

We do need to leave behind the direction we were following, but by no means should we permanently disown or relinquish the essential aspects of our self in the process. Ultimately, we must embrace all levels of self, including who we were in the past. The goal is to recruit and include all of our unique strengths, traits and talents in the quest for healing and wholeness — not just for us, but for all of creation.

PRACTICE

SUBMIT, SEPARATE AND SWEETEN

This is a powerful three-stage practice of teshuvah:

- First, there must be *hachna'ah* — the process of submission, acceptance and humbling. This requires a full accounting and taking responsibility for one's current state of being. This also means fully recognizing the gap between your actions and your essential self — be honest. Where are you? Where would you like to be? What would you need to do to get there? Once you have accepted personal responsibility for your past, you can progress to stage two:
- *Havdalah* or 'separation' — in this case, from your past. This means unburdening yourself of what you have done or who you have become. This requires a reinforcement of the difference between the doer and the deed. Remember that you are not your mistakes and shortcomings. You are a pure and righteous soul. It is time to forget your past and turn your life around in a new direction.
- Stage three is *hamtakah* or 'sweetening'. This is the stage of forgiveness, loving acceptance and re-integration of your entire self. Once you have transcended your past, you can include it.

What stage are you in right now?

REGRET
& Acceptance

L ove is an essential component of teshuvah; love for oneself and love for others. The first step to loving and being kind to others is to be kind and gentle with yourself — believing in yourself and viewing your past with compassion, openness and acceptance. A person who continuously harbors negative feelings toward themselves will never be able to properly reorient and evolve toward becoming a better person.

This fundamental understanding provides us with a beautiful way to understand the mitzvah of 'loving another as yourself'. Seen from this perspective, we are not only charged to love another as much as we love ourselves, but we are alerted to the existential reality that, ultimately, we will only be able to love another as well as we love ourselves — it starts with us. However loving, supportive and forgiving we are able to be toward ourselves, will determine the quality of love and attention we will be able to direct toward another.

We need to learn, or relearn, to see ourselves in a positive light. This allows us to view the present as a perpetual opportunity for transformation. There is no way out of negativity's chokehold when we lack a positive evaluation of ourselves in the present. Self-loathing and degradation are counterproductive to any type of spiritual growth or positive development. Love and respect for oneself are pre-requisites for genuine and healthy teshuvah.

We need to cultivate a belief in the inherent goodness of ourselves and of others, thus attracting even more goodness into our lives. If one thinks he is bad, negative or soiled, then he will attract people, ideas and experiences of that kind. As Rashi says *Arur mistabek b'arur*, "curse cleaves to the cursed and blessings cannot attach themselves to a curse" (Bereishis, 24: 39). Inwardly this means that if you truly believe that you are blessed and good, at least at your very core, you will attract blessings into your life. The converse is also true: if you go about knocking yourself down in a barrage of self-loathing, you will end up being knocked out. It all begins with self-love and appreciation.

Clearly self-love is not intended to eclipse a thorough and genuine evaluation of the reality of your self and soul; there is always more work to be done. Instead, a healthy balance of self-love and belief in your innate goodness will allow you to honestly assess your past and recommit yourself in the present to make a better future.

Constructive criticism of oneself can, if taken to an extreme, devolve into unhealthy self-loathing. When this occurs it can often be traced to a person's upbringing, whether at home or at the mercy of whatever 'system' they were subject to while growing up. Sadly due to poor parenting skills and misguided social engineering, many people from the time of infancy are negatively affected and paralyzed by a lack of self-esteem.

Authoritarian criticism is not always verbal. Sometimes parents or teachers are just too over-demanding, overprotective, or overbearing; leaving a child feeling that they are not 'good' enough to deal with the challenges of life. As a result the child may begin to develop subtle feelings of self-doubt, feeling the need to shelter or punish himself. This can ultimately devolve into a form of chronic depression. Occasionally these feelings are so deeply ingrained and lodged into a person's unconscious that they may feel quite badly about themselves without even knowing why.

Teshuvah offers us a new lease on life. Part of reclaiming your self is to be accepting of your self, realizing your gifts and unique potentials. Self-love is crucial for healthy teshuvah, though this love is not meant to eclipse the fact that there is still much work to be done — to accept is not to condone. We need to rationally assess, not judge, choices made in our past that have not worked out in life in order to determine what we can do now in the present to make our life better.

Everything that happened in life was meant to be, but that is only true in the past tense. In the present tense, however, we continually have the freedom to make choices. Yesterday was meant to be, but today and tomorrow are completely dependent upon our own free choice in the moment. And yet, it is precisely because of our past that we have in the present the appropriate energy, resources and wisdom to implement a new choice or pattern of behavior.

Internal healing is fully realized only when one is able to include all of themselves, without any unpleasant feelings or hang-ups, within their present path of teshuvah. A person may lovingly accept their past and acknowledge its purpose, while still remaining diligently focused on the labor of transforming themselves and their actions in the present to create a brighter future.

Beyond inclusive assimilation on an intrapersonal level, the holistic integration of teshuvah must now extend to the realm of the interpersonal. Unilateral severance in the realm of one's relationships, particularly with regard to parents, siblings or family, should not be an option. (There are of course extreme cases such as abuse, which warrant a definitive break in order for one to heal and evolve.) It is tragic and unfortunate when teshuvah creates a situation wherein a person finds their newfound path and then deems it appropriate to cut themselves off from all those who love them but do not share their opinions or convictions.

Imagine being a good and loving parent investing untold physical, mental and financial energy into your child, and one day your child walks into your house and tells you that he now knows that in order for him to live a more meaningful life, he must abandon all the ways you taught him and commit to a very different lifestyle. The pain that parent may feel, the rejection and resentment, the feelings of inadequacy are very real and highly acute. These feelings must be taken into account by one on the path of teshuvah in order to avoid acquiring more negative energy and baggage in the process of self-discovery and refinement. For one may inadvertently end up hurting others, even while engaged in such a lofty project as 'turning one's life around'.

True, the child may feel that he was the one who was cheated out of a spiritually meaningful or purposeful education. The trick however is for both children and parents to be mature enough to realize that it is no one's fault. The issue is not 'who is right' and 'who has been wronged'; but for all involved to learn to be accepting, respectful and supportive of each other.

This is addressed directly in the fourth of the Ten Commandments — to 'honor your parents'. There is no subtext in this commandment, it is not conditional upon where your parents sent you to school or what synagogue your family attended. It is imperative, especially for the baal teshuvah as they strike out on a new path, to honor and respect the choices and sacrifices that were made by one's parents throughout the course of raising their child. If your teshuvah ruins or rips apart your family or loved ones, then there is something faulty or lacking.

One's teshuvah does not occur in a vacuum, and if one's awakening does not include a deeper sensitivity to their affects upon others — especially loved ones — than it may be that their teshuvah is just as self centered as their previous actions they are so desperately running away from. This is a serious and sensitive dynamic within the process of teshuvah, and one that deserves much contemplation and careful counsel.

Each person's character and present personality is seamlessly intertwined with their past experiences and actions — the constructive and positive, as well as the destructive and negative. What we have done in the past inexorably shapes, forms and molds who we are in the present. Dwelling solely on the negativity of the past can be a great detriment to one's honest desire for change. If regret and guilt permeate our consciousness in the present then the past can only serve as a stumbling block and great impediment, thereby stifling all growth and suffocating any hope for spiritual maturation.

We need to peer into our past and acutely observe what can be positively utilized from those experiences for assistance in the present. Re-

garding the purely negative — that which cannot be applied in any way
— the best solution would be to simply forget it and not to give it any
more consideration. The past can have a chokehold on the present only if
we unconsciously desire it to; it has power only if we give it power. What
is real is this present moment — now is where we really are.

Life should be lived on a level devoid of any regrets or self-recrimi-
nation. The implication of this is twofold: First, we should seek to secure
a degree of foresight and clear conscience regarding our present actions in
order to assure that whatever is done in the present will not be regretted
in the future. A life lived unintentionally and haphazardly inevitably sows
the seeds of a lifetime of guilt and regret. We will therefore attempt to act
in ways that will not generate negative repercussions, whether psychically
or physically.

Secondly, even if we have done something in the past that evokes regret, simply feeling regretful as an end unto itself is pointless and often
counterproductive. Regret is only useful if it catalyzes one toward transformation, if not then our regret becomes a perverse form of self-indul-
gence.

Looking back on your life and saying, "I should have done this or I
should not have done that" is meaningless and inane, or as the Chassidic
Rebbes say, heresy. On its own what can possibly be the result of regretting past deeds, other than cultivating ill feelings toward oneself? What
was done in the past is passed, at this point it is mere memory. There
seems to be no good reason to entertain ideas of 'could have' or 'should
have'. These thoughts only germinate hostile feelings toward the one
thinking them, and when people feel bad about themselves, they end up
doing less for their current situation, not more.

Alternatively, the favorable aspect of regret is that it does have the
potential to inspire a review of the past and serve as a guide for the present. Though the past event cannot be changed, the way we tell the story
about it can, and we can then come to see the past as a staunch protector
of a more conscious future.

In order to do this we need to emotionally detach ourselves from the
past through objective observation so we can identify potential dangers
that lie ahead if we were to select the same course of behavior. When

used to inspire an examination of our past actions and intentions, the feeling of regret is positively charged. Transformation occurs when the negative past becomes a beacon of light in the present that illuminates the path toward a promising future.

Classic Torah commentators such as the Rambam contend that the principal ingredients of teshuvah are *charata*, 'regret', and *kabbalah* or 'acceptance', literally, accepting upon oneself to do better in the future, and on a deeper level, 'acceptance' and 'receptivity'. In order to regret we must first clearly recognize what was wrong with our behavior and how our lives have become misaligned from our deepest soul reality. A firm resolution for the future appears to be the best regret.

Put differently, genuine charata is manifest as a determined kabbalah. A true kabbalah in this sense would not be just an acceptance of the past 'as it is', but a resolve to be receptive toward a redemptive future, with an absolute faith that the All Merciful One will liberate us from the bitterness of our condition and give us the strength to choose our paths wisely and with expanded consciousness. Kabbalah in this context then comes to mean, 'openness to receiving the Creator's mercy and guidance'.

Though regret can be a good initiator and catalyst toward leading a life of intentionality, ultimately spiritual progress is better served if this resolve stems from a desire to create a better future. A true state of kabbalah is not merely a resolve to being open to grace, but rather that we project ourselves into the future and imagine doing things differently. As such, in the place where negativity and ill feelings of regret once predominated and suffused our inner space, there is now a positive and life-affirming energy that permeates our consciousness and engenders genuine growth and further spiritual development.

The ultimate purpose of *kabbalah*, which literally means 'to receive', is to receive in order to give. In this sense, we receive the truth of the past 'as it is' and then open ourselves to receive the gift of Hashem's kindness and mercy in order to give ourselves, and the rest of the world, the gift of our fully realized and integrated self.

Toward this end, distraction can work wonders. Warring against negativity may in fact only bolster it and add more fuel to the fire. One of the ways to combat negativity is to shift our focus from the negative to an unrelated positive. Rabbi Mendel of Kotzk once remarked that when the armies of Napoleon were surrounded by their enemies and on the verge of collapse, Napoleon initiated a great commotion away from the battlefield. The enemy turned and was caught off guard; Napoleon and his men were saved. Similarly, the best remedy for ridding ourselves of a damaging past is not by going up against it in direct battle, but rather through a refocusing on some positive aspect that situates us in a completely different context.

When the Torah employs the word *ve'atah*, 'and now', it is referring to teshuvah, as the most consequential aspect of time is now, the eternal present. Of course 'what is' directly results from 'what was', yet the most empowered ingredient of teshuvah is the now. In the now, we have the ability to transcend that which has been done in the past and to look at the present as a fresh starting point for a future filled with meaning and purpose. The power to behold the present as a clean slate, unmarked or unsoiled from the past is available to us in this very moment.

The full potential of teshuvah is attained when a person feels completely forgiven — forgiven by himself, forgiven by others and forgiven by Hashem. At the peak of teshuvah a person can reclaim a sense of freedom from all limitations and step into a future unimpeded by the negativity of yesterday.

There is negative freedom and positive freedom; there is 'freedom *from*' and 'freedom *to*'. The former is a freedom from everything oppressive — socially, economically, culturally or inwardly. The second however is a freedom to choose the course of one's life, to manifest that which one deems as good and necessary. In a state of teshuvah, we not only function from a place of negative freedom — freedom from the negativity of our past, but also from a place of positive freedom — freedom to choose all that is positive in our lives and in the world.

By truly living a life of teshuvah — a life of freedom, renewal and rebirth — the present moment becomes the most important dimension of time, for the present moment is the only real time-reality that we live in. Now is the moment that contains both the seeds of our future and the transformative power to redeem our past.

SYNOPSIS:CHAPTER 22
Think of Yourself As a Blessing

The foundation of all positive movement in life is the fundamental belief that we can change, that we can make a difference, and that we have the ability to bring blessing into our life. Yet if there is merely a passive acceptance of the past, with no real honest accounting of its potentially negative repercussions, we may then begin to condone our past, no matter what forms our actions have taken. What is needed is a delicate balance between a healthy self-love coupled with a healthy regret, without allowing the feelings of regret to demoralize us. The past can then be utilized as a guide to inform our present in terms of what to do and what not to do, thus reshaping our future for the positive.

PRACTICE
ACCEPTANCE OF SELF

Acceptance means acknowledging the reality that you are who you are; although to accept is not to condone. Acceptance leads to empathy and encouragement, cheering yourself on to live at your highest potential, from the place of your innate goodness. When we live from a place of acceptance while simultaneously regretting certain earlier actions without berating ourselves, the assimilation of past into present brings rectification. From here we discover the positive core of the very traits that initially led to our past mistakes.

Meditate on your day and notice one character trait that keeps resurfac-
ing — impatience for example, or not having the ability to focus on or do
more than one thing at a time. You may want to write down that trait. In
the initial stages of teshuvah it is best to be gentle with yourself; instead
of lamenting your shortcomings or hating yourself for succumbing to
them, aspire to overcome these traits.

In accord with the paradigm of acceptance, you may want to identify pro-
fessions or circumstances where these qualities would be valuable. An inability to engage in more than one activity at a time could be great for
personal prayer, and a love for adrenaline thrills is perfect for rescue work.
This redemptive practice can be done with all character traits.

CHAPTER TWENTY-THREE

LETTING GO OF
Guilt

For many people, feeling guilty is an unfortunate fact of life. Whatever the source maybe, guilt can be a crushing emotion that, when experienced in its full force, has the power to take over one's life. People often make decisions based solely on their feelings of guilt. To varying degrees of intensity, guilt appears to be an inevitability of the socially conditioned human being.

In the quest for personal transformation, the issue of guilt must be confronted. While some are able to use guilt as a catalyst toward rehabilitation, often it is precisely these very feelings of guilt that we must overcome in order to arrive at a genuine desire for change. For the most part, the burden of this puritanical emotion is a colossal impediment along the path of teshuvah. Only after achieving some measure of innocence and inherent goodness can we consciously choose the path of teshuvah. Until guilt has been transcended, the desire to change may be a subconscious reflex born out of negativity.

Guilty feelings are generally accompanied by the emotion of shame. These two are inextricably connected to each other, emerging out the depths of our consciousness. We begin by feeling guilty for doing or not doing something, and then the emotion of shame immediately follows — a feeling of embarrassment over what has been done or not done.

Upon reflection, a more subtle difference between the concepts of guilt and shame emerges. Guilt is inwardly directed, whereas shame is outwardly oriented. Guilt is an ill feeling harbored against oneself, arising after one breaks a code of conduct. Shame on the other hand is an emotion generated by our perception of other people's expectations, real or imagined. We may feel judged by others and subsequently we feel shame.

Guilt, on the other hand, is a self-referential emotion resulting from the psychological tension that stems from a perceived discrepancy between one's actions and one's intentions or ideals. To feel guilty, there first needs to be a standard that one aims to adhere to. Guilt can only exist within the context of a behavioral template.

Guilt is negative emotional baggage that, when held on to, becomes heavier and more difficult to relinquish, eventually weighing down the person completely. It invades, pollutes and destroys any positive feelings one may harbor toward oneself.

In extreme cases, guilt can be so burdensome that it can lead one to believe that he is in fact soiled or contaminated. Sustaining this feeling is the polar opposite of taking oneself lightly. It is an anchor that drags us downward and perpetuates self-resentment. The end result is a devastating sense of immobility, of being trapped. Slowly, spiritual suffocation sets in under the strain of looming guilt.

One of the most prevalent manifestations of guilt is within the parent/child relationship. Often parents idealize their role and, when faced with the imperfections of their own parental or general behavior, a sense of guilt develops for not living up to the expectations they had for themselves. The guilt emerges because an inner ideal was transgressed. Children experience this same emotion when the unrealistic expectations of their parents become their own and they fall short of these ideals. There is a sense of guilt for not being their best. The inevitable conclusion of this paradigm is a life plagued by guilt.

Guilt follows the feeling that we have broken a standard that is not our own, a model of behavior that has been imposed upon us. One who has been instructed by society, educators, or parents on how to behave in certain circumstances, only to misbehave when in those same circumstances, falls short of those standards and will unavoidably feel guilty.

The feeling itself piggybacks on a sense of having transgressed the enforced standard of behavior. There is self-questioning: "How could I do this when this is not the thing that I am supposed to be doing?" The key phrase in this question is: 'Supposed to'. This implies a sense of externally imposed expectations such as persuasion, education, environmental standards or social norms that were never owned as one's own inner code. Guilt is triggered when one deviates from these perceived expectations.

The burden of guilt is often only present in response to others' demands or desires. A person in this condition works very hard to think, feel or act in the way others believe he should think, feel or act. With guilt there is a total eclipse of the authentic I. The I of the self becomes the other. In this estrangement of I, one lives to actualize an image of self which others demand and shape for him. The super-ego, as some would call it, becomes externalized and one's sense of identity come from external impositions, rather than from an internally generated connection to the seed of self. Expectations and directions come from without of oneself, as an external authority, rather than from within, as an internal conviction.

When we consciously set our own standard of behavior — mindfully determining our conduct according to what we believe to be right — then if, and when, we do happen to transgress our code of conduct, neurotically charged feelings of guilt are not engendered.

When we do indeed transgress, we may be disappointed with ourselves, and we should be, but these feelings will not be coupled with the heavy burden of guilt. Certainly we will not wallow in our disappointment if we truly understand that whatever we can damage, we can fix, — and it is up to us to change our behavior and realign our priorities.

Fascinatingly, there is not one Hebrew word that accurately defines the sense of guilt. In Biblical Hebrew, there is a word for 'shame', *busha* and for 'regret', *charatah*, but there is no word for guilt. Guilt is not a Torah idea. Regret yes, as regret can be a positive emotion if it is focused on a deed done or not done, and coupled with a resolve to amend or alter behavior. But guilt is irredeemable as it seeks to turn the harsh judgment inward upon the doer himself, with no resolve for action. Guilt is a purely a negative feeling in and of itself, with no resulting impetus to do anything about that which makes one feel guilty. When these feelings are not accompanied by a resolve to evolve, this characterizes the static sensation of guilt.

On a deeper level — in a Torah-filled existence — there is no room for guilt, as the Torah's desire is that we consciously choose the Torah's standard of conduct as our own, and hence to not feel that Torah is something imposed upon us from the outside. Being Torah-committed should not feel as if it is an external way of life imposed upon us with no choice in the matter. But rather, we should be open to feel how the Torah resonates within us and complements our very own personality. In this way the Torah becomes essentially, our Torah.

There is a spiritual movement upwards and inwards from a place of "I must" to "I am able", from "I have to" to " I can", and from "I feel forced to fulfill the mitzvos because of an external injunction thrust upon me" to "I am able to and would like to fulfill the mitzvos because it is who I am."

The choice is a free choice that rises up from deep within: "I am able". And yet the choice is so eminent, so powerful and so real that you feel like there is actually no choice in the matter.

At first, we were asked if we wanted to receive the Torah and we answered enthusiastically — yes! Then afterwards, as the Gemarah explains the verse (Shabbos, 88a), "They stood under the mountain," Hashem overturned the mountain and held it above their heads like an inverted cask and said, "If you accept the Torah, good; if not, here shall be your burial."

Why the imposed force? This seems to be inconsistent with previous teaching of how the Israelites chose to accept the Torah through our own free choice — willingly and with love.

The inner meaning of this passage is that, the acceptance of Torah is so deep and real to us, that it is as if there is no choice. There is no choice, because it is who we are.

This is much like life itself. Life is who we are, and in life we do not have the choice whether to have choice or not. We have the freedom to choose, but we don't have the freedom whether we choose. We can make a choice not to choose, but we are still making a choice.

The same is true with Torah. Torah is our life. Torah is not additional to life — it is *chayeinu* — it is 'our life'.

So we move from the lower level of "I must — I feel forced", to the higher paradigm of "I am able — I feel free and open to choose", to the highest paradigm of "I am". At this level, "Torah is so real to me it is as if I have no choice".

This highest level of choice does not derive from any external force imposed upon me, but rather it comes from within me. Torah is my essence, and to me, it is life itself.

So there are three movements of growth:
•"I Must"
•"I Could"
•"I Am"

Parenthetically, the stages from "I must", to "I could", to "I am" are not a linear progression from one step to the next. One does not achieve a particular level and remain there, but rather these are states that occur throughout one's life. We come from a place of "I must", then we are able to reach the place of "I could", and finally we arrive at the higher "I am"; and there we can stay for a while until we must again move through this succession of stages in order to access a more subtle and elevated plane, or perspective.

Ultimately, the higher "I am" is the deepest realization that Torah is who we are, and it can then even be called "our" Torah. The Torah was transmitted to each one of us so that it can become ours. So much so, that when we contemplate and master Torah, it is referred to in our own name. Being in a state of *deveikus* or 'cleaving' and 'exalted adhesion' to Torah, the Torah becomes our own.

When our actions or attitudes are not in line with Torah, the resulting dis-alignment is felt as an inconsistency with our own nobler self. The Torah desires for us to reveal our inner-most will, aligned with the

LETTING GO OF GUILT

will of the Master of the Universe, and to live in a way that makes manifest our individual 'i' as an expression of the Ultimate I of creation.

Whether we perceive the deeper/higher voice of Torah as coming from within or from without depends on how integrated we are with our soul, our deepest self. The reason some people may hear the Torah's voice as unwelcoming, harsh, or alien is because they are not vertically and horizontally integrated. They are separated and alienated from their inner selves and thus sense these truths as coming from an Other — from Outside of themselves.

This will not be the case when we become fully unified with our own higher Selves that are rooted in Ultimate Unity. When we reveal these levels and live from that place of integration, these truths will be who we are, and not what we need to or not do.

In life there are many natural laws we accept as absolute, without any type of resistance. Certain laws appear not as impositions, but rather as necessary activities to ensure our survival. Breathing, eating, drinking and sleeping are all 'calls of nature' that are simply accepted as reality — they are considered standard operational procedures. We do not rebel against them, and when we do, if it is not for a "cause" such as fasting, this indicates a condition of illness.

Torah aspires to flow within and through us with at least the same measure of organic ease — without the resistance of the ego. True, for some the initial relationship with Torah may seem a bit forced. A person may feel infringed upon, and occasionally may even feel a desire to rebel against that which seems to be imposed upon them. Overall fear may precede love. But gradually as a person becomes more integrally aligned, he realizes that 'It is' who 'he is'. Progressively, Torah life becomes synonymous with life itself.

This level of self-integration and unity is perhaps a distant aspiration for most people. Unfortunately for many, guilt continues to be an active and pervasive, driving force of life. But there is no reason to despair. As with everything else in life, guilt is neither altogether good nor entirely evil. It is contingent upon how we interpret and utilize it. The fact is that often guilt can propel people toward good deeds.

There are two extreme approaches in understanding human behavior. One understanding suggests that the outward is a direct reflection of the inward, and that energy flows in only one direction. Thus a negative cause cannot be the source of a positive effect, and vice versa. According to this perspective if you act from a place of anger, even if what you have done seems to be positive, inherently it is negative. For example, if you witness an injustice and you feel anger toward the perpetrator of that injustice, any action you take based on that anger will be deemed negative. We will call this modality of behavior *Spiritual Ethics*.

Just to illustrate, this perspective would see no redeeming quality in any aggressive action taken to stand up for the oppressed, such as Moshe's killing of the Egyptian Slave-master. It's judgment and interpretation would only be based on the impulsive anger and violence that gave rise to the act, thereby completely ignoring the social, political, or revolutionary context in which the action arose.

The other extreme is simply consequence-based, suggesting that what matters most are actions and not their intentions. This we will call *Pragmatic Ethics*. If your actions are positive, helping to alleviate injustice for example, even if they are rooted in anger or arrogance, they are nonetheless positive. If you do a positive deed, it does not matter what your intention was — it is only important that you did the good deed.

The Torah is both pragmatic and spiritual — outwardly action-based and inwardly spiritually-oriented — an ethic of *Spiritual Pragmatism* or *Pragmatic Spirituality*. 'Torah spirituality' unfolds within a context of *Halacha*, 'practical law'. Do good deeds, be disturbed, even angered by injustice, and then do more good deeds. Yet the process does not end with the actions; because when your hand opens in kindness eventually your heart and mind opens as well.

Whatever the source, a good deed is a good deed and it should be valued as such. To the poor man who receives charity, it makes no difference if you had ulterior motives or gave money out of a sense of guilt. Yet, our inner state follows our outer actions, and any positive projection outward does indeed have real potential to open us up to inner transformation.

When you perform physical acts of loving kindness, your heart and mind open, for as the Chinuch writes, "The heart follows actions". Good

actions help to create a good heart. Positive behavior opens us up to positive perspectives. Our good deeds expand and transform us internally.

Every outward action has an effect on our inner reality. The *P'nim*
or 'interior' follows the *Panim*, the 'face' — the exterior. There is a symbi-
otic relationship between the internal and the external.

The internal normally projects the external, the Panim normally reflects the P'nim, yet the movement can also be reversed: the exterior can
also effect the interior, and good deeds can transform one's mind and
heart.

Ultimately both the intention and the action are highly valued and
validated within a Torah worldview. It is of the utmost importance to
simply do the action, and also the intention and internal echo of the action or mitzvah is of the utmost importance.

Marirrus is the Hebrew word for the feeling of 'bitterness'. Quite
often, it is precisely marirrus, as opposed to guilt, that assists many in
their quest for change. Let us just clarify that marirrus is not depression.
Depression is feeling hopeless and helpless without any motivation to rise
above, or out of, that status. This can eventually lead a person to become
so deeply depressed that he ceases to feel anything at all.

Marirrus, on the other hand, is a vital, pulsating emotion: the person
is devastatingly unhappy and discontent with his existential condition —
so much so that he is motivated to change. Marirrus has the power to release the individual from his spiritual complacency and awaken him to
the reality that change is imperative. Marirrus is a soul pain that arises
when we feel cut off, and at odds with the deepest part of our self and
soul. Spiritual bitterness is the experience of feeling our alienation and
loneliness so deeply that we are inspired and resolved to transform. This
anguish and discontent is itself the stimulation that impels positive reorientation.

An analogy can be drawn between marrirus and the feeling of pain.
Pain is an experience that can be viewed from two diametrically opposed
perspectives. The first and most obvious reaction to pain is the shock of
the hurt — it is uncomfortable and irritating, but does not necessarily
lead to any constructive action; this is analogous to guilt.

Yet there is a positive aspect to pain as well. Without pain, we would not be aware that we were suffering from an ailment. Pain is the means through which the body informs the mind that danger or dis-alignment looms. If, due to the absence of pain, we were unaware of an injury we would risk leaving it untreated, thereby endangering ourselves further; this is analogous to marrirus.

Simply speaking, pain guards the body. The biological purpose of pain is to prompt a positive reaction within the body to heal itself, or to go seek help.

The same holds true with feelings of bitterness. It is possible for someone to be spiritually, or emotionally unhealthy and to not recognize his own illness, taking the feelings at face value without investigating any deeper. This can be likened to the western medical approach that only focuses on the symptoms of an illness, while ignoring the potential root causes of an imbalance.

Conversely a person feeling this very same pain — or bitterness — may ponder the hurt, evaluate it, and identify its source, thereby redirecting the negative feelings into a positive orientation toward healing and empowerment. We have the ability to employ all of our energies toward further awakening and spiritual development. This means that even bitterness can be a potential springboard toward a more positive, healthy and life-affirming existence.

In this paradigm the negative quality of guilt is not allowed to fester; only its essence is distilled and re-contextualized as a catalyst to do what is correct — to re-align ourselves. The individual utilizes this bitterness to redirect his life's path, sifting out the positive impetus from within the guilt, and employing the bitter emotions as building blocks for spiritual development.

Ideally the healthiest course for spiritual growth is to fully release oneself from all negative emotions, never allowing any internal tension to foster, ferment or grow. Whenever there is tension or guilt, instead of feeling down or incapable of acting differently, try to take a positive stance. Do something good and productive and observe the negativity slowly evaporate.

SYNOPSIS:CHAPTER 23
Let Go of Guilt

Many people walk around with a heavy burden of guilt that pollutes their joy and self-regard. Many also have a mistaken belief that guilt will help them turn their lives around. Guilt almost never helps. Very different from guilt are the emotions of bitterness and regret which can move us toward joy, empowerment and responsibility for our own lives.

PRACTICE
NOTICE

Whenever a guilty thought arises, notice the energy it carries.

Notice the tone of the inner monologue that underlies it. Notice what kind of influence it exerts upon your consciousness and upon your choices. Does it move you toward joy and empowerment or toward depression and disempowerment? Now, vividly imagine an action that you could do that would be in alignment with your own core values. Notice the energy or emotional tone this thought brings you.

CHAPTER TWENTY-THREE

Overcoming SHAME

Having placed the notion of guilt in its proper context, we can now proceed to explore its companion — the idea of *busha*, 'shame'. How are we to relate to shame? Is our ultimate aspiration to transcend shame altogether? Fundamentally, the question is whether or not shame is a feeling that can be utilized for the positive or is it an entirely negative emotion that warrants total eradication?

Guilt is the experiential result of an existential tension generated by a cognitive dissonance between one's actions and one's expectations. Shame on the other hand is a sense of disdain and hostility directed toward oneself. More succinctly — guilt is a self-generated emotion, while shame comes from an internalization of other people's judgments. Essentially, shame is an emotion that arises when we feel judged from an outside source, be it other people, or even a more removed part from within ourselves.

"And they (Adam and Chava) were both naked...and were not ashamed" (Bereishis, 2:25). Shame is an emotion that can only exist when there is awareness of an 'other'. Since they did not yet eat from the

Tree of Knowledge and Duality there was no strong sense of separation, and thus they were not ashamed to be in their natural state.

From among all the living creatures that roam this earth, humans appear unique in that we are the only ones who blush. As animals are integrated creatures whose behavior is congruent with their inner beings, they do not have a need to blush. Animals *do* what they *are*; there is never an inconsistency between their internal nature and their external behavior. Humans however, have free choice and can thus be in conflict with their inner nature, which may then bring them to blush. The blushing occurs because, in addition to our freedom of choice, we also possess a strong sense of self-awareness. The former gives us the ability to be at odds with ourselves, the latter causes us to be aware of it and consequently, to blush.

Human beings have the intellectual sensitivity to recognize when there is an incongruity between what we are and how we behave. Complex intellectual capacity is a pre-requisite for fully realized freedom and therefore, we are the only creatures to blush due to the foolish choices we may make that run contrary to our deeper conscience. When a person who is at odds with himself does not blush upon becoming aware of his own disharmony, he is either lacking in intellectual awareness or is simply callous.

Shame is not an altogether negative emotion. It can actually be quite helpful, at least in the initial stages of one's spiritual journey. The Hebrew word *busha*, 'shame', is comprised of the four letters *beis, vav, shin, hei* and has the exact same letters as the word *shuva*, 'return'. *Busha* may inspire *shuva*.

Shame can potentially catapult an individual into developing good character traits. In fact, in early development, human conscience is largely founded on a child's sense of shame. As young children we come to learn what is positive and what is negative behavior by observing which behaviors seem to disappoint the people we love and which behaviors make them proud. When we misbehave, we feel embarrassment in the face of the people we love, having let them down. Even as we grow older, we demonstrate our sensitivity to other people's feelings by blushing and exhibiting our shame to others. In a way, blushing itself provides the observer with a sort of apology for any behavior that may have offended them.

For practical purposes the idea of shame can be divided into three categories. 1) The so-called lowest level would be experienced because of, and in front of, other people. 2) A higher level of shame would be derived from a superior order — a code of conduct that we have come to accept. 3) The uppermost level of shame would be from within our own deeper self. The higher we climb up the rungs of self-empowerment, the less pronounced shame becomes. In due course, we can aspire to reach a place where neither shame nor guilt exert their hegemony over us.

The more self-assertive and confident we become the more inner-directed and self-referential we are, the less we live to impress others. Eventually a healthy dose of *hishtavus* or 'equanimity' evolves, and praise, condemnation, admiration and scolding all slide right off our backs, un-able to penetrate and alter our self-perspective or sense of self-worth. In this way, we do not take anything personally that is directed toward us from another, whether for the better — as in approval, or for the worse — as in ridicule.

As young and powerless children it is inevitable that we come to value our selves based on what other people think of us. Perhaps this is even a built-in mechanism of our bio-survival, as we are initially depend-ent on others for our nourishment and survival. The trouble is however, that some people never grow beyond this stage — they are perpetually looking elsewhere for validation and confirmation. Their measurement for gauging proper behavior is defined by what other people think they should or should not do. It is never based in their own experience — how they feel or how they think.

The level of shame these people experience is intense embarrass-ment when amongst others. Living in such a manner leaves them in a perpetual state of shame waiting to happen. As the only motivating factor for good behavior at this level of development is shame, if a person wishes to do something amiss he will make sure that no one is around to see him. When no one is around he will do as he pleases, as his ethical index is determined solely by others' observations and assessments; as such there is no internal compass that guides him.

A less intense shame is one that is brought about when a person feels estranged from a higher order that he has come to accept as a way of life. Still this is not the most refined level of shame, for it is still prompted by external stimulus.

The most refined shame is when we feel so self-assured that we function without the need to impress others and the only shame experienced is from within our own self. This is known as literally 'letting yourself down'. There is something within, a conscience or inner voice that tells us when there is an inconsistency, when what has been done is inappropriate – it is from this awareness that we sense shame. Being open to ourselves and to the still, small voice within ensures that we will remain consistent, and when we do deviate from our internal reality we will feel the appropriate degree of internally-oriented shame that will assure that this less-than-ideal behavior will not reoccur.

The best course for genuine growth would be to elevate ourselves to a state where we do not need the experience of negative or hostile feelings to become more spiritually oriented. The foundation of this space would be built on a base of inclusion and love. At this level it is not guilt or shame that guides us to Hashem and to our deepest self, but rather it is love — the greatest unifying agent of all that re-engages and challenges us. In place of hostility and bitterness, where the individual may feel disempowered and disenfranchised, there is now an active and empowered human being who feels good about life and about himself. He seeks with passion and enthusiasm to connect with his Creator — to enter into a relationship with the Ultimate Partner via the greatest life-affirming energy of the universe — love.

Gratuitous feelings of guilt and shame are not productive or supportive to the individual, so the question must be: If we do experience shame, how can it be transcended? Better yet, can we absolve ourselves of these inferior feelings on the journey toward a life free of negativity? And, if so, how?

There are countless suggestions that have been offered to assist people in overcoming shame. It appears that the common thread unifying them all is that shame is brought about when a person feels that he has

stumbled and is imperfect. In this case the advice is: When we feel defi-
cient, instead of being ashamed, we should realize that imperfection is
part of the human experience. Errors are what make human beings
human.

Stated differently, shame is transcended by realizing that there is
nothing to be ashamed of. The source of shame is a belief in perfection.
By recognizing and accepting that we are not meant to be perfect, and
neither is anybody else, we will cease to be ashamed.

Shame is introduced in the Torah after Adam and Chava ate from
the Tree of Dualistic Knowledge — it was then that they realized their
nakedness and were ashamed. This indicates that the tikkun of shame is
to return to a form of 'Garden' consciousness — to put the fruit of
knowledge back onto the Tree of Life — to initiate and experience a re-
unification and re-integration within the world and within oneself.

Theologically speaking, people are told not to feel ashamed in the
Presence of their Creator. The logic follows that because Hashem created
you, Hashem knows better than anyone or anything else, the reality of
your condition. And due to this intimate knowledge of the Creator con-
cerning creation, there is no need to feel shame.

Though there is some truth to this perspective, the trouble with this
method is that the underlying emotion beneath shame is a sense of inadequacy, incompetence or lack of power. This is our very position in relation to the Source of all Creation. Though this approach may provide
short-term relief by alleviating the symptoms of shame; in the long run it
may actually reinforce and exemplify these identifications with inadequacy.

By telling ourselves that there is nothing to be embarrassed of in the
eyes of Hashem, the immediate sense of shame may be alleviated, but
long-term feelings of inadequacy are likely to increase. By feeling validated from within a disempowered state we risk sinking even deeper, believing less in ourselves, not more.

A more inclusive approach would be to contest shame, to respond to
it with a life-affirming force and vitality. By choosing not to examine or
wallow in the shame, and instead doing something positive, we neutralize

the negative feelings we have toward ourselves and thereby begin to feel good.

Shame stems from feeling ineffectual and disempowered. It compounds the negative affects on a person by reinforcing a low self-esteem. Feeling shame causes an individual to feel worse about himself and even more inept then before — it is a downward spiral. In the end, a spiritual lethargy sets in and one degenerates into a state of complete immobility. Clearly the most appropriate tactic would be to combat shame by taking direct action and feeling the surge of empowerment.

If you feel embarrassed because of the deeds you may have committed or omitted, and you feel weak for having surrendered to temporary temptations, accept these feelings and then redeem yourself by taking strength in a positive act. Internal change eventually occurs when we take one step at a time. These actions will slowly change the doer within.

If however you want to do something instantly powerful — enter the world of teshuvah and in place of feeling powerless, inefficient and incompetent, begin to feel powerful, competent and capable. From the highest level of teshuvah, an internal shift occurs in which proper actions organically follow. Teshuvah transforms the doer's dynamic within, which automatically transforms the actions and projections that flow outward.

Ultimately the height of spiritual development is to live life without having to experience embarrassment, as did Adam and Chava in the Garden of Eden before eating from the Tree of Knowledge. There is no room for embarrassment when we are living an integrated 'Tree of Life' reality, when our inner being is evident in our outer behavior.

In the case where a deviation does take place and we are at odds with our soul, we should immediately answer these feelings with positive actions and with teshuvah. Instead of allowing negative emotions to take hold and cause immobility, take action and eliminate these feelings in their inception. The best antidote for ill feelings toward oneself, be they self-loathing, puritanical guilt, self-laceration or condemnation is to take positive action and be productive, thereby countering these feelings by feeling courageous, worthy and able.

SYNOPSIS:CHAPTER 24
Drop Shame

When shame overwhelms a person it can lead to total self-imprisonment. This is the eventual result of the confusion between what we have done and who we really are. Not only is shaming yourself based on an inaccuracy, it is also unjust. In the same way that you would stand up for a victim of injustice, you must stand up for the essentially good person that you truly are.

PRACTICE
ACT!

If you are ashamed of what you have done or if you angrily called yourself weak for surrendering to your ego, stand up now for who you really are.

With the same emotional intensity that you or others might have used for blame, do a good deed — perform a significant mitzvah. You could even do it with righteous anger, like a political activist demanding the release of an unjustly held prisoner.

HUMILITY
& *Confidence*

S adness, joy, melancholy and euphoria are some of the feelings that
typically arise whenever one desires to alter his path of life. Teshuvah
entails a degree of breaking from the past, and as such it can be quite a
poignant undertaking. No matter how happy and exhilarated a person
may be in having chosen a new, more meaningful way of life, there always
lingers in one's memory a nostalgic sentiment for 'what once was'. Separation in any form is a source of pain, be it physical or emotional. Being
happy with the present condition does not negate the feelings of sadness
and pain that may arise when one strays from the ways in which one was
brought up.

A new phase of birth or rebirth is always accompanied by a corresponding form of death or dissolution. No beginning ensues without
marking an end of something else. In human development, a transition
or attainment of a new height connotes the end of an old one. For this
reason, many of us continue to labor in stifling and unpleasant situations,
rather than making the definitive move toward change. Transitions almost always give rise to ambivalent feelings — even if they are for our
benefit.

Whenever we experience internal or external change, even if it is for
the better, it is almost always mixed with feelings of pain or loss. Gradu-

ating from high school and knowing that we are moving on from careless adolescence causes great joy and excitement, but may also bring about sadness or nostalgia. So it is with teshuvah.

Graduating from the past and moving on with one's life, even if one consciously chooses to do so, can still be a journey sprinkled with sadness. Once a person becomes accustomed to a certain behavior or perspective, even if it is detrimental to their inner wellbeing, it becomes all the more emotionally challenging to break away from it.

Humiliation is another psychological condition that must be confronted while in the process of teshuvah. Teshuvah can be a truly humiliating experience. Unquestionably, honesty is an integral component of teshuvah. The trouble is, however, that whenever we are in a position that requires honesty with ourselves regarding the negative aspects of our behavior, there is always room for either self-deception or inordinate honesty. Undergoing a major life transition and stripping down to our barest self, may stimulate extreme conditions of vulnerability.

The internal humiliation experienced from descending into the darker dimensions of self, which is necessary to objectively analyze all misdeeds, mistakes and missed opportunities, can at times, be too intense to correctly assimilate. Good and positive aspects of one's personality may be eclipsed by the overwhelming encounter with negative and unsatisfactory character traits.

Due to this potential dynamic, there is always the danger that we may end up viewing ourselves as unworthy or inadequate. These are negative and immobilizing emotions that will hinder our willpower or even the very belief in our ability to climb out of our abyss and make a better life for ourselves. These detrimental feelings ought to be confronted and overcome so that there can be a cohesive movement toward an inclusive and integral teshuvah in which all previous negativity as well as potential talents and particular genius are re-contextualized within our new spiritual commitment.

In order for us to live a healthy and well-adjusted life, we need our self-worth and self-esteem to be in tact as we acknowledge and admit our past mistakes and misdeeds. We need to learn to be brutally honest about our shortcomings, but also equally as honest about our strengths.

The deeper part of our self is always whole, while the more external aspects of self are at times in need of teshuvah. The proper *derech* or 'path' is to be both a *baki* or 'master' in the higher self and a *baki* in the lower self as well. Master your ups and your downs with a creative ability to navigate and balance your dual nature.

The numerical value of the word *derech* is 224 (dalet=4, reish=200, ches=20). The gematria of the word *baki* is 112 (beis=2, quf=100, yud=10). Thus, being a baki in both worlds equals 224. This is truly the integral path, walking in both worlds at once, as one holistically integrated being.

During the process of an honest and thorough self-accounting, a person may become overwhelmed when they uncover devastating feelings of disgust and humiliation for things they may have done or neglected to do. To counter these sentiments one must remember that there is an indestructible inner point that is always a perfect *tzadik* or 'righteous one'. The superficial self may have transgressed, but the inner reality of self is always perfect — needing nothing to be subtracted or added on to it. We need to learn to maintain a delicate equilibrium between these two aspects of self — the one being in constant need of refinement and the one being in a state of perpetual perfection.

There are various grades of teshuvah. For some, it is truly life-altering — a complete 180-degree turnaround. While for others it simply involves a further deepening of their previously chosen path of development. The more drastic the change, the more chance there is for one to feel humbled by the experience. Additional by-products of teshuvah, though perhaps only when rooted in fear, may be feelings of inferiority, meekness or lowliness.

When a person decides to embark on a new path and change the course of his life trajectory he may feel that whatever he has done in life up until this point was a complete waste of time or of no significance. This may cause him to feel disheartened or inadequate.

These feelings arise particularly when the individual compares his own level of Torah involvement to that of one who was born into a Torah life. He thereby may suffer from an inferiority complex resulting in a feeling that other people who have been 'born into it' have a head start in life.

This inferiority neurosis is one of the more common, though unjustified, feelings that can be experienced on the road of 'return' or *teshuvah*.

The reverse can also transpire. Often those who have experienced a spiritual epiphany begin to feel mentally and spiritually superior to all those who have not shared such an enlightenment. Smugness and self-righteousness can then become the norm.

Healthy teshuvah occurs when all of one's emotions are well balanced, feelings of regret for the past as well as a sense of inner joy in becoming more conscious in the present. This means that, together with feelings of surrender and submission, there is a good dose of confidence and self-esteem. The individual on the path of teshuvah, while perhaps feeling unworthy and inadequate for what was done in the past, should also cultivate strong feelings of self-worth and sufficiency, enabling him to transcend any potential despair and empowering him to move forward in life.

A healthy person is well adjusted and balanced physically, emotionally and spiritually. Balance implies personal liberation. Interestingly, the Greek word *libra*, which is the root of the English word liberation, means 'balance'. To be liberated is to live life in a balanced manner.

Ancient philosophers spoke of physical health in terms of balancing and harmonizing the four basic elements of the body. Everything within creation, mankind included, is comprised of four basic elements: fire, air, water and earth. To live harmoniously these four elements need to be stabilized, and it is only when we secure a state of equilibrium between them that can we truly be healthy.

The premise is that physical health is dependent on the inner balance of these meta-physical elements. This also holds true mentally and spiritually. To lead a healthier and more well adjusted lifestyle it is important to have a proper emotional balance. We must strive to be humble without becoming a doormat, self-assertive and confident without becoming conceited or pompous. We must also learn to be happy without feeling superior to others who are not, and also to be levelheaded about our condition without embracing melancholy.

On the holiday of Rosh Hashanah there is a mitzvah to blow the *shofar*, a 'ram's horn'. The Torah does not explicitly offer a reason as to why the shofar is blown. The verse simply says, "It shall be a day of *Teruah* (shofar sounds) for you". Nevertheless, the Rambam writes that the sounds of the shofar awaken a desire for teshuvah within the listener.

Today the blowing of the shofar consists of three sounds:
- *tekiah*: a 'firm and sustained blast',
- *shevarim*: a 'tripartite sound of a person sighing', and
- *teruah*: the 'broken sound of a person sobbing in quick outpourings'.

Before and after every staccato succession of shevarim and teruah, there must be a powerful blast of the tekiah. This is a *remez* or 'hint' that, before and after any period of intense self-reflection with the intention of recognizing our misdeeds, we should tap into the steady and unwavering sense of connection with Hashem that is always available to us. Like a current that is always flowing, we just need to flip the switch to access this energy.

The long steady notes of the tekiah remind us that our eternal and unchanging nature is constantly connected and creative. This gives us the inspiration and encouragement to delve into the sighing and sobbing of the shevarim/teruah that is necessary to do the real hard work of teshuvah and transformation.

Humility is the most evident emotion experienced when embarking upon the path of teshuvah. Whenever our self-image is manipulated or altered, whether for better or worse, we will inevitably feel some measure of meekness or vulnerability as represented by the sounds of the shevarim/teruah sequence. Then comes the surging sound of the tekiah that builds with intensity and lifts us up with strength and stamina to pick ourselves up and journey forward.

Some may experience harsh realizations, or negative awakenings, while in the process of teshuvah, they may feel broken and smashed into little pieces as the broken sounds of the shevarim/teruah. And so, these sentiments need to be cushioned from both sides with confidence and self-assuredness, a blast of tekiah. If we allow humility to flow without borders or boundaries, it can lead to a debilitating state of self-flagellation and humiliation. Without a healthy dose of self-worth, humility can lead to feelings of inadequacy or inability. These sentiments will only further repress the spirit and dull the zest for life — certainly an undesired result of an inspiring moment.

Rav Saddiah Gaon teaches that blowing the shofar on Rosh Hashanah is similar to the blowing of trumpets at a king's coronation. On Rosh Hashanah, we are given the tremendous honor and awesome responsibility to crown the Transcendent Creator of the Universe as the Immanent Master of the World. This is achieved by blowing the shofar.

This is an enormously empowering feeling — knowing that it is all dependent upon us, a finite and seemingly insignificant creature, to acknowledge and crown the Infinite One as the Master of the Universe. And although these feelings of joy and self-empowerment, along with the awareness that we are in dire need of a spiritual re-alignment, may seem to be diametrically opposed emotions — they are all aroused while listening to the shofar. Far from being opposites, they prove to be complimentary.

Humility experienced in teshuvah should not be confused with humiliation, as there is a marked distinction between the two. Humiliation is self-destructive and stifling. Humility, by contrast, is quite empowering and liberating. To live with humility is to live a much larger life, to go beyond the constraints of the ego, which stonewalls genuine growth, and to stand in awe of the Creator and creation.

In this way, humility does not convert us into doormats. On the contrary, it allows us to see with a degree of openness, un-muddled by the protective ego, that there is still room to grow and evolve. With humility we are able to behold how the world is truly infinite in the opportunities it offers us to spiritually progress ad infinitum.

"Just as we need to know our faults and shortcomings", said Reb Yoseph Yitzchak, the Sixth Chabad Rebbe, "we need to acknowledge our strengths and merits". The challenge is to balance the acknowledgment of our weak points with the recognition of, and focus on, our good points.

> There are normally at least two pockets in a pair of trousers. In one pocket, suggests Reb Simcha Bunim, we should keep a scrap of paper with the words, "The entire world was created for me alone" (Sanhedrin, 37a). The second pocket should contain another piece of paper inscribed with the words of the Midrash, "Even the mosquito preceded you in the order of creation".

We ought to carry these two polar perspectives with us at all times. The first one: "The world was created for me", implies that — '*it is all for me that the sun will rise, and for me too that it will set; my mission in this world is crucial and I am a unique and indispensable person, essential to the fulfillment of the Master Plan of Creation*'. The other: "The mosquito preceded me", reminds us that, '*we entered the scene of creation after even the most minuscule of insects came into being*'. Even the mosquito was created before the human.

These contrary acknowledgments, one in each pocket, will create a greatly needed balance of self-worth and humility. A person who balances these polarities will achieve genuine teshuvah without ever losing his sense of importance within the world.

Earlier we mentioned teshuvah's intricate bond with *viddui* or 'confession'. Colloquially, the word confession has come to represent a recounting of something that was wrongfully done or not done — a verbal recognition of mishap or misdeed.

Yet in addition to the recognition of one's misdeeds, the Torah also makes room for a verbal confession of our positive and meritorious behavior. This is referred to as 'seeking out one's good points' — openly acknowledging how virtuous we are, or have been.

One of the mitzvos of the Torah is to tithe one's earnings. During Temple times when the Temple stood gloriously in Jerusalem, people would bring their various contributions and recite a prayer as they would tithe their income. This prayer is called *viddui ma'aser* or 'confession of tithing'.

Oddly it is not a negative confession of wrongdoings, but rather a declaration of positive behavior. The person giving the charity would list all the exemplary acts done in the process of this particular mitzvah and say: "I have removed...according to Your commandments that You have commanded me. I have not transgressed...I have hearkened to the voice of Hashem, my God". At the conclusion of the prayer, one would say: "Gaze down from Your Holy abode...and bless Your people" (Devarim, 26:13-14).

The supplication is for mercy and blessings to be bestowed upon the giver in response to the worthy deeds he has performed. In this instance, confession is by no means a personal recitation of negative thoughts or actions. Rather, it is an opportunity to focus on one's accomplishments, thereby recognizing the positive in one's life as well as the potential for growth. This mitzvah offers one the chance to reach an expanded awareness of being in the Presence of the Creator of the Universe and to demand blessing based on merit — a mark of truly balanced humility.

Many times people begin to punish themselves when they repeatedly make mistakes, flagellating themselves and slowly beginning to think of themselves as bad people. Overtime, nurturing such sentiments reinforces the perspective that one is unequivocally bad and incapable of doing anything right or good. The negative actions begin to reflect back onto the person to the extent where one may begin to feel irredeemable — literally forgetting all traces of goodness. Of course, the moment we stop believing that we are capable of any goodness is the very moment that we surrender our humanity, our Divine image.

Equally, if we were to simply brush under the rug all the errors we commit, if we would never stand up to claim responsibility for our actions, there would be no accountability. A delicate balance is needed, a balance between total recognition of one's actions and a healthy dose of awareness that the negative acts he may have committed do not define who he is.

A person whose actions are in the realm of a *rasha* or treacherous and 'immoral person' may experience a deep sense of regret. Simultaneously, he should never lose focus on the deeper *tzadik* or 'righteous person' within, the Divine aspect of self. Otherwise he will be left paralyzed, feeling awful for what he has done — unable to change and move forward.

It is healthier and more productive to see yourself as a tzadik and aspire to live up to that image, than it is to see yourself as a rasha and continuously struggle to overcome that image. We become what we imagine ourselves to be.

People who argue in favor of their limitations — whether they feel themselves powerless because of previous actions or decisions, or perhaps because of a low IQ, negative upbringing, or lack of education — remain in that limited space. Defending your limitations will make you even more limited.

Life is best served when we envision ourselves at our best and most genuinely righteous, as a tzadik — a perfect and whole being — which we potentially always are. Living with the image of a tzadik in mind, we won't transgress simply because *Es Past Nisht*, 'its not fitting'. Coming from a place of spiritual pride, one will brush off temptation and say to himself — 'how could I?'

If we truly envision ourselves as Tzadikim, than so much of what we robotically and reactively do will cease to be an option simply because *Es Past Nisht*, 'it is not fitting'. We will say to ourselves, "I am much better than this. How can I lie, I am such an honest and true person? How can I get into petty fights with others, I am a patient and compassionate tzadik? I am much bigger than all this".

And even if, or when, we do slip up, we will automatically know that these actions are out of character and are not aligned with who we truly are. Eventually, the image of self as tzadik will imprint itself into our deepest psyche and our natural and instinctive behavior will be a reflection of this perfection.

SYNOPSIS:CHAPTER 25
Be Confident, You Can Change

Humility should be balanced with self-confidence. Just as we need to recognize our shortcomings, we need to acknowledge and enhance our strengths and merits. We will behave as we imagine ourselves to be. If we think of ourselves as weak, we will probably manifest weakness. If we think of ourselves as strong, we can strengthen ourselves and others. Therefore, instead of allowing yourself to passively daydream, identifying with fantasy and nonsense, harness your imagination for holiness. Visualizing yourself as a perfect tzadik — and we are all potential tzadikim — can empower you to begin living at your spiritual optimum.

PRACTICE
VISUALIZE

Set aside a few moments today to vividly imagine yourself in a noble, happy and highly elevated state.

Visualize yourself doing what you really want to do, in a place where you really want to be. When you pray or perform a mitzvah, imagine yourself as a great and humble tzadik, joyfully connecting with Hashem. When you go about your daily life continue to visualize yourself as a tzadik, elevating the world through every action.

LIVING LIFE
Deliberately

W e would be amazed to realize how much of life simply occurs, whether or not we are ready or equipped. Even internally — our thoughts, emotions and reactions seem to just happen, almost accidently. Often our lives are lived haphazardly and unintentionally. Intellectual decisions and life choices are made at the spur of the moment and without any real conscious thought. Emotions as well seem to simply rise and fall on a whim. A person may feel love for one person and hate for another simply because of the geographical space they occupy, which the other does not.

Eventually this autopilot becomes a tyrant and overrides all individuality and free choice we may have access to. The quest of teshuvah is liberation, unburdening ourselves from these confining shackles so that we may begin to live with intention, awareness and expanded consciousness.

While it is true that some situations in life cannot be changed, such as where we were born and into which family, there is still a lot that can. Our ability to change our circumstances lies in how we respond to what life presents to us; i.e. — how we respond to the situations we find ourselves in.

This is part of being a responsible person. To be responsible is to lay claim to your life, whether positive or negative, to own it, and therefore to live with the awareness that it is only you who can mend or alter your life as needed.

Glancing through the Books of the Prophets, one may notice that while King David seemed to have slipped spiritually numerous times, and King Shaul appears to have misjudged only once, it was David who was forgiven while Shaul was not. Why?

The answer, says the Gemarah, lies in their response when informed of their wrongdoing (Yumah, 22b). When the Prophet Shmuel rebukes Shaul for not listening to the word of Hashem, Shaul replies, "I did not transgress for I have done as I was commanded" (Shmuel, 1:15). His first response to the accusation was to become defensive; only later did he reflect and acknowledge his wrongdoing. On the other hand, when David was confronted by the Prophet Nathan and told that he had deviated, David immediately conceded, admitting to having done something inappropriate. (Shmuel II, 12:9-13).

By taking responsibility for his actions King David placed himself in a position of teshuvah. Willing to see his own missteps, he was able to seek their perfection. This can only be done if we can face our failings openly, honestly and with a healthy dose of humility.

Conversely, Shaul was not yet prepared to be accountable for his actions. Therefore, he closed himself off from the transformative energies of teshuvah. He denied himself in the present, the possibility of redirecting his future through the process of redeeming his past.

During the times of the Temple, a person who committed certain accidental wrongdoings was obligated to bring a *korban*, an 'offering'. This seems puzzling. Why would the Torah require a person to bring an offering for an act committed inadvertently? Yet this is precisely the point. The Torah, writes Rabbeinu Bachya, aspires to educate us as to how to live life deliberately, rather than haphazardly — mindfully, not mindlessly. The Torah teaches us how to take control of our lives and to not allow life to take control over us. As a result, one who follows the dicta of the Torah and is rigorous in the discipline of its teachings "will

rarely encounter mishaps" (Mishlei, 12:21). And if they do in fact encounter an accidental eclipse of their tzaddik-self, then it is precisely this
experience, which the Torah would like us to utilize as an imprint opportunity.

For if we are honestly attempting to live a disciplined and conscious
life of connection and cleaving to Hashem and the Torah, then what better time to reflect upon and deeply integrate the Torah's teachings than
when we are in the vulnerable and humble state of shortcoming — in
need of return. We are often at our most receptive in moments of defeat
or mistake.

There is also a qualitative difference between the mindset of one
who transgresses, or damages on purpose, and one who sins inadvertently.
There is more likely to be a sense of openness to constructive criticism
and re-alignment of consciousness within one who has merely fallen
short of their ideal, rather than one who has knowingly acted outside of
their best interest.

Most of us, however, do not live life in a disciplined, deliberate, or
integrated fashion. We often find ourselves at the effect of internal and
external forces that we are not even conscious of and that can be conflicting in nature. At times, we may even surprise ourselves by our own actions.

Occasionally, we will look back at our day and wonder how we even
said certain things or acted in a particular manner. An action, a thought
or an emotional outburst from a moment ago, may at times seem to us to
be completely uncharacteristic of our true nature in the present.

Lack of consistency, not to be confused with honesty, results in a
misalignment between the varied aspects of a person's character and personality. For this, the Torah holds us accountable by demanding an offering for accidents.

Through the internal process of teshuvah and the physical act of
bringing an offering, we are returned to our pure and perfected self and
become whole once again. In wholeness, nothing is left out. Nothing has
a claim over the person who enters the world of teshuvah. In this context
we are not subject to the *effect* of someone or something else, but rather
we are the *cause* of our life, and the creator of all future effects — to the

extent that we can be as a finite being.

If we desire to understand ourselves in a real way and objectively observe our spiritual standing and mindset, we must take notice of how and
when we behave reactively, or impulsively. What is our immediate response when faced with an unexpected challenge? What are the first
thoughts that spring to mind? These are indicators. These are guides,
helping us to understand what is really going on within us. Those very
feelings, which arise automatically, and are then felt and observed, are the
aspects of our self that are most real to us right now.

In this way an unintentional act demands an even greater teshuvah
than a calculated act. For unconscious and negative behaviors demonstrate more clearly that, deep down the person is still associated with
negative tendencies.

What organically springs to the surface of one's mind are not ran-
dom thoughts operating within a void. On the contrary, there is always a
context to one's thoughts. All acts, and certainly non-premeditated ones,
are manifestations of where a person is holding at that particular moment. And as a result, these are the very areas that need the most refocusing if we truly want to grow.

Did you ever notice that after people with bad tempers go into a
rage and throw a tantrum, they will always remark, "I simply couldn't
help it, I just lost myself"? It may be true that they did not consciously
choose to behave that way, and their anger was simply triggered. Still,
this is no excuse. Through proper re-orientation, a measure of self-mastery can be attained, shifting our psychological roles from being helpless
puppets dangling on the strings of our emotions to shadow-puppet masters — owning the direction and intensity of our feelings, and having the
presence of mind to deploy them appropriately and deliberately.

A disciple of Rabbi Yisrael of Ruzhin once came to confess
and seek the Rebbe's advice for finding the best possible road
toward teshuvah. The Rebbe smiled and gently said: "When
you did what you did, did you ask anyone how to do it? —
Probably not. You simply did what you desired to do at that
moment. The same is true with teshuvah. Do not ask questions

of how to do it, or of when and where to do it — just do it".

Transformation on the deepest level occurs when you can honestly say: "I did this person a favor and I don't even know why. I simply lost myself". In the place of losing yourself to the negative and self-centered impulse, you assume a second nature — which is also your truest nature — and begin to lose yourself to the natural flow of the positive. We find ourselves doing good deeds without forethought or premeditation. It becomes as natural to do positive deeds and mitzvos as it formerly was to mindlessly react or pursue vain desires.

Although, as mentioned earlier, the aim of Torah is to train ourselves to live life deliberately and consciously — sometimes automatic is good. Not everything in life needs to be an existential dilemma. Whether we enter the house through the door or the window does not, and should not, necessitate conscious deliberation. Autopilot can be good if one is conditioned to do good and positive deeds. If we are inevitably going to be running on autopilot some of the time, then it is better to automatically do good deeds than to unconsciously commit negative or damaging acts.

One of the mitzvos of the Torah is that, when you are gathering your sheaves in the field and you forget one, you must leave it for the poor. This mitzvah of *Shikcha*, 'forgetting', can only be performed by an act of forgetting (Devarim, 24: 19). One cannot perform this particular mitzvah by consciously leaving bundles of produce behind in the field on purpose. As altruistic as that act may be, it is something altogether different to 'forget' something and then decide to let go of one's ownership over it — this is what constitutes this particular mitzvah.

The Tosefta recounts that once there was a *Chassid* — the Talmudic term for a 'righteous individual' — who forgot a sheaf in the fields and was able to perform this mitzvah of 'forgetting' by then leaving it for the poor. In his great excitement he sent his son to the Temple to bring an offering, while at home he threw a lavish and festive banquet in honor of this momentous occasion. This Chassid was a scrupulously mindful human being to whom mishaps did not often occur. Therefore, when something was done unintentionally and by mistake, the result was surely a mitzvah.

Part of training oneself to behave in a reflexively virtuous manner is simply to do as much good as possible. Slowly, external behavior becomes one's inner nature, the action transforms the doer.

In Temple times, a person offered a sacrifice to atone for unintentional mishaps. Today when there is no Temple, we should aspire to do as many good deeds and mitzvos as possible, even if they are not done intentionally to counter any inadvertently negative acts.

Every thought, word and action creates our environment, including careless ones. A positive mitzvah creates an environment of *Gan Eden* or 'paradise', a sense of being enveloped and encircled with a light of *kedusha*, or 'holiness', whereas a negative action creates an environment of *Gehenom* or 'hell', becoming enveloped and encircled with darkness and deceit. When we perpetuate good deeds, even those that are mechanical and monotonous, we create a context of goodness — a surrounding cocoon of light and holiness. This light guides us along our way, and this cocoon can eventually be filled with noble and mindful activity. By doing good we train ourselves in becoming good.

The doing of mitzvos enhances our spiritual selves, revitalizing us with an open heart and thoughtful awareness. The positive acts themselves, though reflexive, create a sensitive and supportive space in which mindful actions, thoughts and emotions can later flower.

Earlier we spoke about different situations that we may find ourselves in without choice, such as when we were born, or to what family and in which environment. There are things that can be done to improve or change this predetermined set of conditions. The most obvious is to follow the footsteps of *Avraham Avinu*, our forefather Avraham, who heeded the prophetic call and journeyed from his own family and homeland.

As grown people we do have choices, such as what type of environment and spiritual atmosphere we choose to live in. We can strive to make our environment one that is more conducive for our spiritual growth and maturation.

According to one Talmudic sage, if a person sees that his evil, or ego-driven inclination takes hold of him, he should travel to a place where no one knows him, dress himself in all black and do as his heart desires — lest he disgrace Hashem's name in public (Moed Katan, 17a). Iniquities flourish in an ambiance of callousness and frivolity. Journeying to a far-away place and wearing black clothes, often associated with mourning, sucks the zest out of the initial inclination to transgress. By creating a literal environment, or circumstances that are not conducive for transgression, one will not be so inclined to transgress.

Our Sages teach that, "a person does not commit a negative act unless a *ruach sh'tus* or 'spirit of folly' enters him" (Sotah, 3a). So once a person is on a path of spiritual self-destruction they become as if possessed, completely enveloped in darkness; it is a "spirit of folly" that is now controlling them. So the question is: 'if it is no a longer a matter of choice, for a 'spirit of folly' has taken the reins of ones' actions, how can one be responsible in such a state'? The answer is that we are ultimately responsible for putting ourselves in those situations, and under those conditions, to begin with. This means that if you allowed yourself to get to the point where you were completely overwhelmed, if you led yourself to that brink, then you are responsible for co-creating the circumstances through which that 'spirit of folly' was able to enter the equation.

It is comparable to when a person feels the onset of anger, and then allows himself to go deeper into that anger, until he is no longer able to control himself. The real responsibility that person has is, to not allow himself to get to that point to begin with.

So, we can see that sometimes physically moving away from a destructive environment is the key to avoiding certain negative situations or temptations.

Controlling one's life and living intentionally goes beyond simply moving from one geographical location to another. Rather it is about moving one's consciousness from a state of weakness and vulnerability to an inner, spiritual location of empowerment.

We have the choice to shift our awareness into a deep space within, from where we can respond mindfully to all situations, wherever and whenever they may be. While actual occurrences and circumstances may be beyond our control, the response toward them, and the attitude regarding them, is up to us — and those very responses will make all the difference in our lives and the lives of those around us. This is the responsibility we must take upon ourselves if we desire to live a life of meaning and purpose.

Life is not about inventing excuses, asking who is right and who is wrong, or finding out who is at fault or to blame. The big question is: Are we prepared to take our life into our own hands or not? Are we willing to take responsibility and accountability for our actions and our life, or are we just going to shift blame on others?

Reactions and responses to occurrences and situations are what really matter in life, not so much the actual occurrences. This is truly our challenge, and here is where we can demonstrate our mastery. How will we respond and interpret that which life presents us? Will we be reactive or proactive? Will we become bigger and more mature by assuming responsibility, or smaller and more adolescent by blaming everything on everyone else, letting life simply pass us by? The choice is always ours. Let us choose wisely.

SYNOPSIS:CHAPTER 26
Be Mindful

Spiritual maturity requires mindfulness — being alert and yet relaxed. Only through the power of active awareness can we effectively take the reins of our lives into our own hands and guide our life's course. We can make good choices when we become conscious of our tendency to react unconsciously, thereby liberating ourselves from the chains of the 'inevitable'. We can then reside at the 'cause' of our life, rather than getting lost in its effects.

The first moments we are aware of being awake in the morning are the headwaters, so to speak, of the entire day to come. We are then in the place of 'cause'; for in these moments we can experience ourselves as we are prior to all circumstance and conditioning, prior even to any thoughts and words — we simply are.

The first time we form thoughts into words is therefore a potent opportunity to influence our day. Knowing this, we can mindfully plant seeds of spiritual success that will blossom and bear fruit throughout our day.

PRACTICE

DECLARE

In the morning, seize the first moment when you first realize you are awake and declare the sage's formula: Modeh ani l'fanecha, *'I offer thanks to You...*Raba Emunosecha, *Great is your faithfulness.'*

As you say this traditional offering of thanks and gratitude for the gift of another day, you can bring to mind the thought that you are in the Presence of the Master of the Universe. Humbly acknowledge Hashem's faith in you, displayed by the merciful act of returning your soul to your body once again after a long night of sleep. Hashem has great faith that each day you can guide your life toward accomplishing your highest purpose.

Here is the full text of the Modeh Ani *with an interlinear translation:*

MODEH ANI — I offer thanks

L'FANECHA — to You,

MELECH CHAI V'KAYOM — living and eternal King,

SHE'HE'CHEZARTA — for you have restored

BI — within me

NISHMASI — my soul,

B'CHEMLA — with mercy.

RABA EMUNOSECHA — Great is Your faithfulness (in me)!

CHAPTER
TWENTY-SEVEN

INTEGRATION
& *Inclusion*

B *aal Teshuvah* is the honorary title bestowed upon one who is in a
state of teshuvah. The phrase *baal teshuvah* is literally translated as a
'master of teshuvah'.

As with anything else, we can either be a master over it or be mastered by it. Notwithstanding the amazing possibilities available through
teshuvah, it is quite apparent that being in the process of teshuvah and
going into a chaotic, and potentially harmful past can be a potentially demoralizing experience.

Teshuvah, which is supposed to bring liberation and freedom of the
spirit, can initially leave the novice in a more depressed state than when
he first began. The experience can occasionally be so overwhelming that
the individual may feel completely exhausted and lost in its enormity. Instead of feeling like a master of teshuvah, they may feel as though they
are being mastered by it.

As ironic as it may seem, it is possible to become consumed by
teshuvah. A person can lose himself in the process and become enslaved
to the majestic unfolding. To manage teshuvah and become a *baal* or
'master', we need to ensure that we are still able to find ourselves within
the process of teshuvah. This is done through integrating, including and

bringing forth all of our life experiences into our teshuvah. We need to bring all of ourselves to the table and from this synthesis of energies, begin our spiritual ascent. There is no part of self that should be left behind.

A master of teshuvah is one who is able to utilize teshuvah to create the context of his life, which he then fills with his own content.

Let us explore this idea in greater detail:

In life there is both content and context. The context normally uses us to expresses itself through us. Life always has a context and either we choose it or it chooses us, usually by way of the culture and environment we live in.

If we choose teshuvah, then everything that is understood as the content of our lives — our stories, talents and pursuits — will gradually readjust to align within our new context — our emerging cosmology, connection and consciousness.

Many who take the leap for the first time into the world of teshuvah, assume that commencing a new life path of Kedusha or 'holiness' and Ta'harah, 'purity', must be done with solemnity and a feeling of gloom. As a result, what often occurs in the process of 'discarding' the undesired past is literally a relinquishing of vital parts of the self. This can at times translate as losing one's sense of humor or lightness of being.

It appears that we have come to identify joy and happiness with frivolity and foolishness, while heaviness and sobriety have become synonymous with *kedusha* and *ta'harah*. Yet this assumption is greatly unfounded. There is no place in a world created, and sustained by Hashem's kindness and love for gloominess, morbidity or self-abnegation.

Mastery is achieved only when all of one's life, both past and present, can be embraced in their newly found paradigm. Of course, rigor and discipline are pre-requisites for the assimilation of a newly embarked upon life path. But ultimately there needs to be a regaining of the zest for life, as well as a reclaiming of one's talents, healthy interests and sense of humor. The return can only be complete when it comes full circle.

Just as tragedy can break a person's rigid self-image to allow for a re-evaluation and re-assessment of life, so too can laughter serve this same purpose — and in a much healthier manner. Laughter can be the opening for teshuvah.

Think of the joyous day of Purim as a day of teshuvah. Yom Kippur, the ultimate Day of Atonement, can be read as *yom k'Purim*, 'a day like Purim'. For what is the essence of teshuvah if not the letting go of one's old mask and image, and revealing of one's inner, truer, and less inhibited self.

As tragedy shatters form, laughter releases us from form; allowing us to break free, to live lightly and to rise above any negative self-image in the quest to reclaim one's true self.

We need to always be joyful, especially for the sake of performing teshuvah. Joy helps us break free from constricted consciousness and gain the clarity we need in order to move forward.

> Once, Reb Simcha Bunim was crossing a bridge and saw someone below struggling to stay above water. The man was so overwhelmed, he was unable to help himself out of the swirling deep. Reb Bunim shouted to him, "Send my regards to the Leviyason," humorously referring to the mythological giant fish of the ocean. The man soon got hold of a plank of wood and was saved. Later on, Reb Bunim explained that the man could not be rescued because of his despair and overwhelm. Once a joke was told, however, a small glimmer of joy enlivened the man and he was able to save himself.

Similarly, when we are stressed, we do not notice important opportunities. A sense of humor can make us lighter, opening the way to effective action.

A baal teshuvah may have undergone a major metamorphosis, yet he need not become sadder in order to become wiser.

As a whole, happiness and joy are to be a constant in our journey through life. It is only through a gladness of the heart that we can penetrate the deepest spiritual truths. With all the strength of our being we must avoid any emotion resembling melancholy or depression. These are spiritual and mentally debilitating emotions, paralyzing action and staggering any positive thought or feelings of growth.

Humility and joy are contingent upon one another. Only when truly humble, can one experience a genuine measure of happiness to simply be alive. An old idiom succinctly expresses this concept: Angels fly because they take themselves lightly. A good lesson in life would be to aspire to mimic the behavior of the angels and take oneself lightly.

If anyone desires to know whether they are in a true state of teshuvah, they should monitor whether they are humbled by their experience or, conversely, if they are left feeling smug and self-righteous. If teshuvah has left you feeling easier, lighter and more understanding, then you know that you are on the right path. If the opposite has occurred, perhaps at some point there was a diversion along the path.

Certainly *tamimus*, 'seriousness and sincerity', is a crucial component of teshuvah; but seriousness and sincerity do not necessarily translate as gloominess or heaviness. Teshuvah is intended to make the person more available for himself, for others and for the world, not less. It is ultimately meant to be a sweetening experience, not an embittering one.

To live in a condition of teshuvah does not mean that we ought to walk about frail, bent over and in an altogether gloomy state. On the contrary, we are to burst forth with energy, excitement, vitality and life. Teshuvah is not supposed to be a terrifying experience, reducing one to feeling insignificant, inept and guilt-ridden. It is meant to be redeeming, reenergizing and rejuvenating. The pinnacle of teshuvah is enjoyed when we attain a healthy sense of being fully alive, empowered and integrated.

Teshuvah Shleima, or 'complete and whole teshuvah', is one that includes the *yetzer ha-tov* or 'good inclination' as well as the *yetzer ha-ra* or 'evil inclination'; the spiritual self — the soul, as well as the physical self — the body.

The natural tendency of those who are altering their life's course is to shy away, and run from anything associated with the past. As a result, many end up doing teshuvah from their yetzer ha-tov alone, accepting upon themselves various mitzvos and positive practices, but completely neglecting their yetzer ha-ra. Their natural character traits and dispositions are utterly ignored and end up rotting over time. Yet this is not teshuvah sheliema, for total teshuvah is achieved *be'chal le'vavcha*, "with all your hearts" (Devarim, 6: 6). This means that one on the path of teshuvah should employ the energies of both of their hearts — the yetzer ha-tov and yetzer ha-ra — the spiritual self that yearns for transcendence together with the striving, stamina and vital energy of our physical desires.

Cheshek, or 'desire', is the source of negativity. Even if we have done teshuvah on the level of action and refined negative behavior patterns, still this is not complete teshuvah for our desire itself has not been transformed.

Complete teshuvah includes harnessing the primal force of cheshek for kedusha. Fortunately, kedusha and connection are what we ultimately desire on the deepest levels. When this ultimate desire is uncovered and unleashed, we surge with passion for the gift of being alive in connection with the Source of Life.

Elul is the Hebrew month of the year that is entirely focused on self-evaluation and honest introspection. Following Elul are the Ten Days of teshuvah dedicated to expiation, atonement and hopefully, transformation. The Ten Days begin with Rosh Hashanah and culminate with Yom Kippur. Immediately following the Days of Awe are the days of Sukkos — a holiday cycle so intrinsically connected with joy and happiness that the holiday itself is referred to in our prayers as "the Season of our Rejoicing".

It may very well occur that following the daunting task of self-excavation during the month of Elul, and in the succeeding Days of Awe, we may need to refresh ourselves to once again regain our sense of wellbeing and joy. The penetrating process of self-examination can sometimes leave one feeling depleted and less 'intact' than before. Therefore, "the season of our rejoicing" that follows is a welcome breath of fresh air. The flow from Yom Kippur into Sukkos insures that our teshuvah will leave us feeling more expansive, and not the reverse. Our innate sense of wholeness and joy that may have been lost in the process of the Days of Awe is restored in the Days of Joy. Sukkos is a time devoted to the rejuvenation and revitalization of our broken and humbled spirit.

Besides the sheer mental exhaustion of Elul and the Days of Awe, the psychological intensity of teshuvah may result in an individual losing touch with his previous self-image and sense of identity — so much so that he may not easily find himself once again. Taking leave of a prior established *weltanschauung* or 'worldview', a person may find himself lost in the abyss of *ayin*, 'emptiness' or void. Honestly opening up and baring the inner self through deep, meditative and thoughtful prayer over the course of the High Holidays may leave one feeling devastatingly vulnerable and utterly defenseless.

To regain balance and assure that we do find our place and regain our footing, the holiday of Sukkos comes along and enables us to regroup and find our bearings. We go outside again —literally and metaphorically — after long periods spent inside of the shul, as well as inside of our heads and hearts. We build, we create, we decorate, we hold, we wave, we smell, we eat, we sing and we sleep under the stars. We are back to life, and we are thankful, and so we pray for Hashem's protection and shelter of peace for the entire world.

To dwell in a sukkah is to live in Divine space. When we enter a sukkah, we become aware that we are entering a sanctified space as we are embraced by a cocoon of kedusha. Now that we have found our footing in the sukkah we can emerge from that inner space as a new person — refreshed and reimagined — with a newly discovered, healthy sense of self. The sukkah is therefore a sort of womb space — the womb of the *Shekhinah*, the 'Divine Presence' — in contrast to the Divine Transcendent.

Elul and the Days of Awe are about transcending our past mistakes and shortcomings. The Days of Joy are about reemerging with a renewed sense of aliveness and awareness. Together they complete the psycho-spiritual cycle of Yesh-Ayin-Yesh: from 'i' to 'You' to 'I'.

Interestingly, but by no means incidentally, the empty month of Cheshvan follows the full and exciting month of Tishrei. Tishrei is a month packed with holidays, ranging from the more somber days of Rosh Hashanah and Yom Kippur, to the more joyous days of Sukkos. Cheshvan is the only month of the Hebrew calendar that contains no celebratory or commemorative days. The root of the word Cheshvan is *Chash*, which means 'quiet'. It is a quiet month.

Confirmation that our transformation is complete is not obtained during the swirling energy that is generated throughout the month Tishrei, but is found precisely in the quiet month of Cheshvan. Only through the transference of such lofty inspiration into the minutiae of everyday life can the lessons and blessings of Tishrei have the space and time to fully integrate.

Being able to assimilate our sentiments and resolve into the normative reality of the days of Cheshvan is a sign that our transformation has reached a state of consummation and fruition. Otherwise, it could be argued that the teshuvah and inspiration was merely a reaction to the moment and not something done out of real conviction, and certainly not a lasting transformation that will translate into real life.

Cheshvan is a month of devastating loneliness. From both a religious as well as a seasonal point of view, it seems awfully dull. Not only is it the empty and 'quiet' month that follows the full and busy month of Tishrei; but with it also begins the cold winter months where sunlight begins to slowly vanish. And even when the sun does shine, it is only through the chilling atmosphere of the ensuing winter.

Appropriately, *scorpio* is the *mazal* or 'zodiac' sign of the month. The venomous and often unpopular scorpion represents the challenges of the new cycle that begins with Cheshvan — a life apparently devoid of spirituality and celebration, as well as an increasingly dark life of coldness that can be corrosive to our sense of wellbeing. But it is here in Cheshvan, and only here, where our teshuvah can be tested and proven as real and lasting.

On a more profound level, the ultimate goal of personal transformation is to attain a degree of self-generated motivation and functionality, rather than being only externally referential.

Normative logic would suggest that if we are inspired by all the holidays, then the converse also holds true: the absence of holidays should be dispiriting. We need to reverse this process.

Responsibility is the signature concept of teshuvah. Real responsible behavior, not blame or guilt, is what guides us on our quest to master and take charge of our lives. For this we need to learn to self-generate and source our actions. Such healthy behavior should not need to be imposed, but rather evoked, for the potential is already present within.

Living in a condition of sustained inspiration throughout the cold month of Cheshvan demonstrates that our teshuvah has been internalized as part of the fabric of our existential reality. Cheshvan is the proving ground for the results of Tishrei.

On Yom Kippur it is highly recommended to remind ourselves of the sons of Aharon who died on this day. The Torah tells us that the sons of Aharon expired "as they approached God" (Vayikra, 16:1). They transcended body, says the Ohr HaChaim, in a spiritual state of rapture and ecstasy — a condition known as *ratzu bli shuv*, 'withdrawal without return'. By recalling their deaths we are reminded that the most important element of the transcendent experience of Yom Kippur is to draw the inspiration down into our everyday reality. The genius of 'running' and then 'returning' is to experience a *ratzu*, 'running' or upward surge and corresponding inward movement, coupled with the ability to later experience a *shuv* or 'return' and reintegration within the body and within the world.

A soul's purpose in descending to this world and becoming embodied is to maximize one's spiritual potential through physical involvement. Actualization of the soul through the tools and desires of the body can only occur in the realm of the here and now. Transcendence serves us well when it is experienced as a 'high' or 'peak experience', which in turn infuses our everyday life with a fresh perspective and embodied vision.

A meaningful transcendent experience is one that offers wisdom and understanding in how to best serve our Creator and all of creation through a revelation of presence and purpose. Otherwise it is merely spiritual candy, which may be nice and pleasant tasting, but ends up being an experience without sustainability, substantiality or lasting relevance.

To discern whether or not our transformation is one of inclusion and integration, we must observe how our behavior is enacted once the high of the holidays has faded and life goes back to normal. Teshuvah, in the truest sense of the word, is about coming full circle and being able to articulate the highs and inspirations of the initiatory and exciting stages of spirituality into our day-to-day life.

A master is one who deeply desires and yearns for *ratzu*, or 'transcendence', yet remains intimately aware of the realization that the very purpose of the process lies in the *shuv*, his ability to 'return' to the immanent.

Genuine transformation is attained when we are able to continue living life in a loving and healthy way with the same spirit and vitality that was displayed when we were merely serving our egos through instant gratification. We are now able to utilize that very intensity toward positivity. By harnessing all of ourselves — the way we think, feel and celebrate — we are able to reveal the deeper, more spiritual and transcendent parts of our self in the here and now.

Internal unity is reached when the two extremes of our existence — the spiritual summit and the material base — are unified within a greater context. To be a master of teshuvah is to integrate all levels of being, and to live life in a well-balanced and adjusted manner.

Self is a synthesis of body and soul, ego and transcendence, finite and infinite, temporal and eternal. Authentic selfhood is only achieved when we are fully aligned and can create a perfect harmony between all aspects of our being.

Ultimately, wholeness is achievable, and throughout our lives teshuvah must be lived day by day, moment to moment. The experiential difference that teshuvah makes in one's life lies in the liberation of the vast reservoir of energy that is being spent on 'holding it all together', pleasing everyone else and living in scarcity — spiritual and otherwise.

By reclaiming who we inherently are — stewards to the Spirit of the Infinite — we lay claim to the awesome and abundant power made available to us. The anomaly is that we struggle to attain what is already ours. Teshuvah shifts our perception to a state of acceptance so that we may enjoy such a gift. All we need to do is affirm and reaffirm this truth, and then choose to live our lives accordingly.

SYNOPSIS:CHAPTER 27
Stay Joyous

Teshuvah means becoming wiser, but not more heavy, serious or sad. On the contrary, teshuvah brings us to joy and light. It is like finding a precious object we have lost — in this case, our own self or soul. It is also joy that brings us toward teshuvah. Therefore, no matter what is happening, it is vital to maintain a sense of the lightness of being. Actively choose to stay happy and optimistic and eventually everything will work out for the best.

PRACTICE
NIGUN/MELODY

Whenever you are feeling down or heavy, sing or hum to yourself a song of joy and happiness.

Perhaps choose a *nigun* or 'melody' that has comforting or uplifting words. Keep singing until you sense a shift in your consciousness. Even without words, a melody has the power to penetrate our souls and arouse a sense of spiritual joy and rapture.

CHAPTER
TWENTY-EIGHT

REFLECT & EXPLORE,
Further and Further

No one says open-heart surgery is a simple process, especially when you are operating on yourself. In the journey of life there are so many paths we can walk. One often crosses over the other and so we are never stuck, as our options are truly limitless. But how do we make the best decisions for our own precious self and soul? How do we ensure that we are being attentive to our entirety, not just to the body or the spirit in exclusion of the other?

We must check in with our whole being on a daily basis. We must make time to be in sacred space — where the noise of the outside world is kept to a minimum — and within this eternal moment we open up to hear our own voice coming forth from our innermost depths. We can use this time to tune the instrument of the self, in order to play the harmony of the soul, in the cosmic symphony.

Having read through the practices, was there one specific practice that really spoke to you? Maybe it sounded unreasonable at first, or maybe too demanding, but after a few applications you found that it offered some deep meaning. Do not stop now! Choose a practice — either one that you connected with, or one that seems intriguing to you but did not deliver the goods when you initially tried it out, or maybe even one that engages your competitive side with a challenge. Let your heart guide you and try to continue the practice for a few weeks, starting now!

THE 28 STEPS

TOWARDS INNER
TRANSFORMATION

{1} BE IN THE PRESENT: *Kavanah - Intention*

{2} LIVE WITH A CONTINUOUS SENSE OF RENEWAL: *Breathe*

{3} BE OPTIMISTIC; NEVER DESPAIR: *Resolve*

{4} TAKE CONTROL: *Control Your Intake*

{5} DON'T FOOL YOURSELF: *Meditate on the Divine I*

{6} RETAIN INDIVIDUALITY IN YOUR RETURN:
Histavus /Equanimity

{7} GROW CONSTANTLY: *Question*

{8} BE HOPEFUL: *Read*

{9} RECOGNIZE YOUR PERFECTION & IMPERFECTION: *Be Honest*

{10} REFOCUS YOUR DESIRES: *Meditate on Desire*

{11} BE OPEN: *Listen Deeply*

{12} ACKNOWLEDGE YOUR GOOD POINTS: *Focus on the Good*

END NOTES

CHAPTER I

* "A person would rather possess one coin earned than nine coins granted."*Baba Metzia*, 38a. Or, "A person would rather possess a lesser amount earned that a greater amount given." *Midrash. Sifri*, Parshas Hazinu.

* There are Torah laws how to tie one's shoes. *Shulchan Aruch. Orach Chaim*, Chap. 2:4. Chanoch (Hebrew for Enoch), was a shoemaker, who was transformed into a heavenly being. This is said to have occurred because while he would stitch his shoes, his intention would be for the sake of the unity of the Holy One blessed be He and the Shechinah. As he would lace up the shoes, he would meditate on 'lacing' the earth with heaven in perfect unity. *Midrash Talpiyos*, Erech Chanoch. R. Yitzchak of Aco (1250 - 1340) *Meiras Einayim*. Parshas Lech Lecha, p. 67. See also R. Asher Ben Dovid. *Sefer Ha'Yichud*. Amudei HaKabbalah 2, p. 70. R. Yaakov Ha'Cohen. *Sefer Ha'orah*, (Ibid) p. 2.

* We do not need to perform mitzvos with a sense of nostalgia or with the hopes of reward over punishment. *Avos*. Chap. 1, Mishnah 3. *Avodah Zarah*, 19a. Rambam. *Hilchos Teshuvah*, Chap. 10.

* Regarding the prisoner who was incarcerated. See: R. Dovid Ben Zimra, the *Radbaz* (1470 - 1572) *Teshuvhas HaRadbaz 1111, Teshuvah* 87. See also:R. Chaim Yoseph Dovid Azulay (1729- 1806) *Chedrei Beten All Ha'Torah*. Shabbos Teshuvah, p. 369. *Nemukei Orach Chayim*. (Munkatch) Hilchos Megilah, 695:4. Note: *Yumah*, 33a. *Pesachim*, 64b. *Rashi*. R. Shlomo Yitzchaki. (1040 - 1105) in the name of the *Mechilta. Shemos*. Chap. 12: 17. *Megilah*, 6b. The *Ran, Moed Katan*, 30a.

* R. Tzvi Ashkenazi - Chacham Tzvi (1660 - 1718) argues an alternative point in his work, he argues that it is better to wait and perform a Mitzvah with Hidur. *Teshuvhas Chacham Tzvi*, Teshuvah 106. See also: *Be'er Heitiv*. Orach Chaim, Siman 90. See also: R. Chaim Chizkiah Medini. (1832 - 1904) *Sdei Chemed. Klalim*. Zayin. Klaal 1 –3. Pei, Klaal 39. Note: *Turei Even* to Megilah, 7b, regarding the opinion of *Tosefos*. Though see, *Divrei Malkiel*. Orach Chaim, Siman 8. Also note regarding waiting. *Shulchan Aruch Harav*. Orach Chaim 94:5.

* Placing the letter Yud before a word transforms the word into a continues act. *Rashi. Iyov*, Chap 1:5. *Tanya*. Shar Yichud V'emuna, Chap 4.

* The question of why there is no explicit mention in the Torah regarding the afterlife was posed by nearly all major Jewish thinkers throughout the medieval period. See: R. Saddiah Goan. (882 – 942) *Emunos VeDeyos*. Maamor 9, Chap. 2. R. Avraham *Even Ezra* (1089 - 1164) *Devarim* 32: 39. R. Yehudah Halevi (1075 -1141) *Kuzari*. Maamor 1. Chapters 104 – 109. R. Moshe Ben Mai-

mon. (1135 - 1204) Rambam. *Igeres Techiyas Ha'meisim*, Chap. 9. R. Avraham Ben HaRambam (1186 - 1237) *Sefer Hamaspik Leovedei Hashem. Erech. HaPerishus*, p. 127. R. Moshe Ben Nachman (1194 - 1270) Ramban. *Shemos*, 6:2. *Devarim*, 11: 3. *Rabbeinu Bachya* (1263 - 1340) *Vayikra*, 26: 9. R. Nisan Ben Reuven. (c.1290 - c.1375) *Derashas HaRan*. Derush 1, pp. 18 – 20. R. Avraham Ben Dovid. (Ra'avad) *Emunah Ramah*. (Berlin, 1919) Maamor 1. Chap. 7, p. 39. R. Yoseph Albo (1380-1435) *Safer Haikkarim*. Maamor 4. Chap. 39. R. Shimon Ben Tzemach Duran. (1361 - 1444) *Magen Avos*. (1785: Livorno) Part 3, p. 87a. R. Meir Eben Aldavia. (14th century) *Shivilei Emunah*. Nosiv 9, pp. 368 – 369. R. Meir Ben Gabbai. (1480 - 1547.) *Avodas Hakodesh*. Part 2. Chap. 17 – 19. R. Yehudah Loew. (1512 -1609) *Tifferes Yisrael*, Chap. 57. See also: *Gevuras Hashem* Hakdamah 1. R. Shlomo Ephraim Lunshitz. (c. 1550 – 1619) *Kli Yakar. Vayikra*, 26: 12, he offers many interpretations. R. Yeshayah Halevi Horowitz. (1570–1630) *Shenei Luchos Habris*. Toldos Adam. Beis Acharon, p. 48. R. Nathan Nate Shapira. (1585 – 1633) *Megalah Amukhos. Al HaTorah*. Parshas Bechukosai, p. 62. R. Menasha ben Israel. (1604 - 1657) *Nishmas Chayim*. Maamor 1. Chap. 2. See also : R. Tzvi Elimelech of Dinav. (1785 - 1841) *Bnei Yissochar*. Maamorei HaShabbos, p. 14. R. Shmuel of Sochatchov (1856 – 1926) *Sheim Me'Shemuel. Vayishlach*, p. 11.

* Another perspective is that the phrase "gathered to his people", which is used throughout Torah, – (*Bereishis* 25:8, 25:17, 35:29, 49:33. *Bamidbar* 20:24. 27:13, *Devarim* 32:50)- clearly implies an afterlife, since in many of the above cases it can not refer to being buried with their ancestors, as they are being buried alone, or are the first to be buried in that place.

* *Abarbanel* Parshas Bechukosai, Teshuvah 1.

*"The foundation of teshuvah is considering today as the day you were born, the first day of your life, and you have no demerits or merits." Rabbeinu Yonah. *Yesod Ha'teshuvah*.

* Teshuvah is about the present moment, the eternal present. R. Pinchas of Koritz. (1726 – 1791) *Midrash Pinchas*, p. 38. Chap. 12. R. Yerachmiel Yisrael Yitzchak of Alexander. (1853 – 1910) *Yismach Yisrael*. Vol. 2. Hagada Shel Pesach, p. 57. See also: R. Shlomo of Radomsk. (1803 – 1866) *Tiferes Shlomo. Al HaTorah. Bereishis*, 45: 5.

* The metaphor of garments that are dirtied. R. Shalom Shacnah of Probisht (1766 – 1803) *Mashmiah Shalom. Lekutim*, p. 208. A negative action is like stain on a garment. *Yirmiyahu* 2:22.

CHAPTER 2

* Every moment is a renewed creation. Touching into this recreation of being offers us the ability to instantaneously refresh our lives. R. Levi Yitzchak of Berdichov (1740 - 1809) *Kedushas Levi, Eicha*. The Arizal teaches that there are no identical prayers from the time of creation until the time of redemption. Each prayer is new and unique. *Pri Eitz Chaim*. Shar HaTefilah 7, p. 17. *Olas Tamid*, Shar HaTefilah, p. 11. *Shulchan Aruch Arizal*, Orach Chaim. 89 :1. See also Ramak *Shiur Koma*. Hakdamah, Chap 13. *Ohr Yakar*. Parshas Kedoshim, 4.

* Whereas the concept of 'Kvar/already' is normally considered a state of exile, restriction, or being stuck, and "newness or novelty" is normally associated with a sense of freedom, openness, and teshuvah; on the deepest level, a transformation of the notion of 'Kvar/already' itself is needed. Meaning that one shifts ones perspective reference to an "already" feeling for teshuvah, indicating that one's teshuvah has "already" been accepted, or that they we "whole/holy" already, and they

just had to 'return' to that state. *Koheles,* 9:7. This is especially true after Yom Kippur, a day dedicated to teshuvah. *Shulchan Aruch. Orach Chaim,* Siman 624.

*"It is prohibited to be old." R. Nasan of Breslov. *Likutei Halachos,* Tefilin 5:5.

* "This Mitzvah that I commanded you today..." *Devarim,* 30: 11. According to many commentaries 'this Mitzvah' refers to the Mitzvah of teshuvah. *Ramban.* Ibid. For an earlier source see the argument by the Gaonim. *Otzar HaGeonim,* Sanhedrin, 514. See also : R. Dan Yitzchak *Abarbanel.* R. Ovadyah *Seforno.* (1470 - 1550) R. Yakov Ben Asher. (c1275 – c.1340) *Baal Haturim. Kli Yakar* Ad loc. See also : *Safer Haikkarim.* Maamor 4 Chap. 25. R. Eliyahu ben Moshe Di Vidas. (16th Century) *Reishis Chachmah.* Shar HaTeshuvah. Chap. 1, p. 101b. According to the Midrash this verse implies that Mitzvas are to be preformed as if they were commanded anew each moment. *Sifri Devarim,* Chap 6: 6, *Rashi* ad loc.

* If we can make a genuine self-evaluation. Because of this it is recommended that one write down each night the negative things that he may have encountered during the day, as well as the positive things that he may have been lax in performing. Rabbeinu Yona of Gerondi. *Sharei Teshuvah.* Shar 1, Chap. 8. See also: R. Yehudah HaChassid. (1150- 1217) *Safer Chassidim,* Chap. 21. The Zohar recommends one to do a '*Chesbon HaNefesh,* an accounting of the soul,' each night before going to sleep. *Zohar 1,* p. 191a. See also: p.p. 198b – 199a. 3, p.178. R. Eliezer Ezcary. (1522 - 1600) *Safer Cheraidim.* Chap. 35:30, p. 152. R. Eliyahu HaCohen. (? – 1729) *Sheivet HaMusar.* Chap. 20 : 17, p. 290. R. Tzvi Hirsh of Zhitachov. (1785 –1831) *Sur Mera V'Asei Tov,* p. 40. The Shalah Ha'Kodesh speaks at length of the need to do Teshuvah on the very same day, or perhaps even in the same hour of the transgression, and thus the need to do a Chesbon Ha'Nefesh every night. *Shalah.* Meseches Chulin. Parek Torah Ohr, Chap 63- 72. Parek Derech Chaim. Chap 17. — Or at the very least to do a *Chesbon HaNefesh* once a week. R. Schneur Zalman of Liadi. (1745 – 1812) *Maamorei Admmur Hazoken.* Haktzorim, p. 359. R. Pinchas Eliyohu Ben Meir of Vilna. (1743 - 1821) *Sefer Habris.* Part 2. Maamor 12. Chap. 1, p. 488. R. Yisrael DovBer of Vilednick. (1788 -1839) *Shearis Yisroel,* p. 21. Preferably on Thursday nights. *Tayna. Igeres HaTeshuvah,* Chap. 10.

* "The world thinks that forgetting is a negative quality. I, however, think it has great value." R. Nachman of Breslov. *Sichas HaRan,* Siman 26.

* Teshuvah is seen as something similar to repairing a broken limb. *Reshis Chachmah.* Shar HaTeshuvah. Chap. 5, p. 116b.

* Even the greatest of spiritual figures must strive for teshuvah. In the time of redemption even the greatest of Tzadikim will need teshuvah. R. Schneur Zalman of Liadi. *Likkutei Torah. Shemini Atzeres,* p. 92b. *Shir HaShirim,* p. 50b. See: *Zohar 111.* p. 153b. Teshuvah is a constant even for Tzadikim. *Tiferes Shlomo.* (Radomsk) Al HaTorah. Parshas Beshalach, p. 107.

* Teshuvah is equated with the process of healing. See eg : *Yeshaya,* 10: 6. 57: 18. *Tehilim,* 41: 5. *Yirmiyahu,* 3: 22. *Hosha,* 14: 5. *Tehelim,* 30 : 3. *Rashi.* See also : *Megillah,* 17b. *Rosh Hashanah,* 17b. *Tosefos. Veshav. Yumah,* 86a. *Rambam. Shemone Perakim.* Chap. 3. R. Bachya Ibn Pakudah. (1050 - 1120) *Chovas Halevavos. Shar HaTeshuvah.* R. Menachem Ben Aharon. (1307–1386) *Kitzur Chovos Halevavos.* Chap. 7, p. 64. R. Menachem Ben Shlomo Meiri. (1249-1316) *Chibur HaTeshuvah.* Meishiv Nefesh. Maamor 1. Chap. 12, p. 216. R. Yitzchak Aramah. (1420-1494) *Akeidas Yitzchak.* Parshas Nitzavim. Shar 100, p. 117b. R. Eliyahu HaCohen. *Sheivet HaMusar.* Chap. 38: 12, p 549. Note: *Pri Kodesh Hilulim,* p. 39.

* Others write that the best metaphor would be that of birth or rebirth. R. Shmuel of Sochatchov. *Sheim Me'Shemuel.* Rosh Hashanah, p. 12.

* Upon entering a state of teshuvah one is considered as a new person. *Sifre. Parshas Vaeschanan*, Chap. 30. *Midrash Rabba Vayikra*, Parsha 30: 3. *Midrash Tehilim*, 102:1. See also: Rambam. *Hilchos Tteshuvah*, Chap. 2. Halacha 4. *Semag*. Mitzvah 16. *Ran*. Cited by the *Maharsah. Rosh Hashanah*, 16b. *Avodas Hakodesh*. Part 2. Chap. 35. *Sheivet HaMusar*. Chap. 38: 6, p. 545. "A Baal Teshuvah is like a new born". Ibid. See also *Pri Ha'aretz*. (Vitepsk) Parshas Reah. *Nesivas Shalom*. (Slonim) Teshuvah, Pesicha. p. 197. Teshuvah is not as simple as a normal healing of the limbs, but it is considered as if one has acquired new limbs. *Sheim Me'Shemuel*. Rosh Hashanaha, p 12. Others equate teshuvah with the revival of the dead. R. Yonathan Eibeschuvetz (1690 – 1764) *Yaros D'vash*. Part 1, p.p. 14 – 15.

* Being that teshuvah is a total renewal of self, there are those who suggest that a person going through teshuvah should immerse himself in a Mikvah. *Ma'haril*. Quoted in *Darkei Moshe. Orach Chaim*, Siman 607.

* It is suggested that one who embarks on the path of teshuvah change his name. *Rosh Hashanah*, 16b. Rambam. *Hilchos Teshuvah*, Chap. 2. Halacha 4

* A person who truly desires to heal and begin life anew needs to place trust in the medicine of teshuvah. *Orchos Tzadikim*. Shar HaTeshuvah. Shar 26, p. 213. See also: *Bnei Yissochar*. Maamorei Chodesh Tishrei, Maamor 4, p. 19c.

CHAPTER 3

* According to the Gemarah, teshuvah pre-dates the creation of this world. *Pesachim*, 54a. *Nedarim*, 39b. *Midrash Rabbah*. Bereishis, Parsha 1:4. *Pirkei De'rebbe Eliezer*,. Chap. 3. The world (mankind) cannot exist without Teshuvah. *Ran, Nedarim*, 39b.

* Teshuvah is drawing all of Creation back to its Divine root. *Likutim Yekarim. Yosher Divrei Emes*, p. 137b.

* Mankind was created only with the condition of teshuvah. *Zohar 111*, p 69b. See also : *Zohar 1*, p 134. *Pirkei De'rebbe Eliezer*, Chap. 3.

* "There is no righteous person…" *Koheles*, 7: 20. See also : *Melachim 1*, 8:46. *Chibur HaTeshuvah*. Meishiv Nefesh. Maamor 1. Chap. 1, p. 23. *Reshis Chachmah*. Shar HaTeshuvah. Chap.1, p. 101b.

* If we were to think that there is no way out, we might just sink lower and lower into the abyss. Rambam. *Moreh Nevuchim*, 3;36. Without Teshuvah the world would have been created in vain. R. Moshe Metrani (1500 – 1580) *Beis Elokim*. Shar HaTeshuvah. Chap. 1, p. 100. See also: *Orchos Tzadikim*. Shar HaTeshuvah, Shar 26, p. 209. *Rabbeinu Bachya*. Kisvei Rabbeinu Bachya. *Kad Kemach*. Teshuvah, p. 438. *Akeidas Yitzchak*. Parshas Nitzavim. Shar 101, p. 121a. R. Yitzchak Abuhav. (? – 1493) *Menoras HaMaor*. Ner 5. Hakdamah, p. 245.

* The soul descends into this realm of existence to experience teshuvah. *Likutei Torah*. Parshas Balak, p. 73a. Teshuvah is seen as the foundation of this world, the bedrock upon which this universe was created. *Safer Hayashar*. (Anonymous. *Shem Hagdalim Marreches Siforim. Chof. 72*.) Shar 10, p. 114. *Sheivet HaMusar*. Chap. 10 : 23, p 161. See also : *Avodas Hakodesh*, Part 2, Chap 35.

* According to the Gemarah, this universe was created with the letter Hei, allowing for teshuvah. *Menachos, 29b*. Note : Yerushalmi *Chagigah*, Chap. 2. *Zohar* Hakdamah. p, 4a. *Zohar* Tehilim, Chap 68:31. See: *Midrash Rabbah*. Bereishis. Parsha, 12:2. *Osyos D'Rebbe Akiva*, p. 108. Though the Midrash also speaks of the world being created with the letter Beis. *Midrash Rabbah* Bereishis in the beginning. See Chida, *Chedrei Beten All Ha'Torah*. Chaya Sarah, p. 41, where it is explained that by positioning the letter Hei sideways these conflicting sources are reconciled.

* "You shall become a vagrant..."*Bereishis* 4:12. Cain responds, "Is my iniquity too great to be borne?"4: 13. The transformative power of teshuvah aroused Adam to compose a song for Shabbos. *Midrash Rabbah Bereishis*. Parsha 22. Chap. 13. *Vayikra*, Parsha 10. Chap. 5. *Pesikta D'Rav Kahana*. Shuva, p, 359. Perhaps the reason he touched his face was because he realized that through teshuvah one can become a new person, represented by a 'new face'(see endnotes to end of chap two) much like Shabbos, which is also considered acquiring a 'new face.' *Tosefos* to *Kesuvos,* 7a.

* The Hebrew word Shabbos is comprised of three letters, the same three letters can spell *Tashuv*- return. R. Yisrael Baal Shem Tov (1698 -1760)*Baal Shem Tov Al HaTorah*. Parshas Yisro, p. 332. *Kedushas Levi*. At the end of *Avos. Tayna*. Igeres HaTeshuvah, Chap. 10. *Shearis Yisroel*, p. 21. *Chedrei Beten All Ha'Torah*. Bereishis, p. 3. See also: *Midrash Rabbah*. Bereishis. Parsha 22, Chap. 13. *Yifah Toar*, ad loc. *Likutei Moharan* Part 1, Chap. 58 :7. R. Moshe Isserles (1530 – 1572) writes that Shabbos is a unique time for teshuvah. *Machir Yayin*, p. 25.

* The three days following Shabbos are still connected with the previous Shabbos. *Pesachim,* 106a. See also: R. Chaim Vital (1543 -1620) *Pri Eitz Chayim* Shar HaShabbos, Chap 1, p. 381.

* Shabbos is an other-worldly manifestation. *Berachos*, 57b. *Zohar 1*. p. 48a. Yet, Shabbos permeates and blesses the entire week that follows. *Zohar 11*, p. 63b, and 88a. Shabbos both concludes the preceding week and blesses the week that follows. *Sheim Me'Shemuel*, Bereishis, p. 8.

* We are not locked into a world of misdeeds. Nothing stands in the path of teshuvah. *Zohar 11*, p 106a. *Zohar Chadash*. At the end of Parshas Bereishis. Jerusalem Talmud. *Pe'ah*. Chap. 1. Halacha 1. See also: *Kiddushin*, 40b. Rambam. *Hilchos Teshuvah*. Chap. 4. Halacha 6. *Orchos Tzadikim*. Shar HaTeshuvah. Shar 26. p 226. *Zohar 111*, p. 122b. Though, there are cases where even teshuvah is deemed ineffective. *Menachos*, 109a. *Tosefos*. *La Yishamshu* . Rambam. *Hilchos Nesias Capaim*. Chap. 15. Halacha. 3. *Yevamos*, 21a with regards to a thief. See also *Zohar 1*, p. 60a. 219b. *11*. p 214b. See however, *Sotah*, 39a. *Tosefos*. *Vechi*. *Taanis*, 27a. *Tosefos. Ei Mah*. "There is no misdeed that cannot be mended through teshuvah." *Tanya*. Igeres HaTeshuvah. Chap. 4. See also: R. Yitzchak Blazer (1837 - 1907) *Chocvei Ohr*, p. 239. See also *Tosefos*. Hasam. *Baba Basra*, 88b.

* Though it says, that if the evil inclination says transgress and Hashem will forgive, do not believe him. *Chagigah,*16a. And when someone says "I will transgress and I will then do teshuvah, the doors of teshuvah are closed." *Yumah,* 85b. *Psikta De'rebbe Kahana*. Parsha 45:1. Rambam. *Hilchos Teshuvah*. Chap. 4. Halacha 1. Nonetheless, while the doors of teshuvah are closed they are not completely sealed and if one really tries the doors can be opened. R. Chasdai Cresces. *Ohr Hashem*. Maamor 3. Klal 2. Chap. 2. *Tanya*. Igeres HaTeshuvah. Chap. 11. R. Menachem Ben Shlomo Meiri. *Chibur HaTeshuvah*. Meishiv Nefesh. Maamor 1. Chap. 3, p.p. 68 – 69. *Nesivas Shalom*. Teshuvah, Maamor 8. Even the most wayward of people have the opportunity to declare teshuvah. *Sanhedrin*, 103a. "The doors of *teshuvah* are forever open." *Psikta De'rebbe Kahana*. Parsha 45 : 8. See also: R. Menachem Recanti (1223 - 1290) Parshas Naso. *Levush Malchus*. Vol 7, p. 35b. *Chibur HaTeshuvah*. Meishiv Nefesh. Maamor 1. Chap. 1, p. 29.

* Teshuvah is theoretically affective even with regards to acts liable to be punished by the courts of man. Though in actuality, man does not know what is in the heart of his fellow man and thus can-

2222222

not conclude that the teshuvah is complete or sincere. R. Chaim Yoseph Dovid Azulay. *Ayin Zocher*. Marreches Mem. (20) See however, R. Yechezkel Landau (1713 – 1793) *Noda BeYehudah*. Orach Chaim, Teshuvah 35.

CHAPTER 4

* The root of the word Mitzvah is Tzavsa – connection. Rabbi Moshe Chaim Ephraim of Sudylkov. (?-1800) *Degel Machanah Ephraim*. Parshas Korach, p. 183. R. Schneur Zalman of Liadi. *Likutei Torah*. Parshas Bechukosai, p. 45c. R. Avraham Yeshoshua Heschel (1745 - 1825) *Ohev Yisroel*. Parsahs Vayera, p. 14. See also: *Safer Cheredim*. Chap. 70, p 268. *Reshis Chachmah. Shar Ha'Ahavah*, Chap. 1, p. 54. R. Yehudah Loew. The Maharal. *Tifferes Yisrael*, Chap. 9. *Shearis Yisroel*, p. 229. Our relationship to Hashem is likened to marriage. *Taanis*, 26b. *Midrash Rabbah Shemos*, Parsha, 15:31.

* Cheit comes from the word meaning decent. See: *Rashi, Yumah, 58b*. Hischil. "There were seven hundred chosen men...could sling stones *ve'lo yachati* – and not miss." The word *cheit* thus suggests being off the mark, missing the target.

* Transgressions are thus symptoms of an inner barrier, an underlying mistaken assumption that the Creator is disinterested with Creation, or even that a Creator does not exist. *Midrash Rabbah. Bamidbar*, Parsha 9:1.

* Every Cheit has a trace of idol worship and heresy. R. Yitzchak Issac of Kamarna. *Heichal Ha'Beracha*. Devarim, p. 88b.

* When a person acts out of misalignment with Divine Presence, he erects an imaginary barrier that keeps It from 'entering' or being sensed. "Your iniquities have separated you..." *Yeshaya*, 59: 2. See: Rambam. *Hilchos Teshuvah*, Chap. 7. Halacha 7. See at length. *Tanya*. Igeres HaTeshuvah, Chap. 5. By transgressing, one disconnects from Hashem who is the source of life and who is the essence of life itself. The Torah says : ... "love God... listen to His voice....for He is your life." *Devarim*, 30: 20. Sin is a Tuma- an impurity. *Midrash Shochar Tov*. Tehilim 51. *Ohr Zarua* 112. *Nesivas Shalom*. Teshuvah, Maamor 2. Tuma is separation.

* One of the allusions the Torah makes regarding teshuvah is about theft. *Bamidbar*, 5: 7. Whenever man transgresses he robs from himself his true potential. R. Yehudah Aryeh Leib of Ger (1847 – 1905) *Sfas Emes. Bamidbar*, Chap. 6:2. Note, see also: R. Chaim Ben Atar *Ohr Hachayim*. Mishpatim, Chap. 22: 6.

* "Man does not commit a transgression unless a spirit of folly..." *Sotah*, 3a. See also : *Midrash Rabbah. Bamidbar*. Parsha 9, Chap. 6. *Targum*. Melachim 1, 8: 47. *Sifri*, 132b. Note : *Avodah Zarah*, 54b. See also: *Likutei Moharan*, 1:1.

* Transgressions themselves are their own worst punishments. R. Chaim of Volozhin. *Nefesh HaChaim*. Shar 1, Chap. 12. See also: *Ohev Yisroel*. Ki Tisa, p. 156.

* The harshest consequence of vice is spiritual suffocation that slowly overwhelms a person. "Transgressions entangle the transgressor." *Midrash Mishlei*, 5:22.

* Without teshuvah, a deep sense of constriction, emptiness and loss gradually creep in. *Ramban* Vayikra, 5: 15. And sin without teshuvah is associated with mourning. *Shemos*, 33:4.

* The ripple effect of transgression is that it often leads to doing more of the same. *Avos.* Chap. 4. Mishnah 2 *Yismach Yisrael* Vol. 2, Shabbos Teshuvah, p 123.

* "One should not agonize..."*Midrash Tanchumah,* Parshas Vayikrah.

* Habitual negativity starts to narrow a person's perspective while desensitizing him to the good. R. Shamson Refoel Hirsh. (1808 - 1888) *Safer Chorev.* Pirkei HaMitzvahs. Teshuvah, Chap. 2. R. After a person has sinned he needs to contend with his Netia –inclination towards such activities. R. Chaim Shmulevitz. (1902- 1978) *Sichas Mussar.* Lamed Aleph, Maamor 14. R. Yoseph Yavatz (1434 - 1507) writes that through accustoming oneself to the ways of vice, one's body parts become attuned to such behavior, and only through detached intellect can one unshackle oneself from this pattern of behavior. *Yavatz. Avos,* Chap. 4. Mishnah 13.

* The tenth utterance (commandment) "Do no covet" is linked to the first, "I am Hashem." If the first is secure, than automatically you will keep the tenth. R. Yitzchak Issac of Kamarna. *Otzer Ha'Chaim,* Shemos, p. 131b.

* The tenth utterance is more of an end result of the previous commands than an actual commandment. R. Michael of Zlotchov. (1731 - 1786) *Malchei BaKodesh,* Yisro, p. 45.

* All the utterances are included in the tenth, do not covet. *Kli Yakkar.* Chaya Sarah, Chap 24: 22. Regarding the directive not to covet many have asked; how can there be a commandment how to feel? See *Even Ezra.* Shemos, 20:14.

CHAPTER 5

* Keri is a word commonly used in the Torah to imply the concept of transgression. *Vayikra,* 26: 21. Keri connotes unexpected and aberrational behavior, one that strays from the normal course. R. Tzodok HaKohen of Lublin (1823 – 1900) *Tzidkas Hatzadik,* No. 156.

* One of the words for transgression in Hebrew is *aveirah,* derived from the root word *avar* - to cross over, going to the other side. R. Schneur Zalman of Liadi. *Maamorei Admur Hazoken. Inyonim,* p. 458. *Maamorei Admmur Hazoken.* Kesuvim, p. 58. R. Yoseph Yitzchak of Chabad. *Sefer Hamaamorim 5708,* p . 114. *Sefer Hamaamorim. Kuntreisim.* Vol 1, p. 75. See also : *Shearis Yisroel,* p. 39.

* Traditionally, these two forces are called the Yetzer Ha-Tov and Yetzer Ha-Ra. See *e.g. Berachos,* 61a. *Sukkah,* 52b.

* It is quite healthy and adaptive to make provisions for our own survival. *Midrash Rabba.* Bereishis, Parshah 9, Chap. 7. See also:*Midrash Rabbah.* Koheles, 3 :11. The *yetzer* is the ego that self-preserves. Although in other sources it seems that the yetzer, even in infancy destroys the person. *Avos D'Rebbe Nason,* Chap 16. Perhaps there are various levels within the yetzer itself. Note: *Ohr HaChayim.* Shoftim, Chap 20:10.

* Just as the dregs are a good preservative for the wine. R. Eliyahu of Vilna *Pirush Ha'Grah.* Yeshaya, 5:6.

* The laws of inertia dictate that our uncontrolled selfishness will lead first to seemingly innocuous vice, and finally to obviously pernicious behavior. "The evil inclination first appears as a modest traveler, then (if not controlled) as a welcomed guest, and finally becomes the master of the house." *Sukkah,* 52a.

* The exaggeration, misalignment or stagnation of its survival instincts is what transforms the ego into an instrument of evil, we make it evil. *Tanchumah.* Parshas Bereishis, Chap. 7. Though see *Kidushin,* 30b. Note: R. Yisrael Salanter. *Igeres HaMusar.* End of *Mesilas Yesharim,* p.p. 160 - 161. *Ohr Yisrael,* p.p. 154-155. Thus, the *yetzer* tries to convince man with regard to a *safek cheit* / a doubt of sin- not when it comes to a certain *cheit. Sanhedrin,* 103a. *Berachos,* 55b, *Rashi* ad loc.

* According to one opinion the Yetzer Hara is similar to a bee, another opinion draws a parallel with wheat. *Berachos* 61a. The argument is whether this inclination is essentially negative, or is it merely a potential for negativity. See *Iyun Yakov* ad loc.

* Another name for this level of self is 'the animal soul.' *Tanya,* Chap. 9. See also: R. Yitzchak of Aco. *Meiras Einayim,* Parshas Emor, p. 226. R. Meir Eben Aldavia. *Shivilei Emunah,* Nosiv 3, p. 107. Nosiv 6, p. 306. R. Chaim Vital. *Arba Meos Shekel Kesef,* p.p. 72b – 73. R. Eliyohu of Vilna in his commentary to the book *Sifra DeZeniuta,* Chap. 4, p. 29a.

* The two forces are the cause of the apparent inner duality; one instructs the person to seek what is rewarding in the moment, the other is transcendent, and it beholds the entire picture, past, present and future at once. *Akeidas Yitzchak.* Parshas Naso, Shar 73 .In a state of spiritual alienation, a human beings thinking is limited and confined, thinking short term, with no regard for the future. Ibid, Shar 72. See also: R. Yisrael Salanter. (1810 - 1883) *Ohr Yisrael,* p 153. R. Yoseph Yuzal Horowitz of Navardik. (1848 - 1920) *Madregos Ha'adam. Maamor* Tikun Ha'midos, Chap 1. The Gemarah teaches that the evil inclination can be sweet and alluring in the beginning, but ultimately it is bitter. Yerushalmi. *Shabbos.* Chap. 14. Halacha 3. *Midrash Rabbah Vayikra.* Parsha 16. Chap. 8. See also: *Chibur HaTeshuvah. Meishiv Nefesh.* Maamor 1. Chap. 2, p. 38.

* Every negative act is rooted in idol worship. *Tanya.* Chap. 24. Note, see *Rashi* Vayikra, Chap 5: 15.

* The feelings that follow the actions indicate from where the action originates. *Sheivet HaMusar,* Chap. 25:8, p.p. 358- 359.

* A person should take notice whether he senses an expanded state of intellectual awareness or not. *Kedushas Levi,* Derush Purim, p. 55.

* The Ramban teaches that we should try to strip away our pleasure, our personal gain and this would allow us to make an informed impartial choice. See: *Ben Peros Yoseph,* p. 9. *Toldas Yaakov Yoseph,* Parshas Shoftim. *Baal Shem Tov Al HaTorah,* Bereishis, Chap 152.

* According to the Zohar, the egotistical inclination is a God-sent messenger. *Zohar 11,* Parshas Terumah, p. 163a. Note see: *Baba Basra,* 16a. The Yetzer Ha'ra is an angel. Though in the Zohar it also speaks of it as being a Shed –demon. See *Shar Kitzur A'b'ya,* Chap 3.

* The metaphor of a king who sends his trusted servant is quoted by R. Yaakov Yoseph of Polonnye (?- 1784) *Toldos Yaakov Yoseph.* Parshas Vayakhel, p. 252. The Yetzer is nothing but an illusion. *Avnei Nezer.* Even Ezra, Siman 232:10. The Baal Shem Tov teaches that evil masquerades in a mask of holiness, so that it can seduce man to follow its path. It always comes disguised, and of- fers many 'good' reasons. *Baal Shem Tov Al HaTorah.* Megillas Esther, p. 640. See also: *Sheim Me'Shemuel. Hagada Shel Pesach,* p. 131. Note: *Yaros D'vash* 1, p. 159.

CHAPTER 6

* Teshuvah as return can either mean returning "to" or returning (breaking away) "from'. Either returning to Hashem or turning away from sin. If the Torah source for teshuvah is the verse "You will return to Hashem, your God". (*Devarim*, 4:30), than, teshuvah is an act of returning "to" returning to Hashem. This is the opinion of the *Semak*, Mitzvah 53. *Reshis Chachmah.* Shar HaTeshuvah. Chap. 1.*Safer Cheraidim*, 9:34. However, the Rambam does not site this verse as the source for teshuvah, fittingly, the Rambam is of the opinion that teshuvah is an act of returning *from*, a moving away, a breaking away from the path of negativity. Rambam, *Hilchos Teshuvah*, 1:1. 2:1. Though, as a by product, breaking away from negativity brings a person closer to Hashem. *Hilchos Teshuvah*, 7:7.

* The word teshuvah can be divided into two, Tashuv-return/ Hei. *Zohar 111*, p. 122a. *Tanya*. Iggeres HaTeshuvah, Chap. 4. *Maamorei Admur Hazoken,* Inyonim, p. 460. See also : R. Naphtali Hirtz Bacharach. (17th century) *Emek HaMelech*. Shar TiKunei Teshuvah, Chap. 9, p. 18d.

* Teshuvah is for everyone, for all souls embodied within physical form. *Likkutei Torah.* Parshas Nitzavim, p. 60d. Shabbos Teshuvah, p. 66c. See also: *Meiri, Yumah* 20a. At the time of the redemption even the most righteous of people will need to enter a world of teshuvah. *Likkutei Torah.* Shemini Atzeres, p. 92b. *Shir HaShirim*, p. 50b. See also: *Zohar 111*, p. 153b.

* Even the righteous need teshuvah. *Tanya*, Iggeres HaTeshuvah, Chap. 8. *Likutei Torah*, Parshas Ha'azinu.

* By declaring teshuvah we return to a state of innocence and purity. R. Yehudah Loew. *Nesivos Olam. Nosiv HaTeshuvah*, Chap. 2.

* Teshuvah brings healing to the world. *Yumah*, 86a. *Nesivos Olam. Nosiv HaTeshuvah*, Chap. 2.

* Teshuvah brings redemption. *Yumah*, 86b.

CHAPTER 7

* Galus is a condition of doubt and quandary. R. Tzvi Elimelech of Dinov. *Bnei Yissochar.* Maamorei Chodesh Tishrei. Maamor 8, p. 11b. See also: R. Kook. *Oros HaKodesh*, p. 205.

* The answer is the certainty. There is the Divine Name of Vadai – certain. The first letters of the words *V*aYevarech *D*ovid *E*s *H*ashem (Vav- Dalet- Aleph – Yud) spell the Divine name Vadai – certain. This name in numeric value is 21, same as the Name 'Ehe-yeh/I will be.' (Paradoxically, the name Ehe-yeh suggests the place of all possibilities, *keser*, not certainty.) And the name through which Moshe, according to the Arizal ascended the mountain. By contrast, the *Shechinah* (which is now in a state of exile) is called *Ulai*-maybe. *Tikunie Zohar*, Tikun 69. *Koheles Yaakov*, Erech Aleph. However, since "the beginning is wedged in the end" (*Sefer Yetzirah*), the highest levels of *keser,* referred to as *radlah* – "*riehsa de'lo aisyadon*- the head which is not fathomed", is the space of the "surprise of doubt" which the Zohar speaks of. It is called *radlah* because it tolerates and sustains diametrically opposed states concurrently, a transcendent reality that houses the fundamental paradoxes of existence. Yet, there is a difference between a doubt where "nothing is

possible", which is Kelipa or non - productivity, and a doubt where "everything is possible", which is the deepest level of Kedusha/ the holy, productivity. Parenthetically, there is also a spiritual practice of entering a place of "doubt" in order to reach true clarification. R. Mordecai Yoseph of Izhbitz (1801- 1854) *Mei HaShiluach* 1. Parshas Toldas. Va'Yehav Yitzchak, p. 34.

* R. Moshe Sofer. *Derashas Chasam Sofer*. Shavuos.

* A Chassid asks, why?. R. Mendel of Kotzk. *Amud Ha'emes*, p. 101.

CHAPTER 8

* The word teshuvah has the letters that spell Tohu U'Vahu – chaos and emptiness, and the Shin stands for darkness. *Sefas Emes*. Shabbos Teshuvah, p. 159.

* "A heavenly voice rings forth each day to awaken mankind to teshuvah." *Midrah Rabbah*. Eicha. Hakdamah. Chap. 25. *Pirkei De'rebbe Eliezer*, Chap. 15. *Zohar 111*, p. 126. See also : *Reshis Chachmah*. Shar HaTeshuvah, Chap. 1, p. 103b. In the Mishnah it says that there is a heavenly voice that rings forth from mount Sinai and says, "woe to the people because of [their] affront to the Torah!" *Avos*. Chap. 6. Mishnah 2. *Midrash Rabbah*. Shemos. Parsha 41, Chap. 7. *Midrash Rabbah*. Eicha. *Tanchumah*. Parshas Ki Tissa, Chap. 16. *Tana Devei Eliyahu Zuta*, Chap. 17. (See also : *Zohar 111*, p. 13b.) There are those who say that there is an actual sound coming from mount Sinai. R. Yisrael Lipschutz. (1782 – 1860) *Tifferet Yisrael*, *Avos* 6:2. While others see the voice as a metaphor. R. Shemuel De Uzeda. (1540 – 1605) *Midrash Shemuel*, *Avos* 6:2.

* The perpetual self-evaluation is through Tefilah, prayer. The word Tefilah is derirved from the root word *yefalel* which means judgment. "...then Pinchas rose and *va'yefalel*- executed judgment. *Tehilim* 106 : 30. *Targum* ad loc. *Sanhedrin*, 44a. Prayer brings teshuvah. R. Yoseph Yitzchak of Chabad. *Sefer Hamaamorim. Kuntreisim.* Vol. 1, p. 121. See also : *Siddur Im Dach*, p.p. 60 - 61.

CHAPTER 9

* The root of the word *Karban* is *Kiruv*, to bring closer. *Sefer HaBahir*, Chap. 109. See also : R. Yoseph Gikatalia (1248 - 1323.) *Shaarei Orah*. Shar 2, p. 63. *Shenei Luchos Habris. Toldos Adam*, p. 6. Note : See *Midrash Rabbah*. Vayikra. Parsha 2, Chap. 12, *Yefa Toar* ad loc.

* The purpose is to include physical Chesek/ desire within a spiritual context. *Mei HaShiluach*. Part 1. Parshas Netzavim, V'Haya, p. 196. See also : *Ben Paros Yoseph*, Parshas Vayechi.

* "An abundance of wheat comes through the power of the ox." *Mishlei* 14: 4. The strength of the ox refers to the animal soul. *Likutei Torah*. Parshas Hazinu, p. 75b. Overall the ox is a symbol of the Yetzer Harah. *Keheles Yaakov*. Os Shin. Shor. Note. *Avodah Zara*, 5b. Thus the word Shor is an acronym for *Sone* –despised, *V'Tamei* –and impure, *Ra*- bad. Some of these are references to the Yetzer Hara. *Sukkah,* 52a.

* Teshuvah brings redemption. *Yumah*, 86b. *Ayin Yakov*. Ad loc.

* The 'yardstick/proving ground' of spiritual attainment is when the fast is over and one is confronted with food. Note: *Reshis Chachmah*. Shar HaTeshuvah, Chap. 4, p. 114a.

* With a new awareness, and a new day comes a renewed teshuvah. *Chovos Halevavos*. Shar Avodas Ha'Elokim, Chap. 3.

* "Man was created to toil." *Iyov*, 5: 7.

* The essence of teshuvah lies in the desire to reach and move forward. R. Avraham Yitzchak Kook. *Oros HaTeshuvah*, Chap. 5 – 6.

* There is an ancient debate whether the actual achievement of desire, or the desire itself is the most important. See: R. Yakov Moshe Charlap. (1883 – 1952) *Mei Marom* Vol 1, p. 136.

* The 14th century philosopher R. Chasdai Cresces writes that the destiny of man lies is his toil and struggle to attain love and adhesion with his Creator. The purpose is not (only) in the serenity and pleasure in having arrived, but rather in the quest. *Ohr Hashem*. Maamor 3, Klal 2, Chap. 2.

* What differentiates humans from angels is their ability to desire. R. Tzodok HaKohen of Lublin. *Tzidkas HaTzadik*, Os 249. See also: R. Meir Simcah of Dvinsk (1843 – 1926) *Meshech Chochmah*. Parshas Behaalosecha, p.p. 404-405. In fact, humans are defined by their movement. *Zecharia* 3:7. We may choose what we want but we can never truly free ourselves from the necessity to want. R. Yakov Moshe Charlap. *Mei Marom* Vol. 3, Chap. 1, p. 9.

* Angels have no Yetzer. *Midrash Rabbah*. Bereishis. On Chap 18:5. See *Rashi* ad loc, animals have no Yetzer. *Avos D'reb Nason*. 16.

* The Gemarah speaks of animals possessing an evil inclination. *Berachos*, 61a. Note also: *Baba Kamah*, 19b. However, the Gemarah seems to be referring to the animals survival instinct.

* The beginning of ones journey towards Torah is the *desire*. *Tzidkas HaTzadik, Os* 184.

* We are to hurry to [perform even] an easy and seemingly insignificant Mitzvah. *Avos* Chap. 4 Mishnah 2.

* The chasing of a Mitzvah is in itself a Mitzvah. R. Chaim of Volozhin. *Ruach Chayim* to *Avos*. Chap. 4 .Mishnah 2. See also: *Reshimos Shiurim- Sukkah* (Soloveitchik), p. 95.

* The search and desire for the truth is a truth in and of itself. *Sichos HaRan*. Chap. 27, p. 23.

* The Gemarah says "Greater is the service of Torah (servicing a Torah teacher) than the learning of Torah itself." *Berachos*, 7b. Thus a teacher should never prevent this privilege of his students. *Kesuvas*, 96a. The '*Teshuka* – striving', desire, to connect with Hashem and the Torah is "infinite"-infinitely expansive- whereas the actual study is "finite." *Mei Ha'Shiluach*. Part 1. Likutei Ha'shas, *Berachos*, p. 230.

* Shalom is not something that we attain, so long as there is more life to be lived we are in constant striving towards *shalom*. Note; *Moed Katan, 29a*. There is always more room to grow. R. Shmuel of Sochatchov. *Sheim Me'Shemuel*, Vayeshev.

* "To lose money is not so terrible, but when you lose courage, you lose everything." *Sheim Me'Shemuel, Yisro*.

CHAPTER 10

* For the metaphor of a prankster see: *Sichos HaRan*, Chap. 6, p 7.

* The princess and the simpleton. *Midrash Rabbah. Koheles,* 6: 7.

* "A lover of money will never be appeased by money." *Koheles,* 5:9. Thus "there is no man who dies with (even) a half of his heart's desires fulfilled." *Midrash Rabbah.* Koheles, 1: 13. 3: 10. See : *Sharei Teshuvah.* Shar 2, Chap. 27.

* Mamon is spelled with the repetition of the same letters. *Kli Yakkar.* Chaya Sarah. Chap 24: 22. See also: Chida. *Midbar Kadmos.* Marreches Mem, p. 37. *Chedrei Beten All Ha'Torah,* Toldos. p. 46.

* Spiritual hunger can manifest in the body as a physical craving. *Otzar Sipuray Chabad.* Vol. 14, p. 183. See also: R. Klunimus Kalmish (Shapiro) (1889 – 1943) *Hachsharas Ha'Avreichim.* Chap. 4, p. 29.

* The Baal Shem Tov teaches that a person can feel inspired and can drown the inspiration in alcoholic drink. *Ramach Osyos.* No. 92, p. 20.

CHAPTER 11

* There are various life situations that can catalyze teshuvah. Rabbeinu Yonah of Gerondi enumerates six reasons or incentives why people turn to teshuvah: 1) tragedy, 2) old age, 3) being inspired by a speaker, 4) reading the Torah, 5) contemplating judgment, 6) contemplating death. *Sharei Teshuvah,* Shar 2. See also: *Orchos Tzadikim.* Shar HaTeshuvah. Shar 26, p.p. 230 – 236.

* If our external self is distant from goodness and spirituality, words of wisdom may fall on deaf ears. Thus the Gemarah rules that just as it is a Mitzvah to speak of that which will be hearkened to, so to it is a Mitzvah to refrain from saying that which will not be listened to. *Yevamos,* 65b. Yerushalmi. *Chagigah,* Chap. 1. Halacha 8.

* The deepest desire for teshuvah arises from an inner space beyond everyday consciousness. R. DovBer of Chabad. *Toras Chaim Shemos,* p. 199a. The Lubavitcher Rebbe. *Sefer Hamaamorim Meluket* Vol. 5, p. 205. See also: *Meor Einayim.* Parshas Vayera, p. 21. *Reshis Chachmah.* Shar HaTeshuvah. Chap. 1, p. 104b. Regarding the question, from where does one who is completely alienated become inspired? See : R. Nachum of Chernobyl. (1730 – 1787) *Meor Einayim.* Yumah, p. 26. *Ohev Yisroel.* Lekutim Chadashim, p. 321. *Shearis Yisroel,* p. 8.

* All attractions, proclivities, premonitions and hunches are a result of the soul's yearning to elevate the sparks contained within the objects involved. *Keser Shem Tov,* p. 50. *Tzavoas Horivash.* Chap. 109, p. 38 . *Baal Shem Tov Al HaTorah.* Parshas Vayechi, p.p. 286 – 288. See also: *Meor Einayim.* Likutim, p. 166. A person is connected with his objects. *Sod Yesharim.* (Radzin) Parshas Teruma, p. 147. Thus a person can elevate his possessions. See eg, *Chulin,* 5b.

* The Midrash records a dialogue between the Creator and the people of Israel. *Midrash Rabbah.*

Eicha. Parsha 5, Chap. 21.

* "Return to Me and I will return..." *Zechariah*, Chap. 2.

*"Return us O God of deliverance." *Tehilim*, 85:5.

*"Bring us back to You...."*Eicha*, 5: 21

* Human beings must make the first move. *Reshis Chachmah*. Shar HaTeshuvah. Chap. 1, p. 102b.

* Hashem first empowers us to do so. *Baal Shem Tov Al HaTorah* Parshas Bechukosai, p. 447. Koheles, p. 649. *Keser Shem Tov*. Chap. 79. *Toldas Yaakov Yoseph*. Parshas Tzav, p. 281. *Ohev Yisroel*. Likutim Chadashim, p. 321. *Shearis Yisroel*, p. 9. R. Tzodok HaKohen of Lublin. *Resisei Layla*. Chap. 28. R. Shalom Dovber of Chabad writes that every movement must originate from Above, though at times the revelation is revealed in a concealed manner. *Beshoo Shehikdimu 5672*. Part 3, p. 1'328. See also: *Likutei Sichos*. Vol. 19, p. 13. The arousal from Above is known to inspire us to teshuvah. *Sheivet HaMusar*. Chap. 19:8, p. 272.

* Teshuvah seems to awaken unexpectedly. At times, the soul of Moshe will descend to assist someone in the process of teshuvah. R. Eliezer Ezcary. *Safer Cheraidim*. Chap. 70, p.p. 267 - 268.

* "Hashem is my light and my salvation...."*Tehilim*, 27: 1.

* There is a level of Hashem that is revealed before transgression and Hashem revealed following transgression. *Rashi*. Shemos. 34: 6. *Rosh Hashanah*, 17b. *Tosefos. Shalosh*. Ad loc. Note: R. Moshe Sofer. *Chasam Sofer. Toras Moshe*. Parshas Nitzavim, p.p. 52-53. Even during transgression the Aleph–Hashem is present. *Baal Shem Tov Al HaTorah* Parshas Ki Tetze, p. 578. *Degel Machanah Ephraim*. Parshas Emor, p. 165.

* Following transgression Hashem of strength is needed. See: The Lubavitcher Rebbe. *Likutei Sichos*. Vol. 9, p. 172. See also: R. Moshe *Alshich*. (1508 - 1600) *Tehilim*, Chap. 27:1.

* The metaphor of a piece of wood. *Zohar 111*, p. 168a. *Tanya*, Chap. 29.

* At that point a person may be open to entering the path of return. *Sharei Teshuvah*. Shar 1. Chap. 1. Shar 2, Chap. 2. *Orchos Tzadikim*. Shar HaTeshuvah. Shar 26, p. 230. *Safer Hayashar*. Shar 10, p. 114. *Chovos Halevavos. Shar HaTeshuvah,* Chap. 6. *Kitzur Chovos Halevavos* Chap. 7, p.p. 68 – 69. *Derashos HaRan*, Derush 6, p.107. Derush 9, p.161. Dersuh 10, p. 175. *Chibur HaTeshuvah*. Meishiv Nefesh. Maamor 1. Chap. 2, p. 49. *Menoras HaMaor*. Ner 5. Klal 1. Chap. 2: 5, p. 254. See also : *Likutei Moharan* Part 2, Chap. 82.

* Positive experiences, however, often enhance and reaffirm the un-rectified ego. "The upright thus became fattened and rebelled." *Devarim*. 32:15. See: *Eben Ezra* and R. Dan Yitzchak *Abarbanel*, ad loc.

* "Our vision comes not from the white of the eye...." *Midrash Rabbah*. Vayikra. Parsha 31, Chap. 8.

* Teshuvah of a higher order is an expression of love. *Sharei Teshuvah*. Shar 1, Chap. 1. *Orchos Tzadikim*. Shar HaTeshuvah. Shar 26, p. 229. *Sheivet HaMusar*. Chap. 6 : 25, p. 108. See also : *Safer Chorev. Pirkei HaMitzvahs*. Teshuvah, Chap. 4.

* Genuine teshuvah is when one comes to teshuvah with the same energy as at the time of transgression. *Yumah*, 86b. *Rambam*. Hilchos Teshuvah. Chap. 2. Halacha 1. *Emunos VeDeyos*, Maamor 5, Chap. 6. *Orchos Tzadikim*. Shar HaTeshuvah, Shar 26, p.p. 222. *Safer Chassidim*. Chap. 20.

Chibur HaTeshuvah. Meishiv Nefesh. Maamor 1. Chap. 2, p. 40. *Reshis Chachmah*. Shar HaTeshuvah, Chap. 1, p. 103. *Menoras HaMaor*. Ner 5. Klal 1. Chap. 2: 2, p. 253. *Sheivet HaMusar*, Chap. 38: 18, p. 551. See also: *Shabbos,* 151b. *Avodah Zarah,* 19a.

* According to the Midrash, Reuven was the first to undertake teshuvah. *Midrash Rabbah.* Bereishis. Parsha 84. Chap. 19. His offense was that he slept with his fathers concubine. *Bereishis* 35: 22. Though, not literally. *Shabbos,* 55b.

* Reuven declared teshuvah simply because he felt that he had done wrong. *Midrash Rabbah, Ibid, Pirush MaHarazav,* ad loc.

CHAPTER 12

* The Midrash interprets the word '*ve'atah*/ and *now*', as a reference to teshuvah. *Midrash Rabbah.* Bereishis. Parsha 21. Chap. 6. The time for teshuvah is now. *Shenei Luchos Habris*. Meseches Yumah. Ner Mitzvah, p. 237

* It is forbidden to remind a person of his shameful past. *Baba Metzia,* 58b. Rambam. *Hilchos Mechira,* Chap. 14 Halacha 13. *Shulchan Aruch*. Choshen Mishpat, Siman 228:4

* Teshuvah retroactively transform past mistakes. *Yumah,* 86a. *Rashi. M'Ahavah.*

* Fear oriented Teshuvah reduces 'intentional acts/*mayzid*', to 'acts of negligence/*shogeg*', while the love based version converts them into merit. *Yumah,* 86b. R. Yoseph Albo argues that this transformation occurs via a kindness from Above. *Safer Haikkarim* Maamor 4 Chap. 27.The idea being that without the distance the person would have not come to such levels of *devikus*. R. Chaim of Tzernovitz. (? – 1818) *Beir Mayim Chayim*. Baaloscha, p. 20.

* Every action that a person takes throughout his life creates an energy that clings to him, the doer. *Sotah,* 3b.

* The power of teshuvah is such that it actually disassociates the transgressor from the transgression. In this way, the acts themselves are not transformed, but rather it is the doer who is transformed. According to the Gemarah on the day of marriage all transgressions are erased. *Yerushalmi Bikurim.* Chap. 3. Halacha 3. *Rashi* Bereishis 36:3. Since until the point of this union each body/soul are considered as half of a whole. *Yevamos,* 63a. *Zohar 1,* p.85b. 91b. Thus, all previously done transgressions are nullified. There is no longer the individual who transgressed.

* Through teshuvah one totally transforms oneself, when looking back at the action committed previously it seems to have been done in error. R. Yoseph Albo, *Safer Haikkarim* Maamor 4, Chap. 27. See also Rambam. *Hilchos Teshuvah* Chap. 2. Halacha 4. *Maharsah. Rosh Hashanah,* 16a. In the name of the *Ran*. Others write that when a person does teshuvah he absolves the desire and the will of the transgressions, and thereby, absolves its derivative, the actions. R. Moshe Chaim Luzzato. (1707 - 1747) *Mesilas Yesharim*. Chap. 4, p. 25.

* In ancient Babylon a person who was found to have stolen would have his hands cut off. Interestingly, though as a whole, this method is not found in the Torah, and it seems to originate from Babylonian law, nonetheless, this method seems to have been employed in the times of the

Gemarah by various Babylon sages. *Sanhedrin, 58b. Niddah*, 13b.

* Regarding a *sign* on the face of the transgressor. Note *Zohar 111*, p. 75b, The Baal HaTurim writes in the name of R. Yehuda Ha'Chasid of making a sign on the face of an adulterous women. *Baal HaTurim*. Bereishis. 38:24. Clearly, however, this is not the Halacha.

* Regarding the law of compensating the value of the brick with money, see: *Gittin*, 55a. Rambam. *Hilchos Gezeila*, Chap. 1, Halacha 5. *Shulchan Aruch*. Choshen Mishpat, Chap. 360. Some codifiers write that this law is implemented even in a situation where the person does not desire teshuvah. *Tur Orach Chaim*, Siman 637. See *Beis Yoseph* regarding the opinion of *Rashi*.

* The story of the thief who decided to return what ever he had stolen is found in Gemarah. *Baba Kama*, 94b. There a number of various details regarding this law. See: *Tosefos, B'Yimei. Baba Kama*, 94b. *Rosh* ad loc. Rambam. *Hilchos Gezeila*, Chap. 2. *Shulchan Aruch*. Yore Deah, Chap. 161. *Choshen Mishpat*, Siman 366.

* The story of Reish Lakish is found in *Baba Metzia*, 84a.

* "This Mitzvah that I commanded you..." *Devarim*. 30: 11. According to the Ramban 'this' alludes to teshuvah. Ibid. Many commentaries align themselves with this interpretation. See : *Rabbeinu Bachya*, Devarim, 30:14. See also the following commentaries on *Devarim*. 30: 11. *Abarbanel*. *Seforno. Baal Haturim. Kli Yakar*. See also: *Safer Haikkarim*. Maamor 4, Chap. 25. *Beis Elokim. Shar HaTeshuvah*, Chap. 17, p. 152. *Menoras HaMaor*. Ner 5. Hakdamah, p.p. 245 – 246. There are commentaries who site the verse "you will return unto Hashem, your God" *Devarim*. 4:30, as the source for teshuvah as a positive commandment. *Semak*. Mitzvah 53. *Reshis Chachmah*. Shar HaTeshuvah. Chap. 1, p. 101b. *Safer Cheraidim*. Chap 9:34. p. 62. See also: R. Yerucham Fishal Perlah, brings n the name of early codifiers of Halacha. *Safer HaMitzvos L'Rabbeinu Saddiah Goan*. Part 3. Parsha 42, p. 375. See also: *Midrash Rabbah*. Bereishis. Parsha 84. Chap. 19. *Yifah Toar*, ad loc.

* There are those who maintain that according to the Rambam there is *no* Torah based Mitzvah for teshuvah. See : R. Yoseph Babad (1801 – 1874) *Minchas Chinuch*, Mitzvah 364. See also: *Likutei Sichos*. Vol. 30, p. 200. Footnote 21. *Likutei Sichos* Vol. 38, p.p. 23-24. The *Behag* does not count teshuvah as one of the 613 Mitzvas. See: *Meam Loaz*. Devarim. Netzavim, 30:14-14.

* Teshuvah transcends the category of Mitzvos. *Likutei Sichos*. Vol. 4, p.p. 1144 – 1145. Footnote 5. This very same reasoning can be used with regards to prayer. There is an argument between the codifiers of law whether there is a Mitzvah to pray each day. The *Rambam* rules that there is a Mitzvah to pray each day. Rambam, *Hilchos Tefilah*, Chap. 1. Halacha 1. While some authorities argue differently. See : *Ramban* to *Safer Hamitzvas*, Mitzvah 5. *Safer HaChinuch*, Mitzvah. 433. *Rash* on *Berachos* Chap. *Mi Shemeisu*, Siman 2. See also: *Rashi* and *Tosefos* to *Berachos*, 17b, and 20b. Note: *Sukkah*, 38a. Prayer is so vital an ingredient to man's relationship with his creator that to a degree it stands above commandments, it is an all comprehensive principle. *Likutei Torah*. Parshas Balak, p.70b. Incidentally, R. Yoseph Albo writes that the concept of teshuvah is more essential to Torah than prayer. *Safer Haikkarim*. Maamor 4 Chap. 25.

* Teshuvah reaches the Baal Haratzon - the one who wills. *Maamorei Admur Hazoken*. Ma'arazal, p. 448. *Sefer Hamaamorim. Kuntreisim*. Vol. 1, p. 126. *Likutei Sichos*. Vol. 4, p. 1145. *Likutei Sichos* Vol. 14, p.146. Footnote 24. See also : *Sefer Hamamorim 5671*, p.18.

* Teshuvah re-awakens the love that goes beyond even the Baal Haratzon. Tzemach Tzedek. R. Menacham Mendel. *Ohr HaTorah*. Bereishis, Vol. 6, p. 2090. See also: *Likutei Sichos*. Vol. 4, p. 1152, footnote 12. *Likutei Sichos*. Vol. 14, p.146. *Sefer Hamaamorim Meluket*. Vol. 4, p.p. 16 – 17. R. Moshe Corodovero writes that only parents can stand the odor of their children's dirtied

clothes and thus only they can clean up the mess. Similarly, a human beings transgressions can only be cleansed by Hashem. *Tomer Devorah.* Chap. 1: 3, p 3. See also :*Yeshaya.* Chap. 4: 4. *Midrash Rabbah.* Bamidbar. Parsha 19. Chap. 4. *Tanya.* Igeres Hakodesh, Igeres 22. R. Avraham of Trisk (1802 – 1889) *Magen Avraham,* p. 274.

* The Midrashic tale of the four who gathered is recorded in Midrash. *Yalkut Shimoni. Tehilim,* Chap. 25. *Yalkut Shimoni. Ezekiel.* Chap. 18:4. *Pesikta D'Rebbe Kahanah.* Parshas Shuvah. See also: Yerushalmi *Makkos.* Chap. 2. Halacha 6.

* There is no room for teshuvah in this world of intellect and rational law. *Beis Elokim.* Shar Ha'teshuvah, Chap. 1, p. 98. *Nesivos Olam.* Nosiv HaTeshuvah, Chap. 1. *Akeidas Yitzchak.* Parshas Vayikra, Shar 57. There is no room for teshuvah in the domain of law. *Safer Haikkarim.* Maamor 4. Chap. 25. Meiri. *Chibur HaTeshuvah.* Maamor 1:1. *Meiri* to Avos, Chap 3. Mishnah 18. *Mesilas Yesharim .* Chap. 4, p. 25. See also : *Sanhedrin,* 103a. *Rashi. Midas Hadin. Ohev Yisrael.* Parshas Metzora, p. 175. R. Elchanan Vaserman argues that teshuvah in the present alters the past and it does so based on strict law. *Kovetz Maamorim,* p. 23.

* To connect with the very essence of Being by revealing the intrinsic unity that exists between the soul and Hashem. *Likutei Sichos.* Vol. 4, p. 1152. See also: *Nesivos Olam,* Nosiv HaTeshuvah. Chap. 1. *Tanya,* Chap. 24.

CHAPTER 13

* A negative action is like a stain on a garment (*Yirmiyahu* 2:22, as in, filthy clothes. *Zechariya,* 1:3)- something external to us- yet a Mitzvah is a Chok- something that is engraved- within us, it is who we are.

* Negativity is superficial. R. Shalom Dovber of Chabad. *Sefer Hamaamorim Ranat* (5659), p. 88. *Likutei Sichos.* Vol 6, p.p. 54 – 55. See also: R. Aryeh Leib Ha' Cohen. (1745- 1813) *Shav Sh'-matasa.* Hakdamah. p, 14. R. Tzvi Elimelech of Dinav. *Bnei Yissochar.* Maamorei Chodesh Tishrei Maamor 2, p. 1b. Maamor 4, p. 14d. R. Yaakov Leiner of Radzin – Izhbitz. (1818 – 1878) *Beis Yaakov.* Parshas Emor, p. 112b. Negativity is contradictory to the nature of the soul. *Zohar 111,* p. 16a.
* The Name of Hashem is comprised of four letters that can, when rearranged, spell out past, present and future. *Zohar 111.* p 257b. See : *Tanya.* Shar Hayichud VaHaEmuna, Chap. 7. Beyond and including all dimensions of time, past, present and future.

* Many commentaries conclude that it is not the actual deed that is transformed, but rather, through teshuvah, the doer is transformed. *Maharsah Yumah,* 86b. Alternatively, there are those who explain transgressions becoming merits this way: through teshuvah man regrets his actions so thoroughly, that he thinks, had he not transgressed at that time he would surely have done Mitzvos. Thus, his thoughts become like actions, and it is as if he had performed those Mitzvos he now regrets not doing. R. Yitzchak Blazer. *Chocvei Ohr,* p. 106.

* The transgression, which brought about teshuvah, causes an elevation by the one who declares a state of teshuvah. *Kapos Tmarim.* On *Yumah,* 86b. Or transforming negativity itself into a Mitzvah. *Nesivos Olam.* (Maharal) Nosiv HaTeshuvah, Chap. 2. Transforming negative energy into positive. R. Aharan Berechyah of Modena. (? - 1639.) *Ma'avar Yavak.* Maamor 3. Chap. 27, p. 291.

* The master of teshuvah has more Mitzvos – good deeds- than the wholly virtuous, since he has also the transformed all of his transgressions. *Chedrei Beten All Ha'Torah.* Toldos 2, p. 54.

* *Dorshei Ye'chudecah* – seeker of Your unity. Part of the Ana B'koach prayer attributed to the first century sage Rabbi Nechuniah Ben HaKana.

* The descent may generate greater ascent, and as a result, they are redefined and reshaped into positive virtues. *Tanya,* Chap. 7. *Sheim Me'Shemuel.* Parshas Yisro, p. 253. R. Tzodok HaKohen of Lublin. *Takanas Hashavim.* Chap. 10, p. 78. See also: *Beis Elokim.* Shar HaTeshuvah. Chap. 3, p. 110. *Sefas Emes.* Parshas Vayigash. *Tzidkas Hatzadik,* Os 40, Os. 100.

* The very same thing one is lacking. *Tzikas Hatzadik,* Os 70, p.p. 10a-10b.

* The tree Adam and Chava ate from was a fig tree. *Sanhedrin,* 70b. The garments they put on afterwards were made from a fig tree. *Bereishis* 3:7.

* *Cheit* is unintentional. *Vayikra* 4: 2. *Avon* intentional. *Bamidbar,* 15:31. *Pesha* is transgressions that are done spitefully. *Melachim* 2. 3:7. These are the basic transgressions, and thus the three forms of sins that need to be detailed during confession. *Yumah,* 36b. *Rambam.* Hilchos Teshuvah. Chap.1 Halacha 1.

* The word *chatah,* from the word *cheit* refer to a state of purity. *Bamidbar.* 8: 21. Cheit from the word meaning cleaning. *Tosefos Yesheinim. Yumah,* 59a, *Haya.* See also; *Chulin,* 27a. Avon means strength. *Yeshayahu,* 40: 26. *Hosea.* 12:9. Though the word Avon which refers to transgression is spelled with an Ayin, and Avon referring to strength with an Aleph, we do find that Avon with an Aleph also implies iniquities. See e.g.: *Bamidbar.* 23: 21 The idea of Pesha transgression becomes the source of Shefa. R. Tzvi Hirsh of Zhitachov. *Sur Mera V'Asei Tov,* p. 49.

* An example where a Hechsher for a Mitzvah is considered as part of the Mitzvah would be the Mitzvah of procreation. Though the obligation lies on the male, nonetheless, since it cannot be performed without a female, thus there is a Mitzvah on the woman as well. *Ran.* Kidushin. Beginning of Chap. 2. *Teshuvas HaRan* Chap. 32. *Birkei Yoseph,* Siman 1:116. *Otzar Hapaskim,* Siman 36:2. See also: *Torah Temima.* Bereishis.

* To come to teshuvah with increased vigor. *Zohar 1,* p. 129b. *Tanya,* Chap. 7. See also : *Ohr Hashem.* Maamor 3. Klal 2. Chap. 1. Teshuvah is a new and fresh way of life, and as with all things new, when done for the first time it is done with excitement. *Baal Shem Tov Al HaTorah* Parshas Nitzavim, p. 592.

* One who declares teshuvah stands on a spiritual rung *unattainable* by even the greatest amongst the righteous. *Berachos.* 34b. In our version of the Gemarah it says, "in the place where the Baal teshuvah stands, the wholly righteous *do not* stand." While this same adage is commonly cited as "in the place where the Baal Teshuvah stands, even the wholly the righteous *cannot* stand." See e.g. : *Rambam.* Hilchos Teshuvah. Chap. 7. Halacha 4. *Safer Chassidim,* Chap. 60. *Chovos Halevavos.* Shar HaTeshuvah, Chap. 8. *Kitzur Chovos Halevavos* Chap. 7, p 71. Rabbeinu *Bachya.* Vayikra, 1: 9. *Kad Kemach.* Rosh Hashanah 1, p. 370. *Beis Elokim.* Shar HaTeshuvah. Chap. 4, p. 113. *Orchos Tzadikim.* Shar HaTeshuvah. Shar 26, p. 252. *Akeidas Yitzchak.* Parshas Nitzavim. Shar 100, p.113. *Sefer Ha'emunos.* Shar 6. Chap. 2, p. 60b. *Menoras HaMaor.* Ner 5. Klal 1. Chap. 2: 1, p. 252. *Avodas Hakodesh.* Part 2. Chap. 35. *Tomer Devorah.* Chap. 1:7, p. 7. *Safer Cheraidim.* Chap. 66:160, p. 257. *Asarah Maamoros. Maamor Chikur Din 1111.* Chap. 1, p. 243. *Sheivet HaMusar.* Chap. 38:17, p. 551. See : *Zohar 11,* p. 106b. See also : *Zohar 1,* p. 129a. See however: *Chovos Halevavos.* Shar HaTeshuvah. Introduction. *Pass Lechem. Safer Hayashar.* Shar 10, p. 111. See also : *Asarah Maamoros.* Maamor Chikur Din. Part 4. Chap. 1, p. 245.

* Through teshuvah one has the ability to elevate sparks the are contained within the forbidden.

Sefer Hamaamorim Meluket. Vol. 1, p. 192.

* One who embarks on the path of teshuvah operates with an additional measure of soul. *Tikunei Zohar.* See : *Reshis Chachmah.* Shar HaTeshuvah. Chap. 6, p. 120a. See also: *Mei Hashiluch 11,* p. 179.

CHAPTER 14

* According to many commentaries there is a Torah command to verbalize teshuvah. Rambam. *Hilchos Teshuvah.* Chap. 1. Halacha 1. *Safer HaMitzvos.* Mitzvah 73. In the name of the Midrash *Mechilta. Semag.* Positive Mitzvah 16. *Safer HaChinuch.* Mitzvah 364. *Semak.* Chap. 53. R. Yehudah HaChassid. *Safer Chassidim.* Chap. 20. See also: Midrash *Toras Kohanim.* Parshas Bechukosai. *Reshis Chachmah.* Shar HaTeshuvah. Chap. 5, p. 118b. Note *Kerisus,* 12a.

* Others assert that the verbalizing of teshuvah is a Mitzvah from our sages. See: R. Yerucham Fishal Perlah. On *Safer HaMitzvas L'Rabbeinu Saddiah Goan.* Part 3. Parsha 42, p. p. 374 – 375.

* The Beis Yitzchak asks why there is no Beracha/ blessing on Teshuvah? (*Beis Yitzchak* Yoreh Deah. 2, Siman 168) One of the answers given is that because the essence of Teshuvah is a movement in the heart, whereas the verbalization is merely the outward expression. *Pardas Yoseph.* Parshas Acharei, 15:30. Upon further reflection it seems that this may also be the opinion of the Rambam. *Hilchos Teshuvha 2:2.* Another answer why there is no blessing on Teshuvah is because it is a Mitzvah that is not completely dependent on the doer, but also on the Receiver of Teshuvah. Note: *Teshuvas HaRashba.* 1, Siman 18.

* According to the Rambam confession is said *following* teshuvah. Rambam. *Hilchos Teshuvah.* Chap. 2 Halacha 2. Others write that through the verbalization the contrite will actually become inspired to teshuvah. The verse says "and he will confess and (he will then) leave (his ways of iniquities.)"*Mishlei:* 28: 13. See: Rabbeinu Yonah of Gerondi. *Sharei Teshuvah.* Shar 1, Chap. 11. See however, R. Chaim of Volozhin. *Nefesh HaChaim,* p. 403- 404. R. Bachya Ibn Pakudah writes that it is through the power of speech that a human being is aroused to teshuvah. *Chovos Halevavos.* Shar Habechinah. Chap. 5. The *Chinuch* writes that through confessing the penitent will be awakened to teshuvah. *Safer HaChinuch.* Mitzvah 364. Both opinions are in agreement that teshuvah is a positive Mitzvah. See also : *Zohar 111,* p. 122a. There are also those of the opinion that teshuvah is *not* a Mitzvah, but rather an inevitability, and when it does occur, the Mitzvah is the verbalization. According to many this is the opinion of the Rambam. *Minchas Chinuch.* Mitzvah 364. *.Mishpat Cohen.* Chap. 128. See : *Rambam.* Hilchos Teshuvah Chap. 1. Halacha 1. See also : *Kiryas Sofer.* Beginning of Hilchos Teshuvah. See, however *Safer HaMitzvas.* Mitzvah 73. *Likutei Biurim L'Tanya* 2, p. 40. Yet, all agree that teshuvah is not complete until one actually verbalizes these sentiments. See however, R. Saddiah Goan. *Safer HaMitzvas 336.* R. Meir Simcah of Dvinsk asks how can there be a separate Mitzvah to do teshuvah?- for even without the mitzvah of teshuvah one would be required to do the Mitzvas? And he answers that the teshuvah is the verbalization and the asking for forgiveness. *Meshech Chochmah.* Parshas Vayelech. p. 618.

* Through speaking of teshuvah and concretizing the contrition, the teshuvah and resolve become stronger. *Safer Hacinuch.* Mitzvah. 364. The speaking endows the thoughts of teshuvah with a tangible reality. *Safer Chorev. Pirkei HaMitzvas,* Teshuvah, Chap. 2.

* "Voice arouses intention." R. Dovid Ben Shmuel Halevi. *Taz.* (1586 - 1667) *Shulchan Aruch.* Orach Chaim, Siman. 101: 3. *Reshis Chachmah.* Shar HaKedushah, Chap. 15. *Shenei Luchos Habris.* Shar Ha'asyos, p. 82b.

* Confession reveals the intention of the person who is confessing. *Safer HaChinuch.* Mitzvah 364.

* The more one speaks about a feeling the more real the feeling becomes. Rabbi Shalom DovBer of Chabad. *Sefer Hamaamorim Ranat.* (5659), p.5. The feelings will follow the vocalization. See: R. Eliyahu Dessler. (1892 - 1953) *Michtav M'Eliyahu* Vol. 4. p. 257. See also: The Maharal. *Derech Chaim.* Avos. Chap. 1: 17.

* The Gemarah advises one who is troubled to speak his heart to a friend. *Sotah,* 42b. *Yumah,* 75a. *Sanhedrin,* 100b.

* Teachers throughout the ages have recommended and advocated being open and spontaneous with Hashem. Rabbi Yitzchak Luria quoted by R. Eliezer Ezcary. *Safer Cheraidim.* Chap. 65, p. 226. R. Nachman of Breslov. *Likkutei Moharan.* Part 2. Chap. 95. Chap. 99. *Likutei Aytzos.* Hitbode-dus. 20, p. 61. *Sichos Haran.* Chap. 229. See also: R. Yisrael Meir Hakohen. Chafetz Chaim. *Michtavei Chafetz Chaim,* p. 96 – 97. Through the power of speech we are able to endure and overcome all challenges. *Sichos HaRan.* Chap. 232. This spontaneity is particularly encouraged in an individual who is on a quest for teshuvah. *Safer Cheraidim.* Chap. 65, p. 226. *Shenei Luchos Habris.* Quoted in *Mishnah Berurah.* Biur Halacha. Chap. 571: 2. See also : *Sheivet HaMusar.* Chap. 20 : 39. p. 196. *Maor Vashemesh.* Haftorah Shabbos Shuvah. p 670. *Sur Mera V'Asei Tov.* p. 43. *Tzav Veziruz.* Chap. 4. p. 327.

* "Return O Israel upon Hashem your God." *Hoshea* 2: 14. Return until Hashem becomes *your* God. *Bnei Yissochar.* Maamorei Chodesh Tishrei Maamor 4, p. 14d. Until you are able to confer with your Creator as one friend confides with another. R. Yisrael the Magid of Koznitz (1773 - 1814) *Avodas Yisroel.* Shabbos Teshuvah, p. 257.

* The Midrash teaches that confession is a means of diffusing the evil inclination. *Midrash Rabbah.* Vayikra. Parsha 9 : 1.

CHAPTER 15

* Teshuvah is the process of diffusing impure vibes. R. Nachum of Chernobyl. *Meor Einayim.* Par-shas Chukas, p. 105. See also: R. DovBer of Chabad. *Biurei HaZohar,* p. 124a. Through the speak-ing of teshuvah the negativity of the actions depart from ones "bones." *Likkutei Moharan.* Part 1, Siman 178.

* He who does – even- one good deed acquires himself an advocate, and he who commits –even - one transgression acquires against himself an accuser. *Avos.* Chap. 4 Mishnah 11. Each good deed creates a positive angel, while conversely, each negative action taken creates a negative angel. R. Ovadiah Yarei *Bertinora,* ad loc. See also: R. Moshe Corodovero. *Tomer Devorah,* Chap. 1:2. R. Chaim Vital. *Sharei Kedusha.* Part 3, Shar 7. *Shar Ruach Hakodesh,* Derush 1, p. 1. R. Avraham Azulay. *Chesed LeAvraham* Part 2, Chap.19. *Ohr HaChaim,* Devarim 13:7. *Sefer Habris* Part 2,

Maamor 11, Chap. 4. *Maor Vashemesh*, Parshas Yisro, 232. Note: *Tanchumah* Parshas Vayetze. These angelic forces are named for the actions that created them, thus through the verbalization of teshuvah the letters/vibrations are disassembled and the angelic vibrations dissolve. *Maamorei Admmur Hazoken.* Haktzorim, p. 585. See also:*Ohev Yisroel.* Purim, p.120. R. Menachem Azaryah De Fano. *Asarah Maamoros.* Maamor Chikur Din. Part 1, Chap. 3, p.10. See the commentary *Yad Yehudah* where he cites the *Zohar* as the source.

* Thinking about positive change cleanses our thoughts; speaking about positive change cleanses us of negative speech; resolving to change helps to cleanse our actual deeds. *Safer Haikkarim* Maamor 4, Chap. 26. See also: *Akeidas Yitzchak.* Parshas Nitzavim. Shar 100, p. 117b. *Reshis Chachmah.* Shar HaTeshuvah. Chap.1, p. 101b. Note: *Ramban*.Vayikra. 1:9. *Chibur HaTeshuvah.* Meishiv Nefesh. Maamor 2. Chap. 13, p. 544.

* Speech is a form of action. *Sanhedrin*, 65a. *Baba Metzia*, 90b.

* The feelings of teshuvah cleanses the soul while the verbalization purifies the body. *Likkutei Torah.* Devarim, p. 37a. *Sharei Teshuvah*, p. 6b. *Derech Mitzvosecho.* Viddui Teshuvah, Chap. 1.

* Transgressions cause defects in the letters of the Torah. *Meor Einayim.* Parshas Vayyetze, p.p. 83-84. See also: *Likutei Moharan.* Part 1. Chap. 4:5. Note *Asarah Maamoros.* Maamor Chikur Din. Part 1, Chap. 3. *Chesed LeAvraham.* Part 4, Chap. 37. R. Ze'ev of Zhitomir. *Ohr HaMeir.* Parshas Vayera, p. 25. The internal letters. The Maharal. *Tifferes Yisrael*, Chap 12.

* Teshuvah should be done with simcha/ joy. *Reishis Chachmah.* Shar HaTeshuvah. Chap.6, p. 119a. The Zohar asks; in the Temple when one brings a sin offering where is the joy in the teshuvah? *Zohar 111*, p. 8a. See also *Shearis Yisrael*, p.p.170 - 171. The Ramak explains that for this reason the day before Yom Kippur is a day of celebration with a festive meal. *Avodas Yom Ha'Kipurim.* See: *Chemdas HaYamim.* Erev Yom Kippur, p. 273.

* In the Gemarah the sages debate whether confession must be detailed or not. *Tosefta. Yumah*, Chap. 4:14. Yerushalmi. *Yumah*, Chap. 8, Halacha 7. See also: *Yumah*, 86b. The argument stems from their position as to what is the source of teshuvah. *Likutei Sichos.* Vol. 24, p.p. 241 – 242. Post-Talmudic scholars continue the argument as to whether one must confess the details. The following opinions argue that one *must* confess the details. Rambam. *Hilchos Teshuvah.* Chap. 2, Halacha 3. And Halacha 5. *Mardechai, Yumah,* 725. *Semag.* Positive Mitzvah 16. *Sharei Teshuvah* Shar 4, Chap. 21. *Safer Chassidim.* Chap. 22. Chap. 42. *Chibur HaTeshuvah.* Meishiv Nefesh. Maamor 1. Chap. 10, p. 198. See also: *Reishis Chachmah.* Shar HaTeshuvah. Chap. 7, p. 127a. *Menoras HaMaor.* Ner 5. Klal 1. Part 1. Chap. 4: 3, p. 261. *Safer Cheraidim.* Chap. 12: 25, p. 73. Chap. 62 : 14, p. 215. Chap. 63, p.217. *Sheivet HaMusar.* Chap. 6 : 24, p.107. *Shenei Luchos Habris.* Meseches Yumah. Ner Mitzvah, p. 223. R. Chaim Ben Betzalel (1515 - 1588) *Safer HaChaim Safer Selicha U'mechila.* Chap. 6, p. 174. While others assert that there is no need to confess the details. See: *Ha'Itur.* At the end of Hilchos Yom Kippur. *Meiri.* Yumah, 86b. *Tur Orach Chaim,* Siman 607. See also *Beis Yoseph* ad loc in the name of the *Rif* and the *Rosh.* See also: *Chibur HaTeshuvah.* Meishiv Nefesh. Maamor 2. Chap. 8, p. 402.

* As we approach the final redemption, our task is to experience the teshuvah of thought. R. Tzadok of Lublin. *Pri Tzadik* , Chap. 23. *Takanas HaShavim,* Chap 10.

* The Zohar teaches that the gate of holiness is through the power of 'imagination' *Zohar 1*, p. 103b. A Chassid is one who has complete control over the mind, and can at will visualize, for example the "giving of the Torah" or the Holy Temple. *Kuzari.* Maamor 3. Chap 5.

* "Hirhur of sin is worse than sin itself." *Yumah*, 29a. The Rambam explains because thinking is a higher faculty of the human being than his actions. *Morah Nevuchim.* Part 3, Chap 8.

* To imagine oneself a Tzadik. See: R. Klunimus Kalmish of Peasetzna. *Tzav Ve'Ziruz* 24, p. 340. See also: R. Eliyahu Dessler. *Michtav M'Eliyahu.* Part 5, p. 38. To imagine that the inner attributes that one is working on perfecting are already perfected. *Michtav M'Eliyahu* Part 4. p.p. 252-253. See also *Chovas HaTalmidim.* (Peasetzna), p. 78. Or, as an earlier source suggests, "imagine oneself as an angel." *Safer HaYashar.* Shar 13. In general, the power of Tziyur –creative visualization-is more effective than intellectual understanding. R. Simcha Zisal of Kelm. *Kisvei Ha'Saba M'Kelm.* Part 1, p. 143-144. R. Yechezkel Levenstein teaches in the name of Reb Simchas Zisal that the difference between a Tzadik and the opposite of a Tzadik is that a Tzadik is someone who has the ability to picture things and visualize them in his mind as if they are real. *Sichas Musar,* 26.

* A person can be a Tzadik in one particular issue. *Tzidkas HaTzadik,* Os 58. This is a person's Nekuda's Ha'tov/points of goodness, in the language of Reb Nachman, and the issues in life that are L'mata M'nekuda's Ha'bechirah / lower than the points of choice, in the language of Rav Dessler.

* It is a much higher Avodah to refrain from food in the midst of eating than to fast. *Yesod Ha'avodah.* (Slonim), p. 148d.

* Rabbeinu Yonah suggests that if you find yourself indulging, stop eating in the midst of your meal. *Yesod Ha'teshuvah*

CHAPTER 16

* "The king into the gutters" *Shir Hashirim.* Chap. 7:6. *Tanya.* Igeres HaTeshuvah, Chap. 7.

* Teshuvah Ila'a is Deveikus. *Tanya.* Igeres HaTeshuvah, Chap. 9 – 10. *Shearis Yisroel,* p.p. 170 – 171. The Rambam writes that through teshuvah the Baal teshuvah becomes *Mudbak* –unified with Hashem. Rambam. *Hilchos Teshuvah.* Chap. 7, Halacha 7. The highest form of teshuvah is achieved through Torah study. *Zohar 111,* p. 123. *Tanya.* Iggeres HaTeshuvah. Chap. 8. See also: *Nefesh HaChaim.* Shar 4, Chap. 31. Through Torah study the mind grasps the subject of Torah and encompasses it while the mind is also ensconced within the subject. *Tanya,* Chap. 5.

* Elul is an entire month dedicated to introspection and teshuvah. *Tur* Orach Chaim. Siman 581. *Beis Yoseph* and the *Bach* ad loc. See also: *Meam Loaz.* Devarim. Netzavim, 30:11-14. According to the *Beis Yoseph's* interpretation of the *Tur,* this idea of doing teshuvah is illustrated in the Midrash. *Pirkei De'rebbe Eliezer* Chap. 46. See also: *Menoras HaMaor.* Ner 5. Klal 2. Part 1. Chap. 1: 2, p. 290. Having undergone this month long process the person's slate is completely cleansed when Rosh Hashanah arrives. *Reishis Chachmah.* Shar HaTeshuvah. Chap. 4, p.115a. See also: *Ohev Yisroel.* Parshas Re'eh, p. 239.

* The zodiac sign for the month of Elul is Besula. *Safer Yetzirah.* Chap 5. Mishna 8.

* On Rosh Hashanah we come to synagogue dressed in our finest most elegant attire, trimmed, and showered. *Tur* Orach Chaim, Chap. 581. See *Midrash Rabbah.* Vayikra, Parsha 29. See also :*Menoras HaMaor.* Ner 5. Klal 2. Part 1. Chap. 1: 5, p. 291. *Shenei Luchos Habris.* Rosh Hashanah, p. 151. Regarding "trimmed" see *Tzemach Tzedek,* Siman 93. *Minchas Eliezer* 2.

Siman 48. *Sdei Chemed* Rosh Hashanah, Siman 1:9. Note *Chasam Sofer,*Siman 159 with regards to the R. Menachem Azaryah De Fano.

* Following Rosh Hashanah are the Ten days of Teshuvah. Yerushalmi. *Rosh Hashanah.* Chap. 1. Halacha 3. *P'siktah Rabsi.* Parsha 40. See also : Rambam. *Hilchos Teshuvah.* Chap. 2. Halacha 6. And they are days when, "the Source of light is drawn to its sparks." R. DovBer of Chabad. *Derech Chaim,* p. 13d.

* Regarding the custom of replacing the words *melech ohev tzadaka umishpat* with the words *ha 'melech hamishpat* see *Berachos,*12b. *Rashi* ad loc. See: *Shulchan Aruch Harav,* Orach Chaim, 582:2.

* There are those who receive substance from a place of benevolence, and there are those who receive upon demand. *Berachos,* 17b.

* There is a place deep within that remains luminous at all times. *Tanya,* Chap. 24. In the words of the Gemarah; "A Yisroel even though he sins, remains a Yisroel." *Sanhedrin,* 44a. See also : *Yismach Yisrael* Vol. 2. *Meoran Shel Yisrael,* p. 29. *Resisei Layla,* Chap. 14. *Nefesh HaChaim,* Shar 1, Chap.18.

* There are three domains, universe/space, year/time, and soul/consciousness. *Sefer Yetzirah.* Chap.3. Mishnah 3. See also: *Kuzari,* Maamor 4, Chap. 25.

* Yom Kippur is a time when the inner core of the soul, the level of *yechidah,* is experienced and expressed. *Likutei Sichos.* Vol. 4, p.p. 1151 – 1152. *Sefer Hamaamorim Meluket* Vol. 4, p.p.16 –17.

* On Yom Kippur a person strives to mimic angelic behavior. *Shulchan Aruch,* Orach Chaim, *Ramah,* Chap. 610:4.

* Regarding Yom Kippur, the Rambam writes that it is a day when we '*rest'* from eating and drinking. Rambam. *Hilchos Shevisas Asor,* Chap. 1, Halacha 4.

* Yom Kippur is a day where a person functions as an angel. *Pirkei De'rebbe Eliezer,* Chap. 46. See also: R. Yoseph Yavatz. *Toras Chesed.* Derush Al Yom Kippur, p. 528. Where he explains that everything on Yom Kipur even for example, the law of not going with leather shoes, is done to mimic angelic behavior. See also: *Kuzari* Maamor 3, Chap. 5.

* There is no Satan on Yom Kippur. *Yumah.* 20a. See also: *Nedarim,* 32b. *Ran* and *Rashi* ad loc. *Zohar 111,* p. 63a. *Chibur HaTeshuvah.* Meishiv Nefesh. Maamor 2. Chap. 9, p. 428. Though in the Jewish calendar there are only 354 or 355 days not 364, see: *Yaros D'vash.* Part 1, p. 177, for an explanation.

* On the day of Yom Kippur there are no transgressors. *Pirkei De'rebbe Eliezer,* Chap. 46.

* Although Yom Kippur transcends transgression, transgressions are mentioned in the prayers, because the intense levels that are revealed on Yom Kippur are manifested even in the lowest places, meaning even in a place where transgressions do in fact exist. *Likutei Sichos.* Vol. 19, p. 303.

* "The essence of the day of Yom Kippur atones." *Shevuos,*13a. See also: *Yumah,* 85b. *Kerisos,*7a. All opinions are in agreement that the essence of the day itself brings exoneration, the question is only whether one needs to activate this dimension through participation, or if the day atones even without human involvement. *Likutei Sichos.* Vol. 4, p.1150. See also: Rambam. *Hilchos Teshuvah.* Chap. 1, Halacha 3 –4. Still, all agree that the bare minimum is needed, so long as the individual is passive and does not interfere with the Teshuvah power of Yom Kippur. Thus, if one desecrates

Yom Kipur by committing a transgression against the day then these types of transgression are not forgiven. *Shevuos,* 13a. What is more, all agree that in order to achieve complete teshuvah one needs to partake in the process of teshuvah. *Tosefos Yesheinim, Yumah,* 85b.

CHAPTER 17

* Rabbi Yehudah once wept "there are those who acquire eternal life…in one hour." *Avodah Zarah,* 17a. One Sha'ah means one *turn* around. *Avodas Yisrael.* Mishanah Avos, Chap 4: 2. Teshuvah can be attained in a single moment. *Zohar 1,* p. 129a. Teshuvah can occur instantaneously. *Meor Einayim.* Lekutim, p. 188. See also: *Meiras Einayim,* Shir HaShirim. *Madregos Ha'adam.* Darkei Ha'Tesuvha. Chap 5, p. 15. *Sefer Hamaamorim Meluket.* Vol. 1, p. 167.

* Teshuvah in Machshava/thought occurs in one moment. What takes an hour to "do" takes two minutes to "speak", and one moment to "think." There is less "time" in the world of thoughts. R. Shalom of Belz. Parshas Shemini. See: *Baal Shem Tov. All Ha'Torah.* Lech Lecah, Chap 32. In fact, the idea of undergoing teshuvah in one moment has legal connotations as well. The law is that if an immoral person betroths a woman on the condition that he is a Tzadik –righteous-the betrothal is valid. For perhaps at that moment he may have contemplated teshuvah in his mind. *Kiddushin,* 49b. Rambam. *Hilchos Ishus,* Chap. 8. Halacha 5. *Shulchan Aruch,* Even HaEzer, Siman 38:31.

* For the most part, people do not, and cannot, undergo sudden drastic transformations. *Chedrei Beten All Ha'Torah.* Ki Tova, p. 326. A sudden physical change in the body can cause a meltdown, or even death, spiritually. Spiritual suddenness works the same way. *Akeidas Yitzchak.* Parshas Nitzavim, Shar 100. R. Moshe Isserles, the *Ramah. Machir Yayin,* p. 101. Teshuvah should be slow. Note: *Baba Kamah,* 80a.

* Reb Mendel of Rimanov teaches, in the name of the Arizal, that in order to undo negative patterns of behavior, a person should assert a positive pattern for forty consecutive days. *Ilanah D'chaya,* Ohr Ha'ner, Os 40

* Initially, in order for one to wake up from spiritual torpor and complacency, his early steps must be taken quickly, with vigor and force. *Tzidkas HaTzadik,* Os 1. The nation of Israel exited Egypt in a hurry, the beginning stages of their spiritual journey were done in haste. *Shemos,* 12:11. Regarding the ultimate redemption, after years of spiritual development, growth and progress it says it will transpire in peace and serenity. *Yeshaya* 52: 12. See also:*Baal Haturim.* And the *Kli Yakar,* Shemos. Chap. 12: 11. The haste of the people is a reflection of the haste of Hashem's Presence, so to speak. As the nation of Israel are not yet ready for their freedom, G-d "leaps over mountains" (*Shir Hashirim* 2:8), disregards the conventional rhythm of history, and redeems them quickly. R. Naftali Tzvi. The Netziv. *Ha'Emek Davar,* Shemos, Chap 12:11. *Harchev Davar,* 1.

* The story of Eliezer Ben Durdayah is recorded in the Gemarah *Avodah Zarah,* 17a.

* "All beginnings are difficult." *Mechilta.* See *Rashi,* Shemos,19:5. *Zohar 11,* p. 187. The first movement toward teshuvah may at times be strenuous and difficult. *Reishis Chachmah.* Shar HaTeshuvah, Chap. 1. p.120b.

* Many feel that after a period of time the old feelings of alienation and estrangement begin to once

again resurface. *Yaros D'vash*, Part 1. p.p. 18 – 19. The Baal Shem Tov explanation for this phenomena is found in *Baal Shem Tov Al HaTorah*, Parshas Noach, p. 103.
"No invigoration compares to when a person first becomes invigorated in a path of piety." But this light is temporary and eventually fades. R. Eliezer *Rokeach*. See: *Pri Tzadik* (R. Tzadok) Parshas Beshalach, p. 31.

* Gadlus/ expansiveness (Rishon). *Kisvei AriZal*. See: *Moer VaShemesh*, Parshas Yisro, p. 215.

* The metaphor of a sample. R. Simchah Bunim of Pshischah (1765 - 1827) *Kol Simcha*, p.123. "Do not say, why were the former days better than these? because you are not asking this from wisdom." *Koheles* 7: 10. Read, says Reb Bunim, do not say the former days were better, more exalted, for they were not a result of your wisdom, rather they were on loan/ Shalata to you. See also *Zohar Chai*, (Kamarna) 1: 1b. *Zoas HaBeracha*. (Kamarna) Bereishis, p. 19.

* For the metaphor of a child learning to walk. See: *Meor Einayim*, Parshas Ha'azinu, p. 143. See also: *Baal Shem Tov Al HaTorah*, Parshas Noach. *Kedushas Levi*, Parshas Shemos, p. 68. *Ben Poras Yoseph*, p. 60. *Tzafnas Paneach*, p. 51b. The grandson of the Baal Shem Tov, R. Moshe Chaim Ephraim of Sudylkov writes this very same parable in the name of another Chassidic teacher. *Degel Machanah Ephraim*, Parshas Behaalosecha.

CHAPTER 18

* When someone has committed an offense against another person he must first ask forgiveness from the person that he has offended. *Yumah*, 85b. Rambam. *Hilchos Teshuvah*, Chap. 2, Halacha 9. Teshuvah is incomplete until one has been forgiven, or until one has made a sincere effort and has requested forgiveness at least three times. *Baba Kama,*60b, and 92a. Rambam.*Hilchos Teshuvah*, Chap. 2, Halacha 9. *Tur*, and *Shulchan Aruch*. *Choshen Mispat*, Siman 422:1. See also: *Menoras HaMaor*. Ner 5. Klal 1. Part 2, Chap. 4: 2. p. 269. However, one is strongly encouraged not to be stubborn and to forgive immediately. *Baba Kama*, 92a. *Midrash Rabbah*. Bamidbar, Parsha 19, Chap. 23. *Tanchumah*. Parshas Chukas, Chap. 19. Rambam. *Hilchos Teshuvah*, Chap. 2, Halacha 10. *Tur*, and *Shulchan Aruch*. Choshen Mispat, Siman, 422: 1. *Tur*, and *Ramah*. *Shulchan Aruch*. Orach Chaim, Siman, 606: 1.

* Hundreds of years ago, some thinkers suggested that a person who transgressed and deviated from his inner balance had to re-focus himself through bitter remedies and sacrifices. See e.g.: *Sheivet HaMusar*. Chap. 25:14 – 15, p. 362. Reference to the idea of fasting to amend sins is found throughout the Gemarah. See e.g.: Yerushalmi, *Beitzah*. Chap. 2, Halacha 8. *Baba Metzia*, 33a. *Chagigah*, 22b. *Moed Katan*, 25a. *Eruvin*, 18b. Fasting was once seen as an integral part of teshuvah. *Reishis Chachmah*, Shar HaTeshuvah. Chap. 3, p. 110a. *Safer Chizyonos*. p. 496. *Safer HaChaim*. Safer Selicha U'mechila. Chap. 7 p 177. *Midbar Kadmos*, Marreches Tof, p. 62. See also: *Safer Cheraidim*. Chap. 63, p.p. 218 - 219.

* Paining the body was the only way believed possible for one to achieve complete rebalance and teshuvah. R. Eliezer of Worms. (c. 1160 - c.1238) S*afer Rokeach*, Hilchos Teshuvah, Chap. 11, p. 27. R. Yehudah HaChassid. *Sefer Chassidim*. Chap. 167. *Reishis Chachmah*. Shar HaTeshuvah, Chap. 5. *Emek HaMelech*. Shar Tikunei Teshuvah, Chap. 12. See also: R. Menachem Recanti Parshas Nosa, *Levush Malchus*. Vol 7, p. 35a. R. Yeshayah Halevi Horowitz. *Shenei Luchos Habris*, Parshas Naso. Rabbeinu Bachya. *Kad Kemach*, Rosh Hashanah 1, p. 371. *Orchos Tzadikim*. Shar

HaTeshuvah, Shar 26, p. 243. R. Chaim Vital. *Olas Tamid*. *Inyon HaTefilah*, p. 46b. *Tomer Devorah*. Chap. 1:7, p. 8. *Mesilas Yesharim*, Chap. 18, p. 83. See however; *Menoras HaMaor*. Ner 5. Hakdamah, p. 245 and p. 276.

* Once a person transgresses he enters a modality of negativity and it is difficult to break free of the desire to further deviate, the infliction of pain on the body breaks down the negative inertia. R.Yoseph Dov Ha'Levi (Brisk) *Beis HaLevi*, Torah Derush 15, p. 286. R. Nacham of Breslov teaches that there is a more simple way to "break the body" and that is through a deep sigh. *Likutei Moharan* Part 1, Chap. 22:4-5.

* For a detailed discussion of these four types of teshuvah see: *Safer Rokeach Hagadol*, Hilchos Teshuvah. Chap. 1 – 15. p.p.25 – 27. *Orchos Tzadikim*. Shar HaTeshuvah, Shar 26, p.p. 236 – 240.

* Teshuvas Ha'ba'ah is a teshuvah that occurs when one refrains from committing a repeat transgression when he is in the same condition or environment as the original sin. Only then can it be asserted that his teshuvah is complete. *Yumah*, 86b. *Avodah Zarah*, 19a. Rambam. *Hilchos Teshuvah*, Chap. 2, Halacha 1. In fact, based on the above statement some sources suggest that the Baal Teshuvah should intentionally place himself in the same initial position of temptation. He should tempt himself and then refrain, to show that his resolve is complete. *Shenei Luchos Habris*, Torah She'beksav. Parshas Ki Tetze, p. 168. R. Yakov Yoseph of Ostro (1738- 1791) *Safer Rav Yeivi*. Parshas Balak, p. 158. See also: *Yaros D'vash*. Part 1, p. 11. R. Moshe Sofer. *Derashas Chasam Sofer*, Chanukah, p. 64 with regard to Yoseph. Note also, *Avodah Zarah*, 17b "I will go..." Yet, most commentaries do not encourage such behavior, and view this statement as a theoretical. R. Schneur Zalman of Liadi. *Maamorei Admur Hazoken*. Inyonim, p. 311. Other sources clearly condemn such practices. R. Shlomo Ephraim Lunshitz. *Olelos Ephraim*. Part 2, Maamor 227. Though see by the same author, *Kli Yakar*, Devarim, 19: 21. Others write that he should tempt himself with that which is permitted. R. Tzodok HaKohen of Lublin. *Takanas Hashavim*. Chap. 9, p. 39. Or that he will be placed in a similar situation, but not by his own doing. *Tzidkas HaTzadik*, Os 73, p.p. 20-21.

* Teshuvas Ha'geder is a teshuvah of refraining. One accepts upon oneself extra precautions. See also: *Chibur HaTeshuvah*. Meishiv Nefesh. Maamor 1, Chap. 12, p. 218. One guards oneself even from that which is permitted. *Kitzur Chovos Halevavos*, Chap. 7, p. 64.

* Regarding Teshuvas Ha'mishkol. See: Rambam *Moreh Nevuchim*, Part 3, Chap. 46. R. Menachem *Recanti*. Parshas Nosa. *Levush Malchus*. Vol 7, p. 35a. Rabbeinu Bachya. Kisvie Rabbeinu Bachya. *Kad Kemach*, Rosh Hashanah 1, p. 371. See also: *Menoras HaMaor*. Ner 5. Klal 1. Part 2, Chap. 1, p.p. 263 - 264. On a lighter note see: *Sefer Hamamorim Eter*, p. 61.

* Teshuvah is *Charata* /remorse and *Kabbalah*/ resolve and it is not about fasting. R. Yechezkel Landau. *Noda BeYehudah*. Orach Chaim, Teshuvah 35. *Tanya*, Igeres HaTeshuvah, Chap. 1. *Maamorei Admur Hazoken*. Inyonim, p. 458. *Nefesh HaChaim*. p. 440. R. Moshe Sofer. *Teshuvas Chasam Sofer* . Orach Chaim, 173 – 175. R. Tzvi Elimelech of Dinav. *Derech Pikudecha*. Hakdamah, p 3. *Bnei Yissochar*. Maamorei Chodesh Tishrei, Maamor 4, p. 16b.

* Charata from the word Charitah. See *Ohev Yisrael*. Zochar /Purim, p. 120.

* The Baal Shem Tov taught a path of love and inclusion. R. Baruch of Mezhibuzh. (1757 – 1810) *Butzina De'Nehurah*, p. 12. *Sham Kuf Zayin*. Baal Shem Tov All HaTorah Parshas Mishpatim, p.p. 368 – 369. *Shearis Yisroel*, p. 180. *Maor Vashemesh*. Parshas Ki Tetze, p. 608. *Haftorah Shabbos Shuvah*, p. 670. See also p. 617. The Baal Shem Tov taught that paining the body causes depression which is the antithesis to the Torah's requirement to be always joyous. *Tzavoas Horivash*, Chap. 56, p. 18. Others write that fasting causes anger. *Yaros D'vash*. Part 1, p. 360.

* In today's day and age it is not recommended to fast. *Tanya*, Igeres HaTeshuvah, Chap. 3. R. Klunimus Kalmish of Peasetzna. *Hachsharas Ha'Avreichim*, Chap. 11, p. 145. *Mavo Ha'Shearim*. Chap. 9, p. 293. *Likutei Sichos*. Vol. 2, p.p. 531 – 532. R. Yakov Kanievsky (The Steipler Gaon) *Kreiena D'Igarta*. Part 1. Igeres16, p. 27. See also: R. Akiva Eger (1761 - 1837*) Shalos V'Teshuvhas*. Second edition, Teshuvah 3. See also for earlier sources :R. Asher Ben Yechiel (1250 - 1327), the Rosh. *Orchas Chaim*. Shabbos, p. 168. *Ramah*. Shulchan Oruch. *Orach Chaim*, Siman, 344:26. Shulchan Aruch. *Yoreh Deah*, Siman 185;4. *Shalah*. Meseches Rosh Hashanah, p. 192.It is quoted in the name of R. Shlomo Molcho, that the word fast – Ta'anis can be divided into two words, *Tet* –give, *Oni* – (to the) poor. *Safer Cheraidim*. Chap. 63, p. 220. See also: *Berachos*, 6b.

* One can refine oneself through Torah. See :*Midrash Rabbah*. Vayikra. Parsha 25, Chap. 1. See also: *Orchos Tzadikim*. Shar HaTeshuvah, Shar 26, p. 241. *Noda Be'Yehudah*. Orach Chaim, Teshuvah 35.

* The aspiration should be to work *with* the body. *Keser Shem Tov*, Chap. 231. *Hosofos*, p. 92. *Hayom Yom*, 28th of Sh'vat. See also: Rambam. *Hilchos De'os*. Chap. 4, Halacha 1.Rambam *Shemonah Perakim*, Chap. 4. *Kitzur Shulchan Aruch*, Siman, 32. *Mesilat Yesharim*, Hakdamah, and chap. 26. *Menoras HaMaor*. Ner 5. Klal 1. Part 3, Chap. 1:3, p. 276.There is a tradition from R. Elimelech of Lizensk that anyone that completes the entire book of Tehilim three times in a row, without speaking, it is as if he has fasted an entire week.

* "A small hole in the body is a colossal cavity in the soul." *Keser Shem Tov*, HoSofos. See: *BeTziel HaChochmah*, p. 28.
* For example, if lying is what needs correction, then allow only truth to pass one's lips. Rabbeinu Yona *Sharei Teshuvah*. Shar 1, Chap. 35. *Orchos Tzadikim*. Shar HaTeshuvah, Shar 26, p. 219. *Safer Cheraidim*, Chap. 62 :10, p. 215. See also: *Midrash. Yalkut Shimoni*, Shoftim 42. *Reshis Chachmah*. Shar HaTeshuvah, Chap. 7, p. 124b. *Shenei Luchos Habris*. Shar Ha'osyos, p. 442. Meseches Yumah. Ner Mitzvah, p. 220. Note, *Midrash Rabbah*, Shemos, 23:3.

* Mitzvos are transcendent deeds which when performed, connects the doer with the Creator. R. Yehudah Loew. *Tifferes Yisrael*, Chap. 9.

CHAPTER 19

* Since we are born uncontaminated it is impossible to suffer or be punished for another's wrongdoings. "A man through his own transgressions shall perish." *Devarim*, 24: 16. See however, *Shabbos*, 32b. Yet, there is also the principle of *Arvus*/surety as in "all of Israel are sureties one for another." *Shavuos*, 39a. *Sanhedrin*, 27b. *Sotah*, 37a. In a case where one is able to prevent another person from negativity and does not, he too becomes responsible. *Shavuos*, 39b. This principle of *Arvus* applies to all mature and sane individuals, both men and women. R. Akiva Eiger. *Haga'as Rabbi Akiva eiger*, Hilchos Shabbos, Chap 271:2.

* The Midrashic story of the person walking through a stream of water is found in Midrash. *Yalkut Shimoni*. Tehilim, 38.

* We have the option to make ourselves heavier by being at odds with ourselves and our world, thus

the verse says, "My iniquities have inundated me." *Tehilim* 38:5.

* We are not able to choose into which family we are born, yet, according to the deeper teachings prior to the soul's descent the soul chooses the parents and the environment into which he will be born into. R. Avraham Azulay. *Chesed LeAvraham* Part 4. Chap. 11, p. 131.

* This ability to choose is a God-like power. As the soul is part of Hashem, or a gift from Hashem, we thus have free choice and can orchestrate our own destiny. Rambam. *Hilchos Teshuvah.* Chap. 5, Halacha 1. This reading is according to the interpretation by R. Schneur Zalman of Liadi. *Likutei Torah*, Parshas Emor, p. 38b. See also: R. Yehudah Chayit to *Ma'areches Elokus.* Chap. 8, p. 106a. Note: *Bereishis,* 3: 22. *Rashi,* and *Sforno,* ad loc.

* Man is part beast and part angel. *Chagigah*, 16a.

* The Rambam calls the belief in freedom of choice "the foundation of the Torah." *Hilchos Teshuvah.* Chap. 5, Halacha 3. See also: *Derashos HaRan* Derush 5, p. 68. *Rabbeinu Bachya.* Devarim, Chap 11: 26. Chap. 30:15. Traditionally, the prevailing opinion is that the Torah can only operate if there is complete freedom of choice. As the Rambam writes, "If the Creator has predetermined that a person be righteous or wicked.....what is then the purpose of the Torah." Rambam. *Hilchos Teshuvah.* Chap. 5, Halacha 4. However, it should be noted that there has been traditional Torah sages who have championed the theory of determinism. For example, R. Chasdai Cresces. *Ohr Hashem*, Maamor 2, Klal 5. A noted Chassidic Rebbe, R. Mordecai Yoseph of Izhbitz, writes that "in the deepest sense, 'everything is in the hands of Heaven' and man's freedom of choice is only apparent and exists only in his mind." *Mei HaShiluach.* Part 1, Parshas Veyera, p. 27. Parshas Korach, p. 154. In other words, the idea of freedom of choice is an illusion, of sorts. *Mei HaShiluach.* Part 1, p. 198. Part 2, 191. See also: R. Nachman of Breslov. *Likutei Moharan* Part 1, Chap. 21:4. R. Tzodok HaKohen of Lublin. *Dover Tzedek*, p. 6a. R. Yakov Leiner of Radzin – Izhbitz. *Beis Yakov.* Parshas Pikudei, p. 234a. Interestingly, when one rearranges the letters of the word '*Bechira*/choice', the letters form the words *Bachar Y-a* – Hashem has chosen.

* It should also be pointed out that the notion of determinism does not necessarily lead to fatalism, nor does it suggest that all human efforts are in vain and senseless. On the contrary, the idea of determinism may in fact lead one to extreme activism and the performance of mitzvos. One may believe in determinism and, precisely because of this belief, be totally devoted to the Torah, for they believe that following the Torah is what they were predestined to do. In fact, some suppose that the highest level a human being can attain is to lose his free choice. See: R. Meir Simcah of Dvinsk, *Meshech Chochmah*, Parshas Shemos, p.p. 75 – 76. Historically this is also true, many who championed a deterministic world-view were not lax in their moral behavior, on the contrary, believing in a determined life they wanted to prove to themselves that they were of the 'elected', the chosen, who were destined for a moral life here on earth and a future heaven in the afterlife. How could they know what their destiny would be? By seeing how they act. They know who they are by the actions that they do, or do no do. So it brought more enthusiasm and alacrity to their devotion. Conversely, many philosophers who argue for free choice actually argue in favor of indeterminism, which if true, would regulate mans actions to absolute chance, thus eliminating any grounds for responsibility. Either way, through further exploration of these texts it becomes clear that these mystics/philosophers are not suggesting determinism or that humans have no free choice, but rather that we do have *independent* free choice. Not that *self* does not exist, and we are merely conduits through which divine will flows through us, but rather that the separate self is the illusion and the real self is 'The Self', the small 'i' is but a shadow of the big I.

* In a world of pure determinism there would be no reason for teshuvah. *Likutei Sichos* Vol. 30, p. 200. The philosophers who believe in determinism argue that teshuvah is also a determined state, and it is bestowed upon man as a gift from Above. R. Chasdai Cresces. *Ohr Hashem.* Maamor 3.

Part 2, Klal 2, Chap. 1. R. Yehudah Aryeh Leib of Ger writes that although when a person trans-gresses he loses his free choice, still Hashem renews his power to freely choose each day from new. *Sefas Emes*, Parshas Re'eh.

* In order to change, the person needs to know what needs to be changed. *Safer Haikkarim* Maamor 4, Chap. 26. See also: *Chovos Halevavos*. Shar HaTeshuvah, Chap. 3. *Sheivet HaMusar*. Chap. 27 : 6, p. 375.

* The story of the Rambam is recorded by his son. See : R. Avraham Ben HaRambam. *Safer Hamaspik Leovedei Hashem*. Erech Ha'anava, p. 68. See also: Chidah. *Lev Dovid*, Chap 12, p. 82. This is similar to the teaching of the Maggid of Kaznitz on the Pasuk "...without blemish, and have never been under yoke." *Bamidbar*, 19:2. One who thinks they are without blemish is one who does not have any 'Yirah Shamyaim/ yoke of heaven.'

* The Human within Adam was banished. R. DovBer, the Mitteler Rebbe. *Toras Chaim*. Parshas Va'Yechi, p. 237c.

CHAPTER 20

* Rabbi Eliezer Ben Durdayah has secured himself a place in the World to Come. Eliezer, the one who has lived a sinful life is called *Rabbi* Eliezer, because he becomes a 'teacher' posthumously to all those who seek teshuvah. Note see *Iggros Moshe*, Yoreh Deah, part 1:135.

* According to the Arizal "Rabbi" Eliezer was a reincarnation of Yochanan Kohen Gadol- the high priest, who for eighty years was a righteous man serving as the high priest, only to stray at the end of his life. For this reason he can be called a Rabbi, for the learned soul he possessed. *Safer Ha'-likutim*. Tehilim, Chap 32, p. 429.

* His soul ignited and in a state of deep rapture, his soul departed from his body. Certainly his death was not considered a suicide. R. Chaim Yoseph Dovid Azulay. *Shem Hagdalim*, Marreches Gedalim, Yud ;17. See also: *Teshuvas Shevus Yaakov*, Part 2:111. Besides for the purpose of teshu-vah it may in fact be allowed. See: *Midrash Rabba Bereishis*, 65:18. *Shita Mekubetzet* on *Kesuvos*, 103b. p. 307.

* The three theories are reflected in the three objects Eliezer Ben Durdayah turned to on his path to-ward teshuvah. See : *Yaros D'vash*. Part 1, p.p. 35 - 36. Part 2, p.p. 247 – 248. See also: *Sheivet HaMusar*, Chap. 18 : 6-7, p. 263. *Meam Loaz*. Devarim, Netzavim, 30: 11-14.

* Mountains, at times refer to the forefathers. *Rash Hashanah*, 11a. *Tikunei Zohar*, Tikkun 21. *Midrash Rabbah* Vayikra, Parsha 30, at the end. *Shir Hashirim Rabbah*, 15. As a metaphor. R. Moshe Corodovero. *Shiur Komah*. Chap. 95, p.186.

* The Gemarah tells us that the mountains, sky and earth, sun and moon, answered him; "How shall we pray for thee? We stand in need of it ourselves." Not that they literally answered him, rather it was an imaginary conversation in his mind. *Tosefos, Chulin*, 7a. *Tosefos, Avodah Zarah*, 17a.

* With regards to the particular signs of the day, and how they effect those born on that day, see *Shabbos*, 156a. Generally, there is a prohibition against the consultation of one's astrological fore-cast. *Pesachim*, 113a. See also: *Nedarim*, 32a. *Shulchan Aruch*. Yoreh Deah, Siman 179:1.

Nonetheless, when a person is notified that a certain action is contrary to his astrological influence he should take the information into account and not act contrarily. *Ramban*, Chap. 282. *Shulchan Aruch.* Yoreh Deah, Siman, 179. *Ramah* 2. See also: *Shabbos*, 129b. *Rashi* ad loc. It should be noted, the Rambam writes that the idea of astrology is nonsense and is viewed by the wise people of the world as idiocy. Rambam. *Pirush L'Mishnayos*, Avodah Zarah Chap. 4. *Shemone Perakim*, Chap. 8. *Iggeres HaRambam*, p. 153. However, many sages affirm the astrological influences, though they argue that possessing a certain zodiac influence our behavior is, nonetheless not predetermined, and if we so desire we can transcend the influence and behave as we wish. Essentially we are not bound to the influence of the zodiac. See: *Zohar 111*, p 216. *Rabbeinu Bachya, Devarim*, 31: 16. See also : R. Avraham *Even Ezra, Shemos*, 20:1. *Devarim*, Chap. 4:19. *Ramban*. Vayikra, 18: 25. *Nimukei Yoseph, Avodah Zarah* End of Chap. 7. *Derashos HaRan*, Derush 8, p. 139. *Chibur HaTeshuvah.* Meishiv Nefesh. Maamor 1, Chap. 6. p. 153. *Ohr Hashem.* Maamor 4, Derush 4. *Akeidas Yitzchak*, Bereishis, Shar 22. *Nishmas Chayim.* Maamor 3, Chap. 17, and Chap. 21.

* With regards to the name Eliezer Ben Durdayah see; Maharal. *Nesivos Olam.* Nesiv HaTeshuvah, Chap 8. p.170. See also: Maharal *Chidushei Aggados*, Avoda Zara ad loc. With regards in general to the name Eliezer. See; *Maharsha*, Hakdamah Chidushie Halachos.

CHAPTER 21

* "One who works in a perfume factory inevitably smells sweet…" Midrash. *Pirkei De'rebbe Eliezer*, Chap. 25.

* "There is no righteous man on this earth…" *Koheles*, 7: 20.

* There is a positive life affirming goodness in all creation. R. Chaim Ibn Attar. *Ohr HaChaim.* Shemos, 11: 5. *Hayom Yom.* Hei Av. See also: *Nefesh HaChaim.* Likutei Ma'amorim, p. 375.

* Nothing is all good and nothing is all bad. R. Tzodok HaKohen of Lublin. *Komtez HaMincha*, Chap. 10, p. 2. See also: R. Yakov Emdin. *Migdal Oz.* Aliyas Yetzer Tov, p. 259.

* The Aleph alludes to Hashem. *Midrash. Osyos D'Rebbe Akiva*, p. 29.

* Hashem is everywhere, sometimes just there silently. *Baal Shem Tov Al HaTorah.* Parshas Ki Tetze, p. 578.

* These three levels of submission, separation and sweetening are taught by the Baal Shem Tov. *Baal Shem Tov All Torah.* Noach, No.110. *Toldas Yaakov Yoseph.* Vol 2, End. No. 13. *Ben Peros Yospeh*, p. 29c-d. The first step in Teshuvah is "separation", and eventually the separation brings one to purity and peity. A teaching by R. Pinchas Ben Yair. *Kallah Rabsi*, 2:6.

* Reish Lakish was initially a thief. *Baba Metzia*, 84a. There is also the opinion that Reish Lakish in his youth was involved in Torah, and only later became a bandit. *Baba Metzia*, 84a. *Tosefos*, E' Hadarta. *Eruvin*, 65b. *Tosefos.* Reish Lakish. *Yevamos*, 57a. *Tosefos*, Asa Gavrah.

* Reb Yochanan was a very handsome man. *Berachos*, 20a. *Baba Metzia*, 84a.

* Reb Yochanan and Reish Lakish became contemporaries in Halacha. When Reish Lakish passed on, Reb Yochanan bemoaned the passing of a worthy scholar. *Baba Metzia*, 84a.

CHAPTER 22

* Love is an essential component of teshuvah. Note see: *Hayam Yom.* The sixth day of Tishrei. Just as one should be kind to others, one needs to be kind to oneself. *Midrash Rabbah,* Vayikra 34:3.

* The ruling of the Rambam and the Shulchan Aruch is that one needs to respect and honor parents, even if they are unrighteous. Rambam. *Hilchos Mamrim,* Chap. 6: 11. *Shulchan Aruch.* Yoreh Deah, Siman 240:18. See also: *Sanhedrin,* 85b. *Rif* to *Yevamos,* 22b. R. Meir Simchah of Dvinsk, the *Ohr Samaiach* to *Hilchos Mamrim* offers proof from *Sanhedrin,* 71a. - This is related to the opinion that honoring one's parents is a mitzvah between man and Hashem, and not primarily between man and man. Other opinions counter this perspective. *Tur.* Yoreh Deah, Siman 240. *Ha'-gahos Maimonnis* to *Rambam* Hilchos Mamrim, Chap 6. *Mordechai.* See: *Ramah* on *Shulchan Aruch* Yoreh Deah, Siman 240: 18. *Aruch Hashulcan.* Yoreh Deah, Siman 240: 39. See also: *Baba Kamah,* 94a. *Baba Metzia,* 62a. Still, all opinions agree that one is not allowed to cause pain to his parents. *Shach* (20) and *Taz* (17) to *Yoreh Deah.* 240. Today the ruling is that most people act out of ignorance. *Titz Eliezer* Vol. 9, 41:15.

*When a person lives unintentionally and haphazardly he sows the seeds of a lifetime of regret. "The wicked are full of regrets."An adage attributed to the sages of the Gemarah. *Tanya,* Chap. 11. *Sheivet HaMusar.* Chap. 25 : 5, p. 357. *Meshech Chochmah.* Parshas Nitzavim, p. 610. R.Yoseph Yuzal Horowitz. *Madregos Ha'adam.* Darkei Ha'teshuvah. Chap 1, p. 136. See also *Nedarim,* 9b.

* The two main ingredients for teshuvah are Charata/ regret of the past, which according to many commentaries includes Azivas HaChet/abandoning the ways of vice, and Kabbalah/accepting upon oneself to become better in the future. Rambam *Hilchos Teshuvah,* Chap. 2 Halacha 2. Rabbeinu Yona. *Sharei Teshuvah.* Shar 1, Chap. 19. *Derashas HaRan,* Derush 6, p. 97. *Safer Haikkarim.* Maamor 4, Chap. 26. Rabbeinu Bachya. *Kad Kemach.* Rosh Hashanah 1, p. 371 – 372. *Chibur HaTeshuvah.* Meishiv Nefesh. Maamor 1. Chap. 8, p. 183. See also : *Chovos Halevavos.* Shar HaTeshuvah, Chap. 4. *Kitzur Chovos Halevavos* Chap. 7, p.p. 66- 67. *Safer Hayashar.* Shar 10, p. p.114 - 115. *Safer Cheraidim.* Chap. 63, p. 217. *Nefesh HaChaim,* p. 441. R. Yoseph Dov Ha'Levi (Brisk) *Beis HaLevi.* Torah Derush 15, p. 285. R. Yitzchak Blazer. *Chocvei Ohr,* p. 245. Most of the above quoted sources include Viddui/ confession as another integral part of teshuvah. There are also those who include in the Mitzvah of teshuvah asking for forgiveness. *Emunos VeDeyos.* Maamor 5, Chap. 5. See also: *Safer Hacinuch.* Mitzvah. 364.

* Genuine Charata is manifested in a determined Kabbalah. *Orchas Tzadikim.* Shar HaCharata. Shar 11, p. 108. In fact, according to the Rambam, the Kabbalah comes before the Charata. *Hilchos Teshuvah,* Chap. 2. Halacha 2. See also: R. Moshe Sheternboch. *Moadim Vezmanim.* Vol. 6. Chap. 19, p. 27. There are those, however, who assert that Charata and Kabbalah are inter-dependent. For if one does not show regret then it can be assumed that his Kabbalah is not because he wishes to mend his ways, but rather for other physical or mental reasons unrelated to teshuvah. R. Moshe Metrani. *Beis Elokim. Shar HaTeshuvah.* Chap. 2, p. 102.

* "The awareness of something, that it is negative is itself half the solution." *Meiri. Safer Hamidos.* Teshuvah, p. 159.

* The best remedy for ridding oneself of the negative past is to focus on something positive in the present. R. Mendel of Kotsk. *Emes VaEmunah,* p. 116. See also : *Sha'arei Halacha Uminhag.* (Chabad) Part 4, p. 52.

* 'Veatah /and now' refers to teshuvah. *Midrash Rabbah.* Bereishis. Parsha 21. Chap. 6. The most important dimension of time regarding teshuvah is the present. Note see *Maor Vashemesh.* Parshas

Bereishis, p. 8. Parshas Bo, p.p. 174 - 175. See also: *Avodas Yisroel*. (Koznitz) Parshas Yisro, p. 100.

* When a person does sincere teshuvah he should envision his past negativity completely erased, and should never entertain the thought that perhaps he has not been forgiven. *Maharil Likutim*. Taamei Minhagim. Inyanei Tefilah, No. 97.

CHAPTER 23

* When a person contemplates and masters his studies the Torah is called in his own name. *Kidushin*, 32b. *Avodah Zarah*, 19a. *Rashi* ad loc.

* The Gemarah teaches "The Holy One, blessed be He overturned the mountain upon them like an inverted casket, and said to them, 'If you accept the Torah, good. If not, this will be your burial.' *Shabbos,* 88a. The inner meaning of this passage is that accepting Torah is not a choice we make, but who we are. Life is who we are, and in life we do not have a choice to have choice. We may have freedom to choose, but we do not have the freedom whether we choose. We can make a "choice" not to choose, but we are still making a choice. The same is true with Torah. Torah is our life. Torah is not additional to life, it is life itself, and thus not given to us by choice.

* "Make that His will should be your will...Nullify your will before His will..." Mishnah *Avos*, 2:3. On one level you have a separate will and you need to nullify your will for the higher will, but on a deeper level, your will is His will, as the Mishnah says "Make that His will should be your will."

* There are commentaries who maintain that Marirrus is a requisite in the process of teshuvah. Rabbeinu Yona *Sharei Teshuvah*. Shar 1, Chap. 12 - 13. *Orchas Tzadikim*. Shar HaTeshuvah. Shar 26, p.p. 215 – 216. R. Eliezer Ezcary. *Safer Cheraidim*. Chap. 62:3, p. 214. See also *Tanya*, Chap. 26. *Igeres HaTeshuvah*, Chap. 7.

* Marirrus can release a person from his spiritual complacency. *Tanya*, Chap. 26. See also *Shearis Yisroel*, p. 20.

* "Whoever experiences pain let him visit a doctor." *Baba Kama*, 46b.

CHAPTER 24

* A Chassid is one who blushes and experiences shame. *Orchas Tzadikim*. Shar HaBusha. Shar 3, p. 48. See also *Safer Chassidim*. Chap. 10. Busha as in "holy shame" actually means Yiras Hashem, the fear or awe of Heaven. The Gemarah speaks of the trait of Busha as Yiras Hashem. *Yevamos*, 79a.

* Intellect is equated with shame. Only creatures that possess intelligence are capable of feeling

shame. *Orchas Tzadikim.* Shar HaBusha. Shar 3, p. 43. R. Yakov Emdin. *Migdal Oz.* Aliyas Ha'-boshes, p. 116. See also *Sheim Me'Shemuel.* Hagadah Shel Pesach, p. 48.

* Shame, as lower shame, can be quite helpful, at least in the initial stages of ones journey. The Gemarah says, "he who commits a transgression and later on is ashamed his transgressions are forgiven." *Berachos*, 12b.

* Many commentaries maintain that Busha is a vital ingredient in teshuvah. Rambam. *Hilchos Teshuvah*, Chap. 1. Halacha 1. Rabbeinu Yonah. *Sharei Teshuvah.* Shar 1, Chap 12 - 13. *Orchas Tzadikim.* Shar HaBusha. Shar 3, p. 43. Shar HaTeshuvah. Shar 26, p. 217. The Maharal. *Nesivas Olam.* Nosiv HaTeshuvah, Chap. 5.
* The word teshuvah has the same letters as the word Ha'boshes. *Shenei Luchos Habris.* Meseches Yumah. Ner Mitzvah, p. 227, Haga'ah.

* Busha, as 'unholy shame', is unbecoming for a mature and older person. R. Shem Tov Ben Yoseph Ibn Falaquera. *Safer Hamevakesh*, p. 47. Shame is a condition of the unrighteous person. Note: *Midrash Tehilim*, 6: 6.

* There are those who try to ensure that no other people see them committing their sins. *Berachos*, 28b.

* A higher level of shame is caused when a person feels that he has transgressed a higher order. Or that he has betrayed a higher 'Being' i.e; Hashem. *Orchas Tzadikim.* Shar HaBusha. Shar 3, p. 44.

* "Love is the ultimate...beyond love there is no further stage and above it there is no further rank." *Chovas Halevavas.* Shar HaAvaha, Chap. 1. This does not negate the Mitzvah of fear (*Devarim*, 6: 13), which in the higher state is actually shame. *Tanya*, Chap. 41. R. DovBer of Chabad. *Derech Chaim*, Hakdamah. And that is because shame is not simply to feel embarrassed, but rather it is to be at awe, in a state of reverence where one is overawed at creation and the Creator. The prophet says that there will come a time "when you will call Me 'Ishi/my man', and no longer will you call Me 'Ba'ali/my husband." *Hosha*, 2:18. Ba'ali means husband but also suggests master. Rashi writes that this means you will serve Hashem from a place of love and not from fear.

CHAPTER 25

* Radical transformation can be both joyful and the opposite simultaneously. Note *Shemos*, 18: 9 with regards to Yisro. *Rashi* ad loc. *Sanhedrin*, 94a. Yisro is V'Yichad, which means both joy and sadness. Ibid. And that is becuase he is becoming Chad/Unified. See; *Baal HaTurim* ad loc.

* Honesty is an integral component of teshuvah. R. Yonathan Eibeschuvetz. *Yaros D'vash*, Part 1, p. 376. R. Pinchas of Koritz. *Midrash Pinchas*, p. 82. # 5. R. Zusya of Hanipoli. *Menoras Zahav*, p. 88.

* Teshuvah may cause one to feel inferior. Rambam. *Hilchos Teshuvah.* Chap. 7, Halacha 8. See also: *Orchas Tzadikim* Shar HaTeshuvah. Shar 26, p .253.

* Healthy teshuvah is when one's emotions are well balanced; coupled with feeling dispirited about

the past one may also feel an inner sense of joy. *Derech Chaim.* Shar Hateshuvah, p. 9. Together with one's surrender/submission there is a good dosage of confidence and self-esteem. *Ohev Yisroel.* Parshas Metzora, p. 175.

* Regarding the balancing of the four elements. See: *Shivilei Emunah.* Nosiv 4. See also: *Degel Machanah Ephraim.* Parshas Bereishis, p. 1.

* Everything is comprised of four basic elements. *Midrash Rabba.* Bamidbar, Parsha 14:12. *Safer Yetzirah.* Chap. 1: 9 - 12. See also: *Emunas Vedeyas.* Maamor 1, Chap. 3. Maamor 2, Chap. 8. Rambam. *Hilchos Yisodei Hatorah.* Chap. 3, Halacha 10. *Ramban,* Bereishis 1:1. *Kuzari.* Maamor 4, Chap. 25. *Rabbeinu Bachya.* Bereishis 1:1. *Derashas HaRan.* Derush 1, p. 1. R. Gershon Ben Shlomo. *Shar HaShamaim.* Maamor 1. Shar 1, p. 5. R. Shimon Ben Tzemach Duran. *Magen Avos.* Part 2, Chap. 1, p. 9a. The Safer Yetzirah mentions only three of the elements, fire, wind, and water, and that is because the element of earth emerges from the other three. *Ma'areches Elokus,* Chap. 12. R. Moshe Corodovero. *Pardas Rimonim.* Shar 9, Chap. 3. *Ohr Neerav.* Part 6. Chap. 2, p. 46.

* According to the Gemarah everything that was created has both a male and female expression. *Baba Batra,* 74b. See also: *Zohar1,* p. 157b. Even fish and trees. *Midrash Rabbah.* Bereishis, 41: 1. Yerushalmi *Ta'anis,* Chap. 1, Halacha 3. See also: *Ohev Yisroel.* Parshas Vaeschanan, p. 230.

* In *Safer Hayashar* the author speaks of the four elements and equates them with the four basic components of teshuvah. *Safer Hayashar.* Shar 10, p.p. 114 – 115.

* The Gemarah asserts that the blowing of the Shofar is a divine decree without any rational reasoning. *Rosh Hashanah,* 16a. Rambam. *Hilchos Teshuvah.* Chap. 3, Halacha 4. The verse simply says, "It shall be a day of Teruah/Shofar/for you." *Bamidbar,* 29: 1. Nonetheless, the rationale could be that the sounds of the Shofar awaken us to teshuvah. Rambam. *Hilchos Teshuvah,* Chap. 3, Halacha 4. See also: *Midrash Rabbah.* Vayikra, Parsha 29. Chap. 6. *Tur.* Orach Chaim, Siman 581. *Chibur HaTeshuvah.* Meishiv Nefesh. Maamor 2. Chap. 3, p. 277. *Beis Yoseph,* and *Beis Chadash* ad loc.

* According to most early commentaries Shevarim is a longer sound while the Teruah is a shorter one. *Rosh Hashanah,* 33b. *Rashi,* ad loc. *Semag.* Mitzvah 42. R. Dovid Ben Yoseph *Avudrham.* Sader Tekios, p. 267.

* Before and after every wailing sound there must be a blast of the Takia. Rambam. *Hilchos Shofar,* Chap. 3, Halacha 1. See also: *Rosh Hashanah,* 33b. For a spiritual interpretation of this law see: *Resisei Layla.* Chap. 36. *Likutei Moharan* Part 1, 22: 5. *Sheim Me'Shemuel.* Zechor Bris, p. 8. R. Chaim Vital writes that the numerical value of the word Takia is the same as the word Tokef – a word which in Hebrew means strength, potency. *Shar Hakavanos.* Inyin Rosh Hashanah, *Derush* 8.

* The blowing of the Shofar is similar to that of the blowing of trumpets at a kings coronation. This reason is offered by R. Saddiah Goan. See: *Avudraham.* Ta'amei HaTekias, p. 269. Reason 1. *Menoras HaMaor.* Ner 5. Klal 2. Part 1. Chap. 5:1, p. 303. See also: Rabbeinu Bachya. *Kad Kemach.* Rosh Hashanah 2, p. 379.

* The Gra of Vilna rules that the blowing of the Shofar should be done with joy, as the coronation of a king. *Ma'aseh Rav.* Hilchos Rosh Hashanah, 206:5, p. 231.

* "Just as we need to know our faults and shortcomings we need to acknowledge our strengths and merits." R. Yoseph Yitzchak of Chabad. *Sefer Hamaamorim 5627,* p.p. 237 – 238.

* "The entire world was created for me alone." *Sanhedrin*, 37a.

* "Even the mosquito preceded you in being created." *Sanhedrin*, 38a. *Midrash Rabbah.* Vayikra. Parsha 14, Chap. 1.

* Teshuvah connotes the idea of Viddui - confession. Rambam. *Hilchos Teshuvah* Chap. 1, Halacha 1. *Safer HaMitzvas.* Mitzvah 73. See also: *Safer HaChinuch.* Mitzvah 364.

* The Torah makes room for a verbal confession of our honorable behavior. Note see : R. Yitzchak of Acco. *Meiras Einayim.* Parshas Ki Tavo, 26:3, p. 305.

* Viddui Ma'aser - a confession of tithing. Mishnah. *Ma'aser Sheini,* 5:10. *Berachas,* 40b. *Sotah,* 32a. *Megillah,* 20b. Rambam. *Hilchos Ma'aser Sheini.* Chap. 11, Halacha 1.

* It is not a confession of transgressions, but rather a reaffirmation and declaration of positive behavior. Yet, there are those that maintain that the term Viddui -which has sinful connotations is used because by giving the offerings and presents to the Cohanim/priests, one is reminded of the sin of the Golden Calf. R. Ovadyah *Seforno. Devarim,* 26: 13. See also: R. Yom Tov Lipman Heller. *Tosefos Yom Tov. Tifferes Yisrael. Ma'aser Sheini* Chap. 5, Mishnah 10. See also *Mishnah Reshonah,* ad loc.

*The prayer and confession is found in *Devarim*, 26: 13 – 14.

*Envision oneself as a tzaddik. R. Klunimus Kalmish of Peasetzna. *Tzav Ve'Ziruz*, 24. p. 340.

CHAPTER 26

* According to the Gemarah Dovid did not actually sin. *Shabbos*, 55b. See also: *Zohar 11*, p. 107a.

* Dovid was forgiven while Shaul was not. *Yumah*, 22b. Shaul says, "I did not transgress, for I have done as I was commanded." *Shamuel 1*, Chap. 15. Dovid, on the other hand, immediately concedes and admits that he had done something inappropriate. *Shamuel 2*, Chap. 12:9-13.

* Shaul was not initially prepared to take responsibility for his action. Note see Chida. *Midbar Kadmos.* Marreches Vav, p.16b. Chida. *Chedrei Beten All Ha'Torah.* Ki Sova, p. 327. Shaul used "reason" to justify his behavior, Dovid did not. R. Chaim Shmulevitz. *Sichas Mussar.* Lamed Aleph, Maamor 11, p.p. 35-36.

* "He who covers his iniquity will have no success, He who admits wrong doing and leaves it shall find mercy. *Mishlei,* 28;13. "He who covers..." this refers to Shaul...He who admits wrong doing...refers to Dovid, who when confronted said "I have sinned." *Midrash Tehilim,* 100.

* In the times of the Temple, for certain accidental misdeeds, one was obligated to bring a Karban Chatas, for even an unintentional act needs correction. *Shevuos,* 2a. *Rashi.* Toleh. *Bereishis,* 9: 5. *Rashi. Meyad Aish.* See also *Makkos,* 10b. The question is with regards to an O'nes/someone who was forced, or someone that never knew that something was forbidden', does he too need Teshuvah? The Rambam rules with regard to Shabbos that even a person who never knew about Shabbos needs atonement. *Hilchos Shegagos,* 2:6. See. *Shabbos,* 68b. See also: *Sifri.* Parshas Ki Sietze. Though see Rambam. *Hilchos Shegagas,* 5:6. *Rashi* on *Yevamos* 87b. Shelo All Pi. *Shulchan*

Aruch. Yoreh Deah, *Ramah,* Siman 185:4.

* There is an argument about whether or not one needs reparation for transgressing a precept of the sages unintentionally. In general, mitzvos from our sages are on the Gavrah/the person performing the Mitzvah and not on the Cheftza –the objects themselves. *Kesef Mishnah.* Hilchos Isurei Biah, Chap. 2, Halacha 12. R. Yoseph Engel. *Asvan Deoraisah,* Klal 10. R. Chaim Eliezer (Shapira) of Munkatsch. *Menchas Eliezer,* Part 3:12. R. Schneur Zalman of Lublin. *Torahs Chesed.* Orach Chaim, Chap. 31. *Teshuvas Beis Ephraim.* Orach Chaim, Siman 112. *Teshuvas Avnei Tzedek.* Orach Chaim, 45. *Minchas Shai.* Siman 62. See also: *Nesivas HaMishpat* Siman 234:2. "In matters of Rabbinic law we carry out the practice, and only later consider possible refutations." *Eruvin,* 67b. See *Nesivas ibid.* See however, *Radvaz* 4:19, at length *S'dei Chemed.* Vol. 1, p.p. 245 -246.

* The Torah aspires to educate man on how to live life deliberately rather than haphazardly. *Rabbeinu Bachya.* Vayikra, 1: 9. *Akeidas Yitzchak.* Parshas Vayikra, Shar 57. R. Moshe Isserles. Ramah. *Torahs Ha'olah.* Part 2. Chap. 1, p. 14. R. Moshe Metrani. *Beis Elokim.* Shar HaTeshuvah. Chap. 1, p. 101.

* One who is rigorous in the discipline of its teachings will rarely encounter mishaps. *Tanya.* Igeres Hakodesh, Igeres 28. " To a righteous man, no accidents occurs." *Mishlei,* 12: 21. See also: *Shmuel* 1:2. According to many commentaries this notion applies only with regards to matters of food. *Tosefos* to *Chulin,* 5b. However, see *Yevamos,* 121a. Midrash *Tana Devei Eliyahu Rabbah.* Chap. 26. Where it seems like this assumption holds true regarding all matters of life. See also: *Nedarim,* 10a.

* That which is immediately felt or observed is who the person is at this very moment. *Maamorei Admur Hazoken.* Maarazal, p. 31.

* An unintentional act demands even greater teshuvah than an act which was intentionally committed. *Shalah.* Meseches Rosh Hashanah, p. 194. *Tanya,* Igeres Hakodesh, Igeres 28. *Likutei Sichos.* Vol 3, p. 944. Unintentional misdeed is an indication of previous intentional misdeeds. R. Moshe Alshich. Vayikra, Chap. 4. R. Eliyahu of Vilna. *Mishlei,* Chap. 13: 6. See also R. Chaim Vital. *Likutei Torah LeArizal,* Parshas Vayikra. *Chemdas Ha'Yamim.* Yamim Noraim, p. 225. And an indication that one is still connected with that negativity. R. Yakov Leiner of Radzin – Izhbitz. *Beis Yakov.* Parshas Shemini, p. 44a. It shows of a lack of attachment, of D'veikus with Hashem. R. Yoseph Yavatz. *Avos.* Chap 3. *Nesivas Shalom.* Slonin. Vayikra, p. 21.

* Incidentally, it is recommended that one do teshuvah for an act committed even while one was young and immature. *Shulchan Aruch.* Orach Chaim. *Rama,* Siman 343. See also: *Sanhedrin,* 55b. *Safer Chassidim.* Chap. 692. R. DovBer of Chabad. *Pokeach Ivrim,* Chap. 22. R. Elimelech of Lizensk is said to have done Teshuvah for the pain he caused his mother when he was in her womb.

* Habit becomes second nature. *Chibur HaTeshuvah.* Meishiv Nefesh. Maamor 1. Chap. 3, p. 70. *Shevilei Emunah.* Nosiv 4, Part 2. Mahara De Fano. *Responsa.* Chap. 36. R. Yoseph Yavatz. *Avos.* Chap. 4. Mishanh 13. *Shalah.* Asarah Hilulim, p. 317.

* Regarding the Mitzvah of leaving a forgotten sheaf see *Devarim,* 24: 19.

* The story of the Chassid is recorded in the Tosefta *Pe'ah,* 22.

* If one transgresses unintentionally he should aspire to do as many Mitzvas as he can even if they are done unintentionally. *Avodas Yisrael.* (Kaznitz) Rosh HaShana, p. 251. See also *Midrash*

Vayikra Rabbah, 25:5.

* The Torah cautions a person to live in a proper environment that is conducive for spiritual growth. Rambam. *Hilchos De'os*, Chap. 6, Halacha 1.

* Every thought, word and action creates our environment, for positive or negative. A positive mitzvah creates an environment of Gan Eden and a negative action creates an environment of Gehenom. *Nefesh HaChaim*. Shar Aleph, Chap. 6. Haga'ah. Note: *Avodah Zarah*, 5a. *Zohar 111*, 31b.

* If a person sees that his evil inclination takes hold of him he should travel to a place where no one knows him, dress in black, and do as his heart desires, lest he disgrace Hashem's name in public. *Moed Katan*, 17a. *Chagigah*, 16a. *Kiddushin*, 40a.

* Journeying to an unknown placeand wearing black clothes, takes the life and zest out of the inclination to transgress. *Moed Katan*, 17a. *Rabbeinu Chananel*. *Tosefos*. Im Ro'eh. *Kiddushin*, 40a. *Tosefos*. Ein Makifin. See also *Orchas Tzadikim*. Shar HaTeshuvah, Shar 26, p. 248.

CHAPTER 27

* Baal teshuvah is the honorable title bestowed upon one who is in a state of teshuvah. R. Moshe Metrani. *Beis Elokim*. Shar HaTeshuvah, Chap. 3, p. 110.

* According to many the very reason the world was created was so that the Creator can manifest kindness,and bestow kindness upon creation. R. Yitzchak of Acco. *Meiras Einayim*. Parshas Haazinu, 32:26. *Eitz Chayim*. Shar HaKellalim in the beginning. *Reshis Chochmah*. Shar HaTeshuvah, Chap. 1. R. Yoseph Ergas. *Shomer Emunim*, 2:13. Ramchal *Derech Hashem*. Part 1. Chap 2:1. *Klach Pischei Chachmah*, Klal 1-4. See also *Emunas Vedeyas*. Maamor 1, Chap. 4 at the end. *Ohr Hashem*. Maamor 2. Kellal 6, Chap. 2. R. Yehudah Ben Yitzchak Abarbanel. *Vikuach Al Ahavah*. (1968), p. 38b.

* Happiness and joy are to be a constant. *Tanya*, Chap. 26. *Likutei Moharan*. Part 1, Chap. 282. Part 2. Chap. 24. *Keser Shem Tov*. *Hosofos*, Chap. 169. Particularly with regards to teshuvah. R. Shlomo of Radomsk. *Tiferes Shlomo*. Torah, Berieshis, Chap. 45: 5.

* The AriZal merited receiving the deepest Torah because he served Hashem with joy. *Safer Cheredim*. Hakdamah L'Mitzvahs 4, p. 16. R. Chayim Yospeh Dovid Azulay. *Avodas Hakodesh*. Morah Be'etzbah. Chap. 10:327, p. 69. *Lev Dovid*. Chap 14:3. *Torah Ohr*. Parshas Toledos, p. 20b. *Sefer Habris*. Part 2. Maamar 12. Chap. 4.(4). Part 2. Maamor 14. Chap. 9. *Toldos Yaakov Yoseph*, Parshas Re'eh. *Sheivet HaMusar*. Chap. 20:8, p. 288. *Mishnah Berurah*, Siman 669:11.

* The most difficult type of teshuvah to achieve is a teshuvah for depression. R. Avraham of Trisk. *Magen Avraham*, p. 258. What's more, depression borders on idol worship. Based on a teaching of the Zohar. R. Klunimus Kalman. *Maor Vashemesh*. Parshas Behaalosecha, p. 421. See also R. Menachem Mendel of Vitebsk. *Pri Ha'aretz*, Mattos – Massei, p. 103. R. Mendel of Kotsk once said, "others call it depression, I call it casting off the yoke (of heaven)." *Emes VaEmunah*, p. 8. Depression is strongly condemned. *Sharei Kedusha*. Part 1. Shar 2, and Shar 5. Part 2. Shar 4.

Avodas Hakodesh. Morah Be'Etzbah, Chap. 10:320. p. 68. *Tzavoas Harivash*, Chap. 15. *Sefer Habris*. Part 2. Maamor 2, Chap. 2. *Moer Einayim*. Hanhaggas Yesharas. *Tanya*, Chap. 1. *Igeres Hakodesh*, Igeres 11. *Likutei Moharan*. Part 1. Chap. 23:1. *Degel Machanah Ephraim*. Parshas Vayichi. *Malchei BaKodesh*, p. 79. *Shearis Yisroel*, p. 25a. Note, all the above sources are speaking of psychological depression not clinical, for clinical depression one most visit a physician.

* Only when one is truly humble can one experience a genuine measure of happiness. Ra'Yatz. *Sefer Hamaamorim 5710*, p.p. 237 – 241.

* Tamimus/seriousness is a much needed ingredient for teshuvah. The word teshuvah is comprised of five Hebrew letters; *Tof -Shin –Vov-Beis- Hei*. These five letters are the initial letters for the following five verses:
"*Tamim…* - You shall be sincere with Hashem your God" *Devarim*, 18:13.
"*Shevisi …*- I have set Hashem before me always." *Tehillim*, 16:8.
"*VeAHavtah…* -Love your neighbor as yourself" *Vayikra*, 19:18.
"*- Bechaal…* -In all your ways know Him." *Mishlei*, 3:6.
" *Hatznah….* - Walk humbly with your God." *Micha*, 6:8.
Hayam Yom. Tishrei. 3 – 8. See also: R. Pinchas of Koritz. *Aimrei Pinchas*, p. 188. *Midrash Pinchas*, p. 84. Chap 1. R. Zusya of Hanipoli. *Menoras Zahav*, p. 181. R. Uri of Sterlisk. *Imrei Kodesh*, p. 110.

* There are various acronyms for the word of teshuvah. For example, R. Yitzchak Luria teaches that teshuvah is an acronym for;
Taanis – fasting.
Sak - (wearing) a sack cloth.
V'eifer – (placing) ashes (on oneself.)
Bechia – wailing- tears.
Hesped – moaning.
Safer Cheraidim. Chap. 63, p 220. *Reishis Chachmah*. Shar HaTeshuvah. Chap. 5, p. 118b.
Shenei Luchos Habris. Meseches Yumah. Ner Mitzvah, p. 228. R. Eliezer Papo. *Pelah Yoetzh*. Os Tof. See also *Emek HaMelech*. Shar Te'Kunei Teshuvah, Chap. 9, p. 18d.
Others write that teshuvah is the acronym for;
Torah- studying Torah.
Shabbos- keeping the Shabbos.
Viddui – confession.
Busha – shame.
Hacna'ah – humbleness.
D'Vash L'Phi. (Chida) Marreches Tof. #8. *Bnei Yissochar*. Maamorei Chodesh Tishrei. Maamor 4, p. 19b.

* With regards to wailing and tears, it is worth pointing out that a person who is crying from a genuine remorse of Teshuvah and a longing to reconnect should take the tears and wipe them over his face and forehead. *Reishis Chachmah*. Shar HaYirah, Chap. 9. *Shenei Luchos Habris*. Meseches Yumah, p. 229. *Kaf Ha'Chaim*. Orach Chaim, 582: 60.

* In the prayers for Sukkos, Sukkos is referred to as 'the season of our rejoicing.' Rambam. *Sader Tefilos Kal Hashanah*. Avudrham, p. 292. The Torah mentions three times that one should be happy and joyous on Sukkos. *Midrash Yalkut Shimoni*. Parshas Emor, 247: 654.

* Being able to extend feelings of teshuvah into the days of Cheshvan is a sign that the teshuvah has reached fruition. *Avodas Hakodesh*. Morah Be'Etzbah. Chap. 9:298, p. 63.

* On Yom Kippur it is recommended to remember the two sons of Aaron. *Zohar. Shulchan Aruch*. Orach Chaim, Siman 421. *Magen Avraham*. They died "when they approached God." *Vayikra*, 16:

1. Died in spiritual ecstasy. *Ohr HaChaim*. Parshas Acharei Mos, 16: 1. See also *Meor Einayim*. Parshas Pinchas, p. 109. Note the story of the Akieda, which speaks of a Ratzu *and* Shuv, "we will prostrate *and* return" (*Bereishis*, 22:5), and an event that occurred on Yom Kippur. *Yalkut Ruveini*.

* A master is one who desires to experience a Ratzu, and yet has realizes that the ultimate purpose of the Ratzu lies in the Shuve. *Likutei Moharan 1*, Chap. 6:4. Teshuvah is called the 'Derech/the way'. *Moar V'Shemesh*. Parshas Ki Tissa, p. 271. " Praisworthy is one who knows how to *come* and *go*." *Zohar 11*, Parshas Vayakhel, p. 213b.

OTHER BOOKS BY
RAV DOVBER PINSON

REINCARNATION AND JUDAISM
The Journey of the Soul

A fascinating analysis of the concept of reincarnation as it appears in the
works of the Kabbalistic masters, as well as how it is discussed by the
great thinkers throughout history. Dipping into the fountain of ancient
wisdom and modern understanding, the book addresses and answers such
basic questions as: What is reincarnation? Why does it occur? and How
does it affect us personally?

....

INNER RHYTHMS:
The Kabbalah of Music

The study of music as response is explored in this highly engaging book.
Music and its effects in every aspect of our lives are looked at in the perspective of mystical Judaism and the Kabbalah. The topics range from
Deveikut/Oneness, Yichudim/ Unifications, merging heaven and earth,
to the more personal issues, such as Simcha/Happiness, expressing joy, to
the means of utilizing music to medicate the sad soul. Ultimately,using
music to inspire genuine transformation.

....

MEDITATION AND JUDAISM:
Exploring the Jewish Meditative Paths

A comprehensive work on Jewish meditation, encompassing the entire
spectrum of Jewish thought--from the early Kabbalists to the modern
Chassidic and Mussar masters, the sages of the Talmud to the modern

philosophers--this book includes them all.

The book is both a scholarly, in-depth study of meditative practices, and a practical, easy to follow guide for any person interested in meditating the Jewish way. The word meditation calls to mind the traditional, obvious associations that society has accumulated, such as the lotus position, the mantras and the like. Meditation and Judaism attempts to broaden our view of meditation, demonstrating that in addition to the traditional methods of meditation ,meditation is prevalent within so many of the common Jewish practices. The book also explores a variety of fascinating and intriguing topics such as; panoscopic vision, spiritual synesthesia, psychic powers. What is black magic? What is the Koach HaTumah – the impure powers? What is the definition of spirituality?

....

TOWARD THE INFINITE:
The Way of Kabbalistic Meditation

'Toward the Infinite – A Kabbalistic Meditation' focuses exclusively on the Kabbalistic – Chassidic approach to meditation. Encompassing the entire meditative experience, it takes the reader on a comprehensive and engaging journey through meditation.

The journey begins with the readying of oneself for the meditation. The preparatory stage is discussed at length, dealing with issues such as the time of day most conducive to the meditation, the meditative positions and the like. The journey continues with the actual meditative experience. The various states of consciousness that a person encounters in the course of the meditation, beginning at a level of extreme self-awareness and concluding with a total state of non-awareness.

'Toward the Infinite – A Kabbalistic Meditation' is deliberately written to appeal to a mass audience and thus does not make use of learned quotations and references. An easy read which will pique the interest of all those intrigued by spirituality and meditation.

....

JEWISH WISDOM OF THE AFTERLIFE:
The Myths, the Mysteries & Meanings

What happens to us after we physically die? What is consciousness? And can it survive without a physical brain? What is a soul? Can we remember our past lives? Do near-death-experiences prove the immortality of the soul?

Drawing from the fountain of ancient Jewish wisdom and modern understanding of what consciousness is, this book explores the possibilities of surviving death, the near-death-experience, and a possible glimpse of the peace and unconditional love that awaits, empowering the reader to live their day-to-day life with these great spiritual truths.

In 'Jewish Wisdom on the Afterlife', Rav DovBer Pinson explores the possibility of life after death, presenting a basic understanding of what it means to be mortal and how an understanding of our immortality can serve us in the present and empower us to live more meaningfully today.

....

UPSHERIN:
Exploring the Laws, Customs & Meanings of a Boy's First Haircut

What is the meaning of Upsherin, the traditional celebration of a boy's first haircut at the age of three? This in-depth answer to that question explores as well the questions: Why is a boy's hair allowed to grow freely for his first three years? What is the kabbalistic import of hair in all its lengths and varieties? What is the mystical meaning of hair coverings? Rav DovBer Pinson answers these questions with his trademark deep learning and spiritual sensitivity.

Includes a guide to conducting an Upsherin ceremony.

....

THIRTY – TWO GATES OF WISDOM:
Awakening through Kabbalah

Kabbalah holds the secrets to a path of conscious awareness. In this com-
pact book, Rav DovBer Pinson presents 32 key concepts of Kabbalah and
shows their value in opening the gates of perception.
A short excerpt from the introduction: Simply translated, Kabbalah
means "that which is received." Looking deeper, the word Kabbalah can
mean to be open and receptive, to challenge one's own internal naviga-
tional system in order to see, hear, and be open to… more. We must be
receptive to a teaching to fully absorb it. We turn ourselves into vessels
and invite within that which we wish to understand or grasp. In this way,
we become receptacles, dispensaries, and a part of the Kabbalah. We become vessels of this tradition by opening the self to a higher reality, and
viewing the spirit within the matter. We raise our consciousness to the
point where the Divine within all creation is revealed. As we pursue a
deeper awareness, we become less ego-centered and more attuned to the
deeper significance of our surroundings.

TEFILIN:
A Guide & Deeper Exploration of the meaning and Practice of Tefilin

This is a booklet that was written as a guide to help people put on
Tefilin, discussing the basic laws and how one puts on Tefilin, and offers
a deeper explanation of the Mitzvah.

THE PURIM READER:
The Holiday of Purim Explored

With a Persian name, a costuming dress code and a woman as the hero-
ine, Purim is certainly unusual amongst the Jewish holidays. Most people
are very familiar with the costumes, Megillah and revelry, but are mysti-

fied by their significance. Rav DovBer Pinson offers a glimpse into the unknown world of Purim, uncovering the mysteries and offering a deeper understanding of this unique holiday.

....

EIGHT LIGHTS:
8 Meditations for Chanukah

What is the meaning and message of Chanukah? What is the spiritual significance of the Lights of the Menorah? What are the Lights telling us? What is the deeper dimension of the Dreidel?
Rav DovBer Pinson, with his trademark deep learning and spiritual sensitivity guides us through eight meditations relating to the Lights of the Menorah and the eight days of Chanukah, and a deeper exploration of the Dreidel.
Includes a detailed how-to guide for lighting the Chanukah Menorah

....

THE IYYUN HAGADAH:
An Introduction to the Haggadah

In this beautifully written introduction to Passover and the Haggadah, Rav DovBer Pinson, guides us through the major themes of Passover and the Seder night. Rav Pinson addresses the important questions, such as; What is the big deal of Chametz? What are we trying to achieve through conducting a Seder? What's with all that stuff on the Seder Plate? And most importantly, how is this all related to freedom? His answers will surprise even those who think they already know the answers to these questions.

....

Printed in the USA
CPSIA information can be obtained
at www.ICGtesting.com
LVHW090918211023
761746LV00023B/167/J